Bringing Bernard Lonergan Down to Earth
and into Our Hearts and Communities

Bringing Bernard Lonergan Down to Earth and into Our Hearts and Communities

JOHN RAYMAKER
and
GODEFROID ALEKIABO MOMBULA

WIPF & STOCK · Eugene, Oregon

BRINGING BERNARD LONERGAN DOWN TO EARTH AND INTO OUR HEARTS AND COMMUNITIES

Copyright © 2018 John Raymaker and Godefroid Alekiabo Mombula. All rights reserved. Except for brief quotations in critical publications or reviews, no part of this book may be reproduced in any manner without prior written permission from the publisher. Write: Permissions, Wipf and Stock Publishers, 199 W. 8th Ave., Suite 3, Eugene, OR 97401.

Wipf & Stock
An Imprint of Wipf and Stock Publishers
199 W. 8th Ave., Suite 3
Eugene, OR 97401

www.wipfandstock.com

PAPERBACK ISBN: 978-1-5326-5795-5
HARDCOVER ISBN: 978-1-5326-5796-2
EBOOK ISBN: 978-1-5326-5797-9

Manufactured in the U.S.A.   10/05/18

Contents

Preface | vii
Introduction | ix

Part I: A Lonergan-Inspired Journey with Jesus: The Kingdom of God and Its Challenges | 1

1 Serving God and Neighbor: Paths toward Building Responsible Communities | 3

Part II: The Roles of Persons in Communities, Cosmopolis, and the Kingdom of God—Toward Making this World a Better Place in which to Live and Share | 23

2 Meaning and the Human Good as Constitutive of Human Communities | 25
3 Further Tensions Affecting Meaning and the Human Good | 53
4 The Importance of Insights, Common Sense in Human Experience | 67
5 Kingdom-Oriented Communities Called to Self-Transcendent Deeds | 88

Part III: Spiritually Enriching Humanity by Living the Two Forms of Interiority—as Explored and Experienced, for Example, by Buddhist, Christian, and Muslim Mystics | 103

6 Restructuring Theology to Focus on Kingdom-of-God and Cosmopolis Priorities | 105

Part IV: The Amplitude of Lonergan's Generalized Empirical Method—Addressing Important, Complicated Philosophical Issues in Twelve Explorations | 131

Bibliography | 181
General, Selective Index | 195

Preface

THIS JOINT ATTEMPT TO bring Lonergan's famously complex writings "down to earth" began with Raymaker being asked to improve the English of Molumba's PhD dissertation written by a French-speaking priest-missionary. After Molumba's successful defense of his thesis in Rome (2017), we decided that it would be well for Raymaker to widen his thesis's focus on communities in Lonergan's opus by bringing in the affective component in Lonergan's lifework. This is in accord with Lonergan's own evolution. Lonergan's initial stress on the role of understanding in *Verbum* and in *Insight* was followed in his post-*Insight*'s explorations of the love of God in his *Method in Theology*. A premise of our book is that insights into both mysticism and community life partly motivated the writings of St. Augustine and St. Thomas Aquinas, as well as of Lonergan himself. As Raymaker set about his task, it was decided we should relegate complicated philosophical issues, which form an important part of Molumba's dissertation, to Part IV of our text so as not to distract from our principal aim of showing Lonergan's relevance to peacebuilding efforts. Lonergan's later focus on human values and on interfaith dialogue means that, in a way, he was reexamining anew his earlier work on theology written during his many years as Professor of Dogma at the Gregorian University in Rome.

We are grateful to Rosanna Finamore who guided Mombula's thesis and for the friendship and cooperation of many in our lives. Mombula thanks his family and friends for their unwavering support over the years, and the Missionhurst order of Belgian origin to which he belongs. After finishing his thesis, Mombula returned to the Congo where he now directs several development projects. For his part, Raymaker, too, acknowledges the support of family, Missionhurst, Gerald and Marita Grudzen, as well as the cooperation of many Lonergan scholars such as Frank Braio, Matthew Lamb, Philip McShane, Terry Quinn, Catherine King, Mike Albertson, Doug Mounce, and Joseph Martos.

Introduction

TRYING TO ESTABLISH A world community may be seen as a utopian goal, but in a globalized world it is worthwhile to consider the possibility of having local and global communities willing and able to work for the common good of all. This book—an attempt to apply Bernard Lonergan's method—argues that, if correctly understood and applied, his method can help humanity build self-transcending communities. Although its two authors are Christian (the book often speaks of the "kingdom of God"), Lonergan's method does provide realistic ideals that correspond to those proposed at various historical times by the Buddha, Jesus, and the prophet of Islam, or by Mahatma Gandhi in modern times. Unfortunately, the realistic ideals of the founders of the world religions have in fact only been lived out by a fraction of their followers. This book seeks ways to implement the ideals of religious founders through the insights into the heart and into community life that Lonergan elucidated in his work. For Lonergan, religious ideals are crucial to building viable communities in our globalized world. In the text, we refer to Lonergan's view of consciousness "as a polyphony with different intensities sung simultaneously." Music, a universal language that appeals to people everywhere, comes in myriad forms. Like music, Lonergan's method is universal. Based on human consciousness, his method is able to bridge opposing religious and philosophical views with the sciences by way of re-harmonizing some of the unacceptable dissonances which mar such views.

One of this book's aims is to show how truth, the good, and faith complement one another. If truth is to be a source of living faith for religious communities, they must open themselves up to hard-to-fathom, seemingly elusive realities. Yet, in today's age of fake news, biased media, and populist regimes, truth is hard to come by. Was Lonergan merely a "voice crying in the desert" when he challenged us to evaluate the problems facing both persons and societies? He systematically studied and wrote on how humans can best function in ethically responsible ways. This book interprets his breakthroughs for the average person so that his deep insights into the human situation and into true love may help us develop strategies to combat modern illusions. Throughout the text, we point to the radical nature of Lonergan's work which goes to the root of problems. He radically rethinks the Christian message to make it accessible and relevant for our age.

Since Godefroid Mombula is a native of the Congo, the book touches on how African forms of spirituality might provide models to address the complex issues facing humanity today. How might forms of social commitment in the West on the one hand, and the traditional forms of community life in Africa on the other, reinforce one another? Our book answers that question by applying the somewhat abstruse elements of Lonergan's profound thought to pressing international problems. It does so in interiority-based, interdisciplinary ways. It develops some of the imperatives of love implied in the kingdom of God as preached by Jesus. Our book's "thy kingdom come" strategy explores the social implications of community life that might offset the West's rampant individualism, while recalling and reapplying its erstwhile viable ethical and spiritual motivations in pluralist ways.

PART I

A Lonergan-Inspired Journey with Jesus
The Kingdom of God and Its Challenges

1

Serving God and Neighbor
Paths toward Building Responsible Communities

SOME PRELIMINARY CONSIDERATIONS

THIS BOOK INTRODUCES READERS to Lonergan's views on community-building. It seeks to "bring Lonergan down to earth" while focusing on the gospel and faith as well as on modern scholarship. Lonergan stressed that to the apostles had been given the mystery of the kingdom of God: "The gospel is the good news, and the good news is the kingdom of God."[1] One of our aims is to find effective ways to read and live Lonergan's message in light of the sixth beatitude, "Happy are the pure of heart" (Matt 5:8). For us, Lonergan's profound views on community are rooted in kingdom-of-God ideals—ideals that have been challenging Christians for centuries. We shall argue that the heart (interiority) affects Lonergan's views on ethics. By doing so, we hope to help readers identify in *their own* personal experience their *own conscious and intentional operations* and the *dynamic relations linking them* together.[2] This sentence gets to the core of what Lonergan discovered over his years of teaching. Our aim is to apply this dynamic, relational focus to the challenge of what it is to be a caring Christian. Following Jesus, Lonergan helps us interiorize religious values. How can we Christians today

---

1. Lonergan, "Redemption," 24.

2. Lonergan, *Method in Theology*, 286. In Parts I and III, we examine how Lonergan helps motivate human hearts—a key to building, inspiring, and linking communities in the world so as to foster peace through mindful cooperation.

share the depth of our interior life, our inner self,[3] with others so as to build better, viable communities? How may we empower one another? The various facets of our inner and outer lives call for a realistic optimism of the type Lonergan offers us.

Lonergan wrote about relating one's inner self with others within communities. Sadly, life in the West has often been lived in flawed ways as evidenced in the work of many leading thinkers. In response to that, this book begins and ends with Jesus' good news as interpreted and applied in Lonergan's ground-breaking method. Our appeal to African notions of solidarity[4] throughout the book is meant to show that Lonergan's method is applicable beyond Western notions of community. The Western world can learn much from African communal solidarity. Our book's guiding principle is one of *transformative bridging*. Since across the planet, people are socially, economically, and politically interdependent (but subject to often conflicting claims), we seek to develop Lonergan's discernment of our times and of spirituality in terms of consistent ideals of mercy as inspired by kingdom-of-God community values.

HOW LONERGAN'S METHOD HELPS US LIVE AND SHARE COMMUNAL KINGDOM[5] VALUES

1a The "Word Made Flesh" and "Bringing Lonergan Down to Earth"

The common sense of Greek mythology eventually gave rise with the pre-Socratics to the philosophy of *logos*—the realm of theory. Through both myth and *logos*,[6] humans have continually sought to transcend or surpass

---

3. "Secrets" and "hiding" are central to *The Diary of Anne Frank*. Anne wonders why people go to such lengths to hide their real selves. As did Anne, Lonergan (*Method in Theology*, 122) prized the value of love both inwardly and outwardly.

4. Solidarity is a key underlying notion in our book: "For where two or three come together in my name, I am there with them" (Matt 18:20). That Africans have a strong sense of communal solidarity can help offset dualist notions.

5. For John Bright, Kingdom, 7, "the concept of the kingdom of God" touches on the heart of the Bible's concerns.

6. *Logos* has historically been used in many senses. It can be translated as "science," "study," "reason," or "word." Heraclitus, a sixth-century-BC Greek philosopher, was the first to speak of *logos* in a metaphysical sense, as being the universal reason immanent in all things and binding all things into a unity. For the Stoics, two centuries later, *logos* meant the active principle in reality. Philo spoke of *Logos* in the first century AD in his effort to synthesize Judaism with Platonism. He was the first to designate *logos* as a mediating principle between God and the world. For him, *Logos* is divine wisdom

themselves and their immediate situation. This striving to surpass ourselves points us to the infinite which alone can fill our inner yearnings. Humans thirst for God because they are created not for themselves but for God. Sensitive persons seek to find the reason for their existence. Having an inbuilt craving for the infinite, they are not free to cut themselves off from this yearning since it is an inbuilt one. Lonergan, as a theologian, spent many years teaching large classes of seminarians in Rome. He had to address complex issues such as the meaning of the *Logos* or Word "made flesh" in John 1:14. How was the Son of God incarnated? This question is discussed with as much intensity now as it has been for the past two millennia. Our book hopes to spare general readers from delving into complex issues in its attempt to "bring Lonergan down to Earth." Many today downplay religion, but they cannot explain away the sense of mystery pervading our lives. The understanding of religion is evolving, but for us, living the good news of Jesus today is a key priority.

1b The Opposing Priorities of the Gospel and Those of the World[7]

In our age of globalization and unparalleled numbers of displaced persons, joining Jesus in his kingdom-of-God teachings is an appropriate starting point for efforts to spiritually enrich mankind. Lonergan, early in his career, undertook his own journey toward kingdom values, being committed from the first to identify the spiritual import of Jesus' teachings in our day. Although not himself a biblical scholar, he did focus on Jesus' commitment to God's justice. In the Gospels, Jesus repeatedly teaches us that God is merciful—a lesson Lonergan took to heart early on and kept developing throughout his life.[8] His many-splendored method can be applied to many diverse fields. He combined his pursuit of truth with an emphasis on living the good news. This twin aspect characterizes the radical nature of Lonergan's achievement. Let us note here the important foundational role that

---

immanent in the world. In St. John's Gospel, Jesus is the incarnate *Logos*.

7. Jackall, *Mazes*, gives an eye-opening account of how corporate managers think. In such a world, people hide their intentions. Accountability, bereft of moral consciousness, amounts to the ability to outrun one's mistakes.

8. Rixon, "Mysticism," 480. Mercy and compassion are core themes in both Christianity and Islam. In Islam, the phrase "In the name of God, the compassionate and the merciful" is often recited before speeches and actions so as to receive God's blessings. "Al-Rahman" (The Merciful) is an attribute of Allah—indicating that it should be mirrored in human affairs. For Jesus: "Blessed are the merciful: they shall have mercy shown them" (Matt 5:7).

"*wordless*" *(apophatic)* realities have in Lonergan's faith-motivated work, a foundation to be developed in word and deed:

> Lonergan's spirituality is a spirituality of "the Word" as it spreads out to all of human culture. Such a spirituality *radiates outward* to focus on the long-term cultural implications of the Gospel. In an empirically inclined culture from which God is often so decidedly absent, Lonergan's thought can open up—even in the midst of scientific and scholarly work—the question of God that lurks just below the surface. The conversion in our understanding of ourselves promoted by Lonergan can break open the hardened symbols and clichés of misunderstanding that so often define our culture. Besides a *wordless "apophatic"* spirituality that loses itself in contemplation, there is also a need today for a *"kataphatic" spirituality that values the Word* and shows how that Word fits into our other human words—sciences, scholarly disciplines . . . —so that God can have a say in the world we construct.[9]

Lonergan reinterpreted the Christian faith in light of the Catholic tradition so that it may better address our human needs today. The Buddha, Jesus, and Muhammad all radicalized the traditions they had inherited—each did so in his own intense way. While Nietzsche sought to undermine Christian notions of values and morality, Lonergan brings us back to a quest for the kingdom of God and the common good—two complementary ideals. The language of the kingdom is rooted in the dominion that God "exercises over creation and which he delegates to humanity" (Gen 1:27).[10] Despite the Israelites' sins and failures, the ideal of the kingdom remained associated with God's chosen people in the Old Testament. Other nations have kings, but Israel "needs no king because God is their King" (1 Sam 8–15). Even when they ask for a king, the language of the kingdom becomes symbolic of God's rule. Ultimately it becomes an anticipation of the perfect peace when God himself will visit his people. Since God's rule is perfect, and humanity is far from perfect, participating in his kingdom requires conversion.

In his teaching on the kingdom,[11] Jesus reprimands the scribes and Pharisees. His message is authentic, having a radical sense of inclusion

---

9. Liddy, "Mystery of Lonergan," 16. With Liddy, our text stresses the *radical combination of the word and wordless* in Lonergan.

10. Paul, "Kingdom and the Common Good," 1.

11. Lonergan retained the traditional Christian view of community: one should "First seek the kingdom of God" (Matt 6:33). See Lonergan, *Early Latin Theology*, 519. In the first-century Mediterranean world, people thought of themselves as members of communities, being conscious of their responsibilities and obligations to their

about it. It calls for transformative change; sinners should repent (Luke 5:32). It contrasts with the Romans' oppressive rule—but it avoids directly setting the kingdom "over against empire."[12] In John's Gospel, his message is not so much spiritualized as made cosmic. The kingdom differs from the rule of this world, having been overthrown by Jesus' sacrifice on a cross (John 19:18). This cosmic contrast is continued in Paul, for whom the kingdom separates those who are "in Christ and those who are not" (1 Cor 6:11). The old creation, dead in sin, under the control of "the flesh," has now been raised to new life (Rom 6:4). It is part of the new creation (2 Cor 5:17), in anticipation "of the transformation of the whole cosmos (Rom 8:19)."

2 Lonergan's Cosmopolis-Influenced Spiritual Teachings

Diogenes the Cynic declared himself to be "a citizen of the cosmos."[13] In *Insight,* Lonergan explores human understanding and its pitfalls; he overcomes the latter by developing a *generalized* empirical method, or "GEM." The present book links Lonergan's GEM breakthroughs in such fields as philosophy, the social sciences, theology, economics, and spirituality. Overall, Lonergan addressed change and effective global transformations in light of his profound, challenging vision of "cosmopolis," a notion which we take pains throughout our text to relate to, but not equate[14] with the Kingdom of God. What is original in GEM is that it relies on both the data of sense *and of consciousness,* a stance that led him beyond Husserl's breakthroughs.[15] As GEM "generalizes the notion of data to include the data of consciousness, so too it generalizes the notion of method. It wants to go behind the diversity

---

community before they thought of their individual rights. Unlike Westerners, Africans remain focused on solidarity.

12. Arcamore, *Violence,* 244, argues that there is a difference between distorted and genuine religion, between authenticity and inauthenticity of the subject. Distorted religion has falsified traditions in ways that have led to violence, while genuine religion heals persons and helps them make difficult moral decisions when confronted with situations of conflict. Our book explores new ways of self-understanding that might positively shape events. Arcamore's dialectical engagement complements this book's attempt to take seriously the gaps between the tensions of the heart and political ambitions. There is great need to establish communities based on true justice.

13. Diogenes, Fragment 7 in Diogenes the Cynic: *Sayings.*

14. Cosmopolis, as a worldview on culture, would break the barriers dividing us. In this book, cosmopolis plays a key role since we assume that all humans should be free to turn toward a transcendent being despite the obstacles.

15. Lonergan's notion of meaning builds on Edmund Husserl. Incorporating the data of consciousness as well as that of sense enabled him to integrate while expanding Husserl's notions of intentionality. See Exploration 5 in Part IV.

that separates the experimental method . . . and the quite diverse procedures of hermeneutics and of history. It would discover their common core."[16]

The data of consciousness involves: 1) a genetically related series that adequately treats data by way of understanding, judgments, decisions, and actions; and 2) an ongoing series of dialectically operative methods grounded in decisions and actions aimed at promoting the good. GEM "does not treat of objects without taking into account the corresponding operations of the subject, it does not treat of the subject's operations without taking into account the corresponding objects."[17] *Generalizing the notion of data to include* those of consciousness enables GEM to function as a reduplicative structure[18] within one's consciousness, and to ground the eightfold functional specialization process explored in *Method in Theology*. In doing so, GEM expands the notion of data by spelling out what *must be added* to the commonly received notion of empirical method. In *Method*, Lonergan applies *Insight*'s lessons to theology. Exploring the role of religion in a cultural matrix, he develops GEM as an eightfold process involving two phases: in the first phase, theologians learn from the past, and in the second phase, they seek to solve contemporary problems. Both phases involve the four levels of a person's conscious and intentional activities: experiencing, understanding, judging, and deciding—activities which Lonergan explored at length in *Insight*.

Method deploys the four levels of our cognitional activities as criteria to distinguish the eight functional specialties in the specific field of theology: research, interpretation, history, dialectics, foundations, doctrines, systems, and the ways of communicating a religious message so that it may bear fruit.[19] The first four functional specialties are restricted to what Lonergan calls "indirect discourse," the phase whereby a theologian learns from the past in a *mediating* manner. These first four specialties challenge both a theologian and his/her reader to decide: "In what manner or measure am I to carry the burden of continuity or to risk the initiative of change?"[20] At

---

16. Lonergan, "Religious Knowledge," 141. GEM finds the missing links that have afflicted Western thought since Descartes.

17. Lonergan, "Religious Knowledge," 141.

18. Crowe, *Lonergan and the Level*, 161. Raymaker, *Bernard Lonergan's Third Way*, 21.

19. Lonergan's *Insight* (on how humans can attain sure knowledge) laid the groundwork for his second major work, Lonergan, *Method in Theology*, which focused more on persons' hearts rather than their minds. *Method*'s eight functional specialties are a values-informed, interdisciplinary bridge which we study and apply in the present book.

20. Lonergan, *Method in Theology*, 135.

stake here is a religious event which leads toward a decision initiating one into theology's second *mediated* phase. It is in this second phase, in the last four specialties, that a theologian moves into *direct* discourse whereby he/she seeks to tackle contemporary and future problems. Lonergan's method is based upon the intentional operations of our cognitional structure[21] and upon the unrestricted desire to know that is present in intelligent persons. His eightfold functional specialization process helps us explore the horizon[22] of our consciences and apply it, for example, to a lived spirituality based on Jesus' teaching. This book argues that Jesus' teaching on community and the Kingdom is one that can help humans forego unethical power politics.

We apply GEM to a dialectic of community, hoping that readers will complement Lonergan's insights into global forms of renewal with personal initiatives to help people remedy some of the woes afflicting humanity. *Bringing Lonergan Down to Earth* does not delve into all of GEM's complexities; it does seek to help humans in spiritual, ethical ways based on Jesus' kingdom of God in *our* "midst" (Luke 17:21).[23] Both Jesus and Lonergan appeal to our hearts, inviting us to transform self and communities.

This book stresses an often-overlooked facet of Lonergan's work, namely the moral intensity[24] that motivated him. Focused on our conscious, intentional operations, Lonergan transposed Nietzsche's intensity of will[25]

---

21. For Colin Brown, *Insight* is "a major restatement of Thomism in a post-Kantian setting. It is Thomist in so far as it builds upon a natural theology on the basis of reflection on what can be observed. It is post-Kantian in that it does so within the framework of a critique of knowledge. . . . Each form of knowledge contains elements which go beyond itself." Ultimately, "we are confronted with the transcendent which is God" ("Wrestled," 47).

22. The notion of horizon is extremely important in Lonergan's work; we explore and apply horizons in many ways.

23. Biblical scholars debate as to whether "in your midst" means "within your hearts" as nineteenth-century scholars held, or whether it means the effect of Jesus' transforming presence. We hold both interpretations as valid. The point is that the Kingdom "is right in front of their face in Jesus. It is 'in their midst' or 'in their reach' in that the hunt for that which represents the Kingdom's presence stands before them" (Bock, "Kingdom of God," 2).

24. Doran calls attention to "a resistance to the prophetic character of Lonergan's work." Lonergan challenged his readers to conversion in everything he wrote. One is reminded of "Rilke's famous line, 'You must change your life.'" This can "arouse not only resistance, but also resentment." Lonergan was able to write the way he did because he himself was "on the receiving end of it" (Doran, "Why Lonergan?," 6).

25. Rather than accepting Nietzsche's theory of decadence and transvaluation of all values, Lonergan replaces that theory with his own sense of "abolishing" one's horizon and setting up a "new horizon in which the love of God will transvalue our values" (*Method*, 106). As opposed to Nietzsche's claim, *Beyond Good*, chapter 4, that "Insanity in individuals is something rare—but in groups, parties, nations and epochs, it is

with the loving intensity of Christian commitment. He perceptively identified the *four biases* that cloud our minds and prevent us from doing good. Lonergan's view on cosmopolis can help Christian communities live the intellectual, moral, and religious conversions.[26] A quote from Vatican Council II reinforces this view on conversion:

> It is imperative that no one . . . indulge in a merely individualistic morality. The best way to fulfill one's obligations of justice and love is to *contribute to the common good* according to one's means and the needs of others, and to promote and help public and private organizations devoted to bettering the conditions of life.[27]

It is crucial to grasp that GEM, a *generalized* empirical method, can help us link the deepest, personal aspects of our private lives to the momentous events that have been occurring in recent history. For Lonergan, being liberated from our biases depends on God's grace and on cosmopolis. Cosmopolis "refers to the links between *cosmos*, the order of nature or the universe, and *polis*, the order of human society."[28] Many cultures have assumed that there is a direct link between the two orders. But tragically, modernity has sacrificed much of previously *existing forms of order* due to its pursuit of progress. Lonergan's cosmopolis would retrieve such forms as it inspires us to build kingdom-oriented communities. The kingdom can only be realized if enough people make it their heart's concern. For Lonergan, cosmopolis goes beyond the practical. It approximates a cultural framework for living values authentically. Based on judgments of value, cosmopolis, as *an ideal cultural community*, transcends the frontiers of states and the epochs of history. It is concerned with the *fundamental issue of the historical process. It stands above* the claims of class or any state. Founded on the detached disinterestedness of every intelligence, "it commands our first allegiance. It implements itself through that allegiance. It is too universal to be bribed,

---

the rule," this book seeks an alternative in the submission to God's love by persons and kingdom-oriented communities. Personal conversion is to be supplemented by addressing complexity and injustice in our world; much flexibility is needed to combat evils.

26. Cosmopolis, like other objects of human intelligence, is an X, "what is to be known when one understands. Like every other X, it possesses some known properties and aspects that lead to its fuller determination" (*Insight*, 263).

27. Abbott, *Documents of Vatican II*, 228; emphasis added.

28. Featherstone, "Cosmopolis," 2. In *Notion of Cosmopolis*, Onyango Oduke argues that cosmopolis, grounded in authentic subjectivity and critical-historical consciousness, is a nonpartisan fact that transcends factionalism. Its critique of culture functions as a creative humanistic framework to undo societal degeneration and decline.

too impalpable to be forced."[29] But it does require interactions between communities and persons to meld a process of unity within diversity. This book seeks to promote cosmopolis inspired by a value-laden intensity based on kingdom priorities.

3 Addressing Future Issues in Light of Past and Present Realities

How can one address a foregone past or the future? Meaning[30] and history connect us to the past and help us anticipate rather than predict future events. Lonergan adapts Augustine's view that meaning can point to the past, the present, and the future. The relation of meaning and time is a developing one. Meaning implies human consciousness which is or should be self-corrective. Key to this is what philosophers call dialectic. There is no past without reference to both present and future, nor a present without the past and the future, nor a future disconnected from past and present events. Meaning is dialectical[31] because it can help us relate the present to both the past and the future.[32] In this book, we relate Lonergan's notions of cosmopolis to the kingdom-of-God ideals preached by Jesus. In so doing, we seek to build transformative bridges between meaning[33] and the good of humanity.

All knowledge involves meaning, temporality, and human development. Because "development occurs principally in the field of meaning, the development of man is principally the development of meaning" which

---

29. Lonergan, *Insight*, 263.

30. Lonergan's interest in meaning started in *Verbum*. When sent to Rome, he had to deal with European students immersed in continental philosophy. "I had to talk meaningfully to them, and it involved getting a hold of the whole movement of the *Geisteswissenschaften* . . . It's, of course, something that stretches one." He links that to his notion of a moving viewpoint ("Interview with Fr. Bernard Lonergan," 220).

31. Dialectic comes from Greek *dialektik*—prefix *dia*, (across, between, through) and the verb *legein* (to say).

32. Lonergan writes of the *spirit of darkness that acting out of bias*, would "justify" its bias by resorting to ideology, using power to get its way. As a result, people "sink into apathy and despair" ("Moral Theology," 305–6). We evaluate how cosmopolis can overcome the existential gaps of conflicting horizons afflicting biased thought.

33 For Lonergan, in *Philosophy of God*, 197, one must form notions about language so as to attain the tools and models giving you access to "the empirical side of the study. There's an intelligibility that can be reached that way." One does not ignore social science, but one sets up "a heuristic structure within which specialists in different fields can construct models that will help people enter into mentalities quite different from their own. Simple description does not suffice." One must use fundamental tools that account for differences in language. One can "start from the empirical and move up to it." This moves you from mere speculation to cognitional theory.

implies time and history.[34] Some approach time as a mere mechanical succession of events. For the ancient Greeks, "social and natural regularities alike were aspects of the same overall *cosmos + polis*."[35] Augustine revised the notion of time: "In the soul, there are three aspects of time. The present considering the past is the memory, the present considering the present is immediate awareness, the present considering the future is expectation."[36] Lonergan refashions and integrates Augustine's view so as to effectively apply it to today's complexities in view of the future:

> Words denote not only what is present but also what is absent, not only what is near but also what is far, not only the past but also the future, not only the factual but also the possible, the ideal . . . for which we keep on striving though we never attain. So, we come to live, not as the infant in a world of immediate experience, but in a far vaster world brought to us through the memories of other men, through the common sense of the community through the investigations of scientists, through the experience of saints, through the meditations of philosophers.[37]

Time and meaning do affect human communities. One can learn from communities which no longer exist. If time and meaning can refer to the past, the present, and the future, so can a community—given the fact that meaning constitutes community. In Africa's cult of ancestors, for instance, "The family is made up of both the living members and the ancestors. The ancestors are still present, watching over the household and the property of the family. . . . It is essential that the living be on good terms with the ancestors."[38] One can also be a member of a community in its future state inasmuch as one helps protect it against rationalized abuses or the creation of myths. This is related to Lonergan's view of cosmopolis *as* community, wherein all collaborate. For Lonergan, cosmopolis, community, and the kingdom of God are complementary realities impinging on the present.

---

34. Lonergan, "Time and Meaning," 94.

35. Toulmin, *Cosmopolis*, 38. We appeal to cosmopolis as a path to kingdom of God values. Mark Miller notes that on the cross, Jesus transforms "the consequences of sin into a twofold communication to humanity of a perfect human and divine (1) knowledge and love for humanity and (2) knowledge and condemnation of sin and evil" (*Why the Passion?* 5). Humans are invited into a twofold human response: the repentance of sin and a love for God and all things.

36. Augustine, *Confessions of St. Augustine*, XI:26.

37. Lonergan, *Lonergan Reader*, 388.

38. Ige, "Cult of Ancestors," 27.

4 Lonergan's Method as Fostering the Kingdom of God

This book cannot address in all its depth and breadth the full dynamism of the knowing process and of spirituality as explored in Lonergan's writings. It does aim to honor Jesus' warning that it is not they who say "Lord, Lord who will enter the kingdom of God but those who do the Lord's will" (Matt 7:21). The Gospels take us on a journey with Jesus—from the announcement of his birth to his ascension. The journey includes Peter's testimony when to Jesus' question "Who do you say I am?," he answers "You are the Messiah" (Matt 16:16). Jesus trained his disciples to preach the good news as they journeyed with him during the three years of his public ministry. The unexpected death of Jesus on a cross eventually led his disciples to establish Christian communities in the Middle East. Our book focuses on loving, caring communities and on a dialectic that can help Christians respond to today's vast needs by living modestly and helping the afflicted. It seeks to show that Lonergan is an effective harbinger of both Christian and universal human values. Mirroring the intensity of Jesus' preaching, Lonergan speaks to our hearts; he motivates us toward reconciliation and community-building. Paul Kidder, drawing from Lonergan, notes that a community always exists in a complex of tensions.

> For every choice that any individual makes, there is the option of promoting the values of the larger community or of merely serving oneself. . . . Conversely, community decisions can violate the rights of individuals. Every choice involves limited knowledge and limited understanding of the issues at stake, of implications of one's thoughts and actions. Every community's history is shaped as much by failed choices and bad deeds as by the realization of good: every society is structured in some measure by incomprehensible social surds which, for all of their absurdity, nonetheless hold sway over common sense and common practice.[39]

Our Lonergan-inspired journey is one of solidarity with Jesus. We shall ask whether, historically, Christians have lived or failed to live the good news. Rooted in history and directed toward a peaceful future based on

---

39. Kidder, "Hermeneutic," 1193. Conflicts are fueled by inauthentic persons. For Lonergan, "The fruit of inauthenticity is decline" whereby conflicts arise within communities. The "conflicts may be overt or latent. . . . Inauthenticity is realized by any single act of inattention . . . irresponsibility" ("Dialectic of Authority," 8). In *Method in Theology*, he notes that a "rejection of the other may be passionate, and then the suggestion that openness is desirable will make one furious. But again, rejection may have the firmness of ice without any . . . show of feeling" (237).

mutual tolerance, our journey requires us to contrast the priorities of Jesus' message with those of the world. Christian priorities are summarized in such gospel ideals as "Seek and you shall find" (Matt 7:7), or losing one's self so as to find one's self (Matt 10:39).

JESUS CHALLENGES THE WORLD'S PRIORITIES WITH HIS KINGDOM OF GOD[40] PARABLES

Just as Max Scheler explored our social emotions such as love and hatred, and the values they are associated with, so this book aims to evaluate the types of sympathy needed in any self-transcendent, religious commitment. With Scheler, we hope to help promote fellow-feeling as a "primary source of our knowledge of one another."[41] Sadly, many Christians *fail* to live gospel priorities, to love neighbor as one's self. Rooted in history and directed toward a future based on mutual tolerance, we set on a journey requiring us to contrast the priorities of the good news of Jesus' gospel with those of the world. Lonergan explored human understanding in *Insight*—the complexities of which we shall try to simplify. We do want to study Lonergan's work so as to evaluate how people of common sense can help bring about the kingdom of God.[42] As Jesus reached out to the despised Samaritans of his day, so *Bringing Lonergan Down to Earth* would foster believers' outreach

---

40. As opposed to Hans Jonas's "heuristics of fear," Patrick Nullens and Ronald Michener's *Matrix* seeks to revitalize Christian ethics through an integrative approach. Their effort may be compared to our kingdom strategy as heuristic structure, and to John Fuellenbach's view that Jesus "raised the phrase the Kingdom of God to a level of a heuristic scheme for understanding God's purpose in human affairs" (*The Kingdom*, 25). Our book seeks with Lonergan to help implement such a heuristic of renewal by building bridges among people of good will.

41. McGill, "Sympathy," 75. Lonergan, going beyond Aristotle, held that achieving the good is itself a good. He adopted Scheler's notion of emotional intentionality which leads to values, but not Scheler's view on the status of values. Lonergan places values on the fourth level of intentional consciousness (*Method*, 31). Scheler illustrates his notion of sympathy: "Two parents stand beside the dead body of a beloved child. They feel in common the 'same' sorrow, the 'same' anguish. It is not that A feels this sorrow and B feels it also, and moreover that both know they are feeling it. No. It is a feeling-in-common. . . . The sorrow, as value-content and the grief, as characterizing the functional relation thereto, are here one and identical." Scheler, *Sympathy*, cited by van Hooft, "Scheler," 18.

42. Exploration 7 touches on Lonergan's economics which helps lay a basis for an economy that does not primarily focus on profit but rather on sensible, equitable forms of production and of the distribution of goods. The Vatican's document "Considerations" decries the myopic egoism of markets. Lonergan suggests viable ways to offset that.

to today's many victims of injustice—despite personal failings or mistaken life priorities. For this purpose, it may be well to recall a few texts from St. Matthew touching on Jesus' core teachings:

Matt 5:9: "Blessed are the peacemakers, for they will be called the children of God."

Matt 13:24: The kingdom of God is like a man who "sowed good seed in his field." But when he was asleep "an enemy came and sowed weeds among the wheat and went away." In Matthew 13:21, Jesus tells us that the seed sowed in our hearts must sink deeply and take root. Seeds sown in good soil refers to those who have understood the message of Jesus, helping them bear much fruit.

Matt 13:33: "The kingdom of God is like a yeast that a woman took and hid in three measures of flour, till it was all leavened." Lonergan's lifework promoting God's kingdom is like a yeast. If yeast is a microscopic, one-celled organism that produces carbohydrates causing a bread to rise, in this book we treat Lonergan's work as a leavening agent that promotes values conducive to the good of all.

Matt 13:44–45: "The kingdom of heaven is like treasure hidden in a field. When a man found it, he hid it again, and then in his joy went and sold all he had and bought that field. Again, the kingdom of heaven is like a merchant looking for fine pearls."[43] Having found one pearl of great price, he went and sold all that he had, and bought it. The parable of the precious pearl helps us express our deepest expectations and even to break through the thick layer of our emotions such as joy, anger, hate, and sentiments "so as to send us back to the present, the daily alternation of the structures of daily lives, to open our hearts to that treasure hidden in the field, to organize the scope of our relationships."[44]

In Matthew 13:41, Jesus speaks of the Son of Man sending out his angels to "gather up out of his kingdom all those who cause people to sin and all others who do evil things." Christians must share their lives with those who are not yet of the kingdom. Jesus uses the image of the kingdom to stress that which humans cannot achieve without God. Jesus asks his disciples whether they have understood his teaching in the hope that they

---

43. St. Matthew speaks of the kingdom of heaven and the kingdom of God interchangeably. In Matthew 19:23–24, for example, when speaking to a rich young man, Christ uses both "kingdom of heaven" and "kingdom of God." Jesus, then says to his disciples, "I tell you the truth, it is hard for a rich man to enter the kingdom of heaven" (Matt 19:23). In the very next verse, Christ proclaims, "Again I tell you, it is easier for a camel to go through the eye of a needle than for a rich man to enter the kingdom of God." Jesus makes no distinction between the two terms. He considers them synonymous. See https://www.gotquestions.org/kingdom-heaven-God.html.

44. Von Kirchbach, "Kingdom of God," 1.

will truly fathom the meaning of his passion and death. In like manner, being a Christian means that one is called to be faithful rather than to fall into temptation. With Ricoeur, we hold that Jesus' parables of the kingdom apply on two levels: *interpreting* them before *committing* one's self to the kingdom of God on personal or ecclesial levels.[45] The Gospels' teaching on the kingdom should inspire believers to live in such a way that they will be transformed on both personal and community levels. In Mark 12:34, Jesus tells a scribe, who had admitted that God's commandment of love is more important than offering sacrifices, that he is "not far from the kingdom of God." Jesus sought to gather God's people so that they might love God, community, and neighbor from the heart.

Contrasting Gospel Priorities with those of the Worldly-Minded

In 1980, Pope John Paul II, commenting on the Sermon on the Mount, refers to Scheler's ethics and its appeal to our hearts. For the pope, Matthew 5:27–28 introduces us to the wider context of Jesus' global teaching. Jesus "fundamentally revises the way we should understand and carry out the moral law."[46] The old covenant refers to such commandments of the Decalogue as the fifth, "You shall not kill" (Matt 5:21–26); the sixth, "You shall not commit adultery" (Matt 5:27–32). The pope continues:

> It is significant that at the end of this passage there also appears the question of the "certificate of divorce" (Matt 5:31–32). Significant, above all, are the words that precede these articles . . . in which Jesus declares: "Think not that I have come to abolish the law and the prophets; I have come not to abolish them but to fulfill them."[47]

The pope notes that Jesus is here explaining the necessity of fulfilling "the law in order to realize the kingdom of God. Whoever observes these commandments and teaches them shall be called great in the kingdom of heaven" (Matt 5: 19). John Paul II adds that fulfilling the law fundamentally conditions this kingdom both in the area of justice in general and in observing individual commandments. "Unless your righteousness exceeds that of the scribes and Pharisees, you will never enter the kingdom of heaven" (Matt 5:20). Jesus condemns the scribes and Pharisees' legal compromises

---

45. Ricoeur, *Essays on Biblical Interpretation*, 182.
46. John Paul II, "Christ Appeals to Man's Heart," 2.
47. John Paul II, "Christ Appeals to Man's Heart," 2. "We find ourselves in this way at . . . the interior form of human morality."

as a "hardness of heart" (Matt 19:8) that distorts the law. Observing the letter of a law while ignoring its inner core is what disturbed Jesus. His intensity as to this issue is clear when he declares that "Everyone who looks at a woman lustfully has already committed adultery with her in his heart" (Matt 5:27–28). Over and over again, Jesus appeals to the interior man. We should focus on the depth of the evangelical ethos and on the true value of the individual person as the needed foundation of Christian communal life today.

In our age of unparalleled numbers of displaced persons, joining Jesus in establishing the justice of God's kingdom is a key to spiritually renewing mankind. Lonergan's lifelong commitment to Christian values reflects Jesus' commitment to God's justice. Jesus repeatedly taught us that his Father is a merciful God who welcomes back sinners,[48] but rebukes the self-centered. Jesus denounced the rigor of the Pharisees which prevented their acceptance of Jesus' preaching on the kingdom.[49] In this book, we emphasize an affective conversion of the heart needed to foster communal conversions.[50] We argue with Lonergan and others that present generations must encounter the past so as to save the future.

In Luke 4:3, Jesus says, "To other cities also I must preach the kingdom of God: for I am sent for this purpose." In his short public life, Jesus taught the good news. Jesus was sent to unite all the faithful in the kingdom. In Luke 10:9, Jesus plainly says that the kingdom is already present as evident in the good deeds he and his disciples perform. In Luke 17:20, he cautions his hearers not to expect any other visible manifestation of the kingdom.[51] When this caution is combined with John 18:36 (where Jesus declares that his kingdom "is not from here") and with other scripture passages that point "to the establishment of God's Kingdom with power at Christ's return, we

---

48. McFarland, "Neighbor?" The parable of the Good Samaritan can serve as a context of contemporary debates over the nature of personhood. Jesus there provides both the model and the source of our own personhood.

49. McKenzie, *Dictionary of the Bible*, 481.

50. A polarized world needs a method that can bridge our differences. This requires collaboration and viable cooperative structures not yet in place—but which GEM's integrative ability does offer. GEM keeps us from self-centeredness in favor of other-centered, spiritual ends as we shall try to show in Part III on interfaith encounters.

51. In Luke 17:21, when Jesus is asked when would the kingdom of God come, he replies that it is not something people will be able to see. Strikingly, he adds: "Neither shall they say, 'Lo here!' or, 'Lo there!' for, behold, the kingdom of God is within you." We find here a timeless, universal teaching emulated in every great religious, spiritual, and wisdom tradition, namely that life's ultimate truth—its ultimate treasure—lies within us.

realize that it is both a present and a future reality."[52] The kingdom is at present mainly a spiritual reality, not yet fully manifested on earth. When preaching the Kingdom, Jesus and his apostles were inviting people to become part of that spiritual Kingdom focused on a radical renewal. It is for the "spiritual minded."[53] This still applies in our digitalized age. The kingdom's agents—now personified in the church of the faithful—seek to *radically renew* the earth by energizing the kingdom's spiritual citizenry.

The Roles of Kingdom-Oriented Communities that We Emphasize and Foster

With Jesus, Lonergan advocates kingdom ideals in the face of conflicts. How can communities best deal with conflicts? This book's twelve explorations examine philosophical views on this theme, but we note here that for Lonergan, "The fruit of inauthenticity is decline"[54] provoked by overt and latent conflicts. Ethical alienation tempts persons to sometimes act in irresponsible ways. The basic forms of ideology seek to justify "such alienation. From these basic forms, all others can be derived."[55] For Lonergan, "As alienation and ideology are destructive of community, so self-sacrificing, Christian love *reconciles* alienated man to his true being, and undoes the mischief initiated by alienation and consolidated by ideology."[56] How realistically counter corrosive power politics in our troubled world?

---

52. The *New International Version* (NIV), *Barnes' Notes*, *Tyndale New Testament Commentary*, *Expositor's Bible Commentary*, *The New International Biblical Commentary*, and *The Interpreter's Bible* all tend to agree that Jesus' primary mission was to renew God's kingdom on earth.

53. Ritenbaugh, "Bible Verses," para. 7. He stresses that it is those who are poor in spirit who will enter the kingdom of God. This implies spiritual qualities of being poor in one's relationship with Jesus.

54. Lonergan, "Dialectic of Authority," 9.

55. Lonergan, *Method in Theology*, 55. Not being attentive, intelligent, reasonable, responsible are the basic forms of alienation.

56. Lonergan, *Method in Theology*, 364; our emphasis. "While the ideal basis of society is community, while society does not survive without a large measure of community, it remains that community is imperfect. . . . To ignorance and incompetence there are added alienation and ideology" (360). We appeal to those of good will. All too many feel frustrated and overwhelmed by the cacophony of self-dealing politicians. Kingdom-oriented communities are called to save the sheep from the wolves.

LIMITS IMPOSED BY IDEOLOGICAL, MACHIAVELLIAN POWER POLITICS

The Hope a Blaise Pascal Brings to Our Hearts and Reason

Our hope that people today can live kingdom values is severely limited by the realities of self-serving power politics. Long gone are the days when politics was conducted in benign, face-to-face relationships. We now live in a quasi-nihilist culture that fosters selfishness. Machiavelli's *The Prince* emboldens political leaders to disregard morality, and yet a century after Machiavelli, the Christian genius Blaise Pascal explored the heart and its reasons. For Lonergan, the heart's reasons are "feelings that are intentional responses to values" felt by persons "in the dynamic state of being in love."[57] He recalls that such responses include the *absolute* aspect of recognizing values and the relative aspect of preferring one value over another. One discerns value through judgments of value. Faith is a type of knowledge a person may experience when God's love floods one's heart.

To our apprehension of vital, social, cultural, and personal values, faith adds an apprehension of transcendent value leading "towards the mystery of love and awe."[58] William Johnston speaks to the mystic's "eye of love."[59] How may we relate an eye of loving faith to today's realities? Since faith and progress have a common root in man's cognitional and moral self-transcendence, to promote either is to promote the other indirectly. In this aspect also, Pascal is exemplary. With his role in the discovery of probability theory,[60] he solved the problem of bringing the superficial lawlessness of pure chance under the domination of order and regularity. Today, we can use the theory of probability to rationally explain things and events that had before been attributed to magic and mysticism.[61]

In the face of the complexities of life today and the forms of alienation they entail, we advocate the creation of a coalition of loving persons who are dedicated to overcoming alienation. Karen Armstrong has shown that in our technological age fundamentalism is a powerful force in every major

---

57. Lonergan, *Method in Theology*, 115.

58. Lonergan, *Method in Theology*, 115.

59. Johnston understands "mystical theology as reflection on mystical experience" (*Inner Eye of Love*, 43). We reflect on mystical experiences in the three world religions as an *interfaith mysticism*, uniting people in heart and mind.

60. Fermat and Pascal created probability theory which has influenced a wide variety of areas of studies requiring the quantitative analysis of large sets of data such as in statistics, finance, insurance, science, and philosophy.

61. See Apostol, *Calculus*, Vol. 2.

world religion. Her approach to compassion[62] helps reinforce this book's optimistic reliance on loving hearts and communities in a secularized world. In Part III, we shall explore the foundations Lonergan laid for living spiritually and ethically in our times. These foundations provide a key to identify the links that can viably integrate liberation theology's method. Such links are parallel to what is needed in authentic community-building.[63] Before turning to these topics in Part III, we examine in Part II the roles of religious and civil communities in our world. Because Lonergan's method has found and applied some of the missing links between science, daily life, religion, and spirituality, it can help us rebuild the world anew, as it were. It can do so because it invites each person—whether they are a believer in one of the world religions or an atheist—to radically revise his/her life while addressing societal problems.

Machiavelli and Descartes almost "destroyed" the ethical-spiritual links between morality, reason, and government,[64] but Pascal and Lonergan

---

62. Armstrong, *Twelve Steps*. Every great religious and spiritual tradition teaches that life's ultimate truth lies within us. Jesus urges "Seek ye first the kingdom of God and His righteousness and all shall be added unto you" (Matt 6:33). This inner treasure of life has had many names. Plato refers to it as the Good and the Beautiful, Aristotle as Being, Plotinus as the Infinite, Ralph Waldo Emerson as the Oversoul. In Taoism it is called the *Tao*, in Judaism *Ein Sof*. One may ask whether Islam's ideal for unity (allowing no separation between faith and cultural norms) is rooted in Islam's failure to study the Koran critically. Some argue that the West's separating church and state has led Christians to silo their belief/actions to the extent that so-called religious politicians say and do things that are at odds with the gospel. Islam has tended to the other extreme. Muslims and Christians should better live out their ideals. Lonergan's notions of authenticity and self-appropriation are basic medicine for religious contradictions.

63. Figueroa-Villarreal, "Gustavo Gutierrez's Understanding," 49. GEM has found and applied some of the missing links between science, daily life, religion, and spirituality. The links can help us rebuild the world anew, as it were, because it invites each person—whether a believer in one of the world religions or an atheist—to radically revise one's life while addressing societal problems. This requires sound communities able to forge the links of solidarity between individuals and governments. For example, one must not falsify Christianity with privatized forms of feel-good Christian escapisms which would shield us from social responsibilities. It is true that Christian mercy prods many churches to cater to disoriented persons so as to comfort them, but this catering is not to be *the* norm, but rather *a* step to spiritual growth. Social ethics is one key needed to adequately share in Jesus' kingdom (Mark 1:14). See Raymaker, "Theory-Praxis of Social Ethics," on a social ethics aiming to retrieve and apply relevant value-judgments links.

64. For Thomas McPartland, Lonergan and Voegelin both viewed "the two leading political movements of the twentieth century, liberalism and totalitarianism in its various guises, in a very dim light, seeing liberalism as, at best, superficial, and totalitarianism as diabolical" ("Lonergan and Voegelin," 1). Lonergan spent much of his life trying to work out a philosophy of history opposing both liberal social engineering and totalitarian practicality. See also, Exploration 12.

help us reestablish the links. In Part II, we turn to identify the "GEM links" which 1) can be personally appropriated by conscientious persons so that, 2) working together in responsible communities, they can jointly apply such links as needed. Jesus' emphasis on the kingdom is one example of what is needed to build responsible communities today. In our view, Lonergan's cosmopolis is very much influenced by Jesus' focus on the kingdom. It is part of Lonergan's genius that his notions of cosmopolis and community on the one hand, and of interfaith, interdisciplinary issues in our multicultural world on the other, reinforce one another in retrieving the links to spirituality and ethics that Machiavelli, Descartes and their followers nearly destroyed.

PART II

The Roles of Persons in Communities, Cosmopolis,[1] and the Kingdom of God

Toward Making this World a Better Place in which to Live and Share

---

1. Dennis Gunn comments: "For Lonergan, authentic cosmopolitanism does not impose a universal, totalizing metanarrative. Rather, it embraces the particularity of one's own cultural, religious, and intellectual traditions, while remaining radically open to dialogue with the other. By doing so, education for cosmopolis fosters both authentic appropriation and reflective critique of one's own traditions, as well as an appreciation for the authenticity of others. Teaching for cosmopolis is an invitation to dialogue which promotes mutual understanding, mutual respect, and mutual interdependence in a globalized world" ("Teaching for Cosmopolis," 1).

2

Meaning and the Human Good as Constitutive of Human Communities

THIS BOOK EXPLORES LONERGAN's community-based transformative potential.[1] It explores the roles of loving hearts in such an endeavor. Suffering, joy, or a leap of empathy can, at times, help transport us into the soul and heart of another person. Where are the communities that are willing and able to engage in leaps of transformative empathy in our troubled world?[2] This is a question we raised in Part I when we appealed to Jesus' beatitudes. Academia often obscures ways for integrating the ways of heart and mind. Lonergan's groundbreaking metaphysics and ethics, if properly understood and acted upon, can help spiritual activists lead the way to community transformations. In Part III, we shall delve further into how GEM foundations can help integrate the hopes and aspirations of people of good will in mutually complementary ways. GEM, foundationally, deploys its eight functional specialties, but in practice, GEM scholars have not yet succeeded

---

1. This potential is well assessed in McCarthy, *Authenticity*, 179. Moral philosophy requires "a normative account of our troubled and uneven moral development and frank recognition of the diverse moral sources on which that development actually depends. . . . It also requires an equally frank recognition of the sources of moral impotence and decline: dramatic, egoistic, group and general bias," as well as "humility and candor."

2. Part of the solution would be to *integrate diversity* as summarized by So-Young Kang: "It starts with understanding and recognizing that everyone is unique, with a different set of strengths, capabilities and experiences. Integrating diversity is about . . . creating environments where you can bring out the best so that when you work together" ("Why Integrate Diversity?" 1), allowing us to expand our horizons and push the boundaries.

in fully integrating GEM's cooperative potential based on the complementary aspects of mind, heart, and spirit. With the aim of helping the Lonergan community fulfill this potential, we proceed to explore a dialectic of community so as to prepare for the foundations Lonergan developed in *Method in Theology*. "Thy kingdom come"[3] remains our central focus.

Ideally, we humans can think and love in the dynamic ways Lonergan outlines in his work. In *Insight,* Lonergan explains how we know through our three basic, interrelated operations of attending, understanding, and judging. Through these operations, persons constitute themselves and interact with one another. Human communities are a pervasive, yet often contested reality[4] which should not be taken for granted. Here in Part II, which focuses on ways to make our world a better place in which to live, we turn to explore some of the important roles communities play or should play in the world. We begin by asking with Lonergan a series of questions as to how our lives, ideas, and ideals can affect the ways humans interact with one another[5] for "better or for worse."

---

3. "Thy kingdom come," as an earnest plea, coincides with our aim to bring Lonergan down to earth and into our hearts. Chapter 2 prepares a ground for Part III's investigation of interfaith inculturation insights into mysticism.

4. Intrinsically linked with the notion of human community is the notion of moral duties. For Lonergan, community places on our shoulders moral tasks based on our common experiencing, understanding, and judging. Our moral duties spring from reflection. Community, far from undercutting freedom, communally fosters it. (*Insight,* 624).

5. Our relationship to God is to be sought in faithful questioning. Lonergan speaks to our hearts, prodding us to commit ourselves to ethical, spiritual interventions in the sociopolitical problems facing us. Such interventions can be rooted in the authenticity common to Buddhist, Christian, Muslim, and secularist traditions. As a bridge, GEM lends itself to the see-judge-act method of liberation theology. In "Redeeming the Academy," Charles Tackney argues that while "grace cannot be empirically assessed," if you posit the prospect for its manifest efficacy in persons and history, "then one can find an empirical model to investigate its effects, insofar as humans respond to the invitation" (3). The "standards of grace" criteria are accessible from religious/spirituality teachings and theological investigation as mediated in cultures. Religious traditions help us assess our innate capacity to be responsive to the invitation of Providence. These include the Aristotelian-Thomistic obediential potency, *fitrah* (the primordial human nature of of Islam, realizing *genjokoan* (actualizing the real) of Japanese Zen, as well as Lonergan's "authenticity" (4).

SOME INTERACTIONS BETWEEN ACTUAL REALITIES AND KINGDOM-OF-GOD IDEALS AS LIVED AND REFLECTED IN LONERGAN'S OWN LIFE

Lonergan, born in 1904, grew up in heart-rending times. Early in life, he was much influenced by Pope Leo XIII's plea of making "all things new," a phrase that was to guide his own life. In the nineteenth century, Christianity had suffered massive losses in Europe when much of the industrial working class left the church in response to the *Communist Manifesto* (1848). At the threshold of the twentieth century, no one could have predicted either the outbreak of the "Great War" or the heady economic speculation of the "Roaring Twenties" which led to the Great Depression (1929). But having seen the writing on the wall, Leo XIII had responded (1891) to social injustices in *Rerum Novarum*—the charter of the Catholic Church's social doctrine. As for the young Lonergan, his mind and heart had been captured with justice issues[6] while studying at Heythrop College, London (1926–29), and during his three-year regency in Loyola College in Montreal. His *Essay on Circulation Analysis*—first sketched in 1944 and many times revised, was published several years later under a different title.[7] It has yet to capture the interest of mainline economists, but it does testify to Lonergan's interest in the theoretical and social problems facing humanity. We argue that the relevance of Lonergan's method will be enhanced to the extent it reaches into the hearts and minds of scholars and administrators who can make a difference.

Insight, toward which all Lonergan's "earlier studies lead and from which all his later ones follow"[8] laid foundations for us to understand ourselves. For Lonergan, if one thoroughly understands "what it is to understand, not only will you understand the broad lines of all there is to be understood but also you will possess a fixed base, an invariant pattern, opening upon all further development of understanding."[9] *Insight* helps a person heighten his/her own consciousness so as to bring to light one's "conscious

---

6. Lonergan took as his motto Pope Leo XIII's call for a "return to the sources of the great traditions of Aristotle, Augustine, and Aquinas, bringing them up to date so as to illuminate modern philosophical and theological issues."

7. Lonergan, *Macroeconomic Dynamics*. McShane, "Detoxing Lonergan Studies," February 14, 2018, para. 2, and February 17, 2018, para. 1, speak of the challenges dodged by theology in past centuries, of apophatic contemplation and of common sense arrogance. Lonergan early focused on what needs to be done to address said problems. He wanted to solve the problem of effective interference in societies through dedicated Christian communities among other strivings.

8. Campbell, "Insight and Understanding," 477.

9. Lonergan, *Insight*, 22.

and intentional operations and thereby leads to the answers to three basic, interrelated questions. What am I doing when I am knowing? Why is doing that knowing? What do I know when I do it?"[10] These questions pertain respectively to cognitional theory, epistemology, and metaphysics.[11]

Method is not to be imitated: it does offer a framework for collaborative creativity. It is

> A normative pattern of recurrent and related operations yielding cumulative and progressive results. There is method, then, where there are distinct operations, where each operation is related to the others, where the set of relations forms a pattern, where the pattern is described as the right way of doing the job, where operations in accord with the pattern may be repeated indefinitely, and where the fruits of such repetition are, not repetitious, but cumulative and progressive.[12]

Since this book prioritizes kingdom-of-God ideals, we stress that Lonergan nuanced his method as he moved from *Insight* to *Method*. His notion of dialectic in *Insight* is mostly philosophical—subtle and to the point. *Method* builds on *Insight*, but goes beyond it in the sense that in *Method*, the notion of dialectic is profoundly transformed. It is no longer a mere philosophical dialectic[13] of the mind but one that can open us to the wonders of foundations—foundations motivating the heart toward committing one's self to kingdom values (hopefully by way of a deep mystic awareness that all is holistically related).

---

10. Lonergan, *Insight*, 25.

11. Lonergan writes: "Questioning not only is about being but is being, being in its . . . luminosity, being in its openness to being, being that is realizing itself through inquiry to knowing that, through knowing, it may come to loving" ("Metaphysics as Horizon," 206). In principle, our book seeks to develop this loving horizon.

12. Lonergan, *Method in Theology*, 4.

13. "Beyond dialectic, there is dialogue. Dialectic describes concrete process in which intelligence and obtuseness, reasonableness and silliness, responsibility and sin, love and hatred commingle and conflict. But the very people that investigate the dialectic of history also are part of that dialectic and even in their investigating represent its contradictories. To their work, too, the dialectic is to be applied" (Lonergan, "Natural Right and Historical," 182).

TOWARD A DIALECTIC OF COMMUNITY-PROMOTING KINGDOM VALUES[14]

1 Philosophical Horizons in Search of Remedying Modern Reductionisms

From Socrates onward, philosophers have reflected on reductionism (reducing the other to sameness) and the opposite tendency that stresses differences. In fact, reductionism and its opposite have complementary aspects which are often overlooked. Instead of focusing on the parts composing a whole, Lonergan speaks of horizons: "A horizon is specified by two poles, one objective and the other subjective, with each pole conditioning the other."[15] Using such a horizon, we explore some of the relations affecting subjects, communities, and cultures. Modernity has placed reason, science, progress, and liberty on a pedestal. For Lonergan, modern man has created his states, sciences, philosophies, histories, and "literatures on the basis of absolute autonomy. There is human intelligence, human reasonableness, human responsibility, and that is all there is."[16] But modernity has proved to be ambivalent. Descartes is the "father of modernity" (see Exploration 3). After him, modernity became oppositional in tone. "Philosophies can straddle, as did Cartesian dualism, or choose one of the alternatives, as did rationalism and empiricism respectively, or reject both, as did Kantian criticism."[17] For Lonergan, opposed philosophies are not merely alternative logics, one being true, the other false. "The thesis and the antithesis have their ground in the concrete unity-of-tension"[18] and in the polymorphism

---

14. Pope Francis in "Rejoice and Be Glad" exhorts us to become holy by serving with mercy within communities. He exhorts us to be holy by skillfully and perseveringly laboring with integrity in the service of our fellow humans.

15. Lonergan, "Metaphysics as Horizon," 213. GEM horizons include moving us from self-seeking to self-giving, from mere immanence to self-transcendence by communally living out the implications of the kingdom, of cosmopolis.

16. Lonergan, "Existenz and Aggiornamento," 247. We might extend the proverb "a sound mind within a sound body," to "sound minds within sound bodies within sound, responsible communities" by applying the soundness of GEM's wisdom to it. GEM's wisdom becomes operative inasmuch as it is aware of the biases of evil, while still reaching out with love.

17. Lonergan, *Insight*, 560. Doubt was Descartes's starting point as indicated in the section "Of the Things of Which We May Doubt" in *Mediations on First Philosophy* (in Meditation I, page 17), where he writes that he was struck by the large number of falsehoods that he had accepted as a child. He began to realize that it was necessary to build a new foundation. Lonergan writes that Hume practiced the universal point "more successfully" than did Descartes (*Insight*, 436).

18. *Lonergan Reader*, 224. The etymologies of tension and intention both imply

of our consciousness. This leads to either basic positions or counterpositions in epistemology. In *De Anima*,[19] Aristotle opposed Plato's one-sided idealism.[20] In modern times, Hegel's absolute idealism sought to reconcile opposites. In the 1950s, postmodernists began to reject the grand accounts of modernists who had claimed that their views applied to everyone.[21] What has come to pass is that our lives are now pulled apart between the exponents of modernity who promise autonomy and those of postmodernity who reject the accuracy of this claim.[22]

2 The Transcendent God and the Realities of Human Evil[23]

In 1933, Dietrich Bonhoeffer, commenting on human weakness, wrote:

> Christianity stands or falls with its revolutionary protest against violence, arbitrariness, and pride of power, and with its plea for the weak. Christians are doing too little to make these points clear. . . . Christendom adjusts itself far too easily to the worship

---

being *stretched* out or a *stretching* toward. For Lonergan, "The existential gap consists in the fact that the reality of the subject lies beyond his own horizon" (*Phenomenology and Logic*, 281). Due to this, what we know and what we think we know differs—we are ever stretching out toward the new. After *Insight*, Lonergan evolved from faculty psychology to intentionality analysis and the development of functional specialties to help scholars-scientists mutually complement their views.

19. The *De Anima* is about soul as an inner principle, a constituent of life. See Lonergan, *Verbum*, 3.

20. Plato was himself reacting to a Parmenidean idealist reductionism which denied any or all differences.

21. "Postmodern" stems from Jean-Francois Lyotard, *The Postmodern Condition: A Report on Knowledge*. It rejects modernist metanarratives as to the autonomy of persons and a belief in progress among other things. (XXVI).

22. In "Postmodernism," Marsh writes of the "modernist" Lonergan "who draws the fire of postmodernism" for being oriented to universality and metaphysics. For Marsh, Lonergan helps us construct a compelling critique of postmodernism "while incorporating valid aspects of its project. . . . Modernism at its best is characterized by (an) orientation to reflexive, self-conscious understanding and critique. Postmodernism is an . . . insightful, profound attempt to undermine that project. In the grip of such a Ratio, being tends to be covered over and difference and individuality tend to be submerged. Western Ratio, in the eyes of postmodernists . . . is oriented toward an identity that excludes difference and an active, conceptualizing stance that inhibits receptivity to being" (149).

23. Ephesians 6:12: "For we do not wrestle against flesh and blood, but against the rulers, against the authorities, against the cosmic powers over this present darkness, against the spiritual forces of evil in the heavenly places."

of power. Christians should give more offense, shock the world far more, than they are doing now.[24]

Paul Ricoeur admired Bonhoeffer. In one essay, Ricoeur cites Bonhoeffer as an ally in his own project to fight against today's idols so as to relativize such masters of suspicion as Nietzsche and Freud. For Ricoeur, religious beliefs are "often subconsciously motivated by such forces as fear, desire . . . and the struggle for power."[25] In his *The Symbolism of Evil*, Ricoeur began to analyze the constitution of symbolic language by deciphering expression, language, and text.[26] In doing so, he found the horizon he later used to evaluate Freud's work. *Symbolism* retraces how the Old Testament prophets stressed the need for justice in human affairs. "Isaiah, in the lightning-like vision in the Temple (6:1–13), discovers another dimension of God, and so a new dimension of sin: after the God of Justice, . . . here is the God of sovereignty and majesty, the holy God."[27] Ricoeur asks, "how can thought be bound and free at the same time? How can the immediacy of the symbol and the mediation of thought be held together?" His reply is that symbols "rescue feeling and even fear from silence and confusion; they provide a language for avowal, for confession. . . . Only a hermeneutics can mediate symbols." This, in fact, leads to the dissolution of myths. The explanation of myths "is the necessary way to the restoration of the myth as symbol."[28] This book attempts a parallel assessment of Lonergan's realist-idealist evaluations of the roles of the heart[29] and of faith in establishing viable communities despite the many tensions in life.

---

24. Bonhoeffer, "Sermon on Second Corinthians 12:9," 402.

25. Ricoeur, "Critique of Religion," 263, as quoted by Brian Gregor, "Ricoeur"

26. Since we moderns cannot go back to a primitive *naivete*, with Lonergan we aim at a second *naivete*—in and through criticism. For more on "pseudo-metaphysical mythmaking" as unscientific, unfounded blind leaping, see Lonergan, *Insight*, 528.

27. Ricoeur, *Symbolism of Evil*, 57.

28. Ricoeur, *Symbolism of Evil*, 350.

29. By "heart" we mean with Lonergan "the subject on the fourth, existential level of intentional consciousness." Faith is the knowledge had when "the love of God floods our hearts," enabling one to apprehend transcendent value and actuating within one an "orientation towards the mystery of love and awe and . . . the truly good" (*Method in Theology*, 115). Analogously to Gabriel Marcel's distinction between problem and mystery, faith is an archetypal ground that enters as a realm of mystery in one's life. In the realm of faith, love precedes knowledge. One accepts God's loving initiative as grasped by faith. The eye of love can then embolden persons to act heroically in times of difficulty even in daily life. This mystical "eye" penetrates beneath the surface of life's sordid aspects.

3 Human Ambivalence Portrayed in Don Quixote and in Conrad's The Heart of Darkness

Recall Don Quixote's ideals at the beginning of modernity and how Joseph Conrad interpreted these ideals at the dawn of postmodernity. At the age of fifteen, Conrad, then known as Korzeniowski, was reprimanded by his tutor for being "an incorrigible, hopeless Don Quixote" just because he wanted to become a seaman.[30] Conrad's *The Heart of Darkness* centers around Marlow, an introspective riverboat captain, and his journey up the Congo River on his way to meet Kurtz, reputed to be a capable idealist. Marlow gradually realizes that Kurtz and his employers are brutal. The native inhabitants have been reduced to forced labor; they suffer terribly from overwork and ill treatment. The cruelty of the imperial enterprise contrasts sharply with the impassive and majestic jungle surrounding the Belgian settlements, making them appear to be tiny islands amidst a vast darkness. The ambiguity in the novel is that Marlow wants us to understand his own story while shielding himself from blame. Conrad is a seer who reveals and veils the truth. Our book seeks to penetrate into the human heart, to assess what might enable persons to build genuine communities despite such ambiguities as those which Conrad exposes. Lonergan's realist-idealism would touch our minds and hearts for, despite the evils colonialism brought to the Congo and other parts of Africa, devoted, prayerful missionaries did establish the church there.

Michel Foucault argued that Don Quixote's quest is to be dismissed as "madness" that forms "a boundary" outlining the beginnings of new relations whereby "the cruel reason of identities and differences make endless sport of signs and similitudes."[31] With Conrad, we look deeper into what Cervantes meant with his feckless hero, Don Quixote. In Cervantes's time, the Western model of capitalism had begun to displace the Catholic medieval synthesis represented intellectually by Aquinas, and spiritually by Europe's cathedrals. It is the rise of capitalism, focused on material wealth, that provokes Don Quixote's madness. Cervantes had anticipated what occurs when a reductionist mindset threatens values and ethics. Shakespeare and Cervantes both died in 1616; both men were aware that in their time the very principle of action had become "the splitting up of the social operations and of the private sense of life into specialized segments."[32] While King

---

30. Romero, "Quixote," 1. Tying his desire to become a sailor to the "knight" of La Mancha seems deliberate.

31. Foucault, *Order of Things*, 327.

32. McLuhan, *Gutenberg Galaxy*, 20.

Lear displays the madness and misery of the new Renaissance life of action, Cervantes and his Don Quixote are hypnotized by the segmentation of life. Like Shakespeare, Cervantes realized the seemingly futility of reacting against the new mentality's fragmentary biases. With Lonergan, we want to help offset modernity's biased fragmentations which often lead to mindless reductionisms in the sciences and in philosophy.

4 The Shortcomings and Failures of Reductionist Thinkers

Following Lonergan, we oppose reductionist shortcomings.[33] For Lonergan, there are permanently valid general schemes which set limits to interpreting historical epochs.[34] He defines dialectic as "a concrete unfolding of linked but opposed principles of change."[35] For Robert Doran, dialectic includes three distinct but related processes with analogous structures, namely the dialectics of the subject, of community, and of culture.[36] In our book, the dialectic of community plays a central role (Part II). This dialectic is related to Lonergan's inner dialectic of the dramatic subject. Both dialectics have to be related to the dialectic of culture. A dialectic of community focuses on human relationships, while the inner dialectic of the subject regards personal development. These two dialectics are linked "for the spontaneous, intersubjective individual strives to understand and wants to behave intel-

---

33. Lonergan Archives, 62200DTEL60 on his early remarks on topics he later took up in his post-*Insight* work.

34. Aiken, "Bernard Lonergan's Critique of Reductionism," 233.

35. Lonergan, *Insight*, 242.

36. Doran, *Theology and the Dialectics*, 144. For Lonergan, "The levels of consciousness are not only distinct but also related, and the relations are best expressed as instances of what Hegel named sublation," that is, of a lower element in discourse being retained, preserved, yet transcended and completed by a higher element. Human intelligence goes beyond human sensitivity, yet it cannot get along without sensitivity. Human judgment goes beyond sensitivity and intelligence yet cannot function except in conjunction with them. Human action finally, must in a similar fashion both presuppose and complete human sensitivity, intelligence, and judgment" (Lonergan, "Subject," 80). Michael Vertin writes that for Doran, a "careful phenomenological analysis brings to light a series of utterly basic and pre-voluntary structural tensions in the concrete life processes of human individuals in community. These tensions may be characterized generically as the resultants of two contrasting human tendencies" (toward limitation and toward transcendence) ("Review of *Theology*," 160). At the level of the individual, at the level of a culture, and at the societal level, these structural tensions constitute occasions of life-shaping decisions, occasions of unavoidable choice among what in fact are alternative, basic personal, cultural, and social values. At each level there is the "'dialectical option' of living in such a way as to do justice to both poles of the tension, or of reinforcing only limitation, or transcendence" (Vertin, "Review of *Theology*," 161).

ligently; and inversely, intelligence would have nothing to put in order were there not the desires and fears,"[37] labors and satisfactions of individuals. "The dialectic of community is concerned with the interplay of more or less conscious intelligence and more or less conscious spontaneity in an aggregate of individuals, while the dialectic of the subject is concerned with the entry of neural demands into consciousness."[38] Such processes constitute the immanent intelligibility of the process of human history and its vast networks of subjects, cultures, and communities. Difference does not undercut unity; in fact, it presupposes it—unity underpins difference.[39] One must correctly understand distinctness-amid-relatedness (complementarity)—a recurrent focus in Lonergan. This principle of complementarity helps one find a surprising unity in his various works, even if these works differ in themes (e.g. his writings on theology, economics, or anthropology being informed as they are by his underlying historical and social concerns).

5 The Tensions and Biases Afflicting Many Communities

Why are communities so often mired in tension and conflict? In search of answers, we deploy two dialectics: one of community in Part II, and one of personal religious foundations in Part III. For Lonergan, "The person is not the primordial fact. It is within community" through intersubjective relations "lived within community, that there arises the differentiation of the individual person."[40] Communal *relations are the mold within which* a person can find one's self. But it is in our minds that Lonergan discerns "a transcendental method..., a basic pattern of operations employed in every cognitive enterprise."[41] The operations involved in doing so are linked—but are prone to ambivalent shadows and to biases:

37. Lonergan, *Insight*, 243. Problems may seem limitless, but GEM helps us find the patience to help reconcile diversity. It probes our innermost hearts, and community policies as these function within cultural frameworks.

38 Lonergan, *Insight*, 243. As to these two dialectics and the kingdom, we do face the dilemma that only a minority of Christians, such as a St. Francis and model Christians, fully commit themselves to kingdom priorities. That is why Lonergan asks us to launch on "a resolute... intervention in history" (Lonergan, *Phenomenology and Logic*, 306).

39. Here, one finds similarities to Husserl's thought. Husserl writes "The world does not exist as an entity, as an object, but exists with such uniqueness that the plural makes no sense when applied to it" (*Crisis*, 143).

40. Lonergan, "Relationship between Philosophy of God," 211.

41. Lonergan, *Method in Theology*, 4. It is a transcendental method, for the results envisaged are not confined categorically to a "particular field or subject but regard any result that could be intended by the completely open transcendental notions. Where

> We are brought to the profound disillusionment of modern man and to the focal point of his horror. He had hoped through knowledge to ensure a development that was always progress and never decline. He has discovered that the advance of human knowledge is ambivalent, that it places in man's hands stupendous power without necessarily adding proportionate wisdom and virtue, that the fact of advance and evidence of power are not guarantees of truth, that myth is the permanent alternative to mystery and mystery is what his hubris rejected.[42]

Postmodernists reject intrinsic values. Lonergan not only develops moral precepts based on his deep insights into intrinsic values, but he also links moral precepts to economic process:

> From economic theorists we have to demand, along with as many other types of analysis as they please, a new and specific type that reveals how moral precepts have both a basis in economic process and so an effective application to it. From moral theorists we have to demand, along with their other various forms of wisdom and prudence, specifically economic precepts that arise out of economic process itself and promote its proper functioning.[43]

While Lonergan relies on other thinkers, he often goes beyond them as he develops his unique ethical, philosophical, and theological projects. Far from being an exhaustive exploration, this book would bring Lonergan down to earth by focusing on persons and communities—and their biases. We hope that good, unbiased persons may help foster values consonant with God's kingdom on earth.

---

other methods aim at meeting the exigencies and exploiting the opportunities proper to particular fields, transcendental method (= GEM!) is concerned with meeting the exigencies and exploiting the opportunities presented by the mind itself. It is a concern that is both foundational and universally significant and relevant. . . . It is a matter of heightening one's consciousness by objectifying it, and that is something that each one, has to do in himself and for himself (14). *Method in Theology,* despite its title, is very much philosophically-oriented.

42. Lonergan, *Insight*, 572.
43. Lonergan, "Healing and Creating in History," 108.

VARIOUS KINDS OF COMMUNITY AND THE DEPLOYMENT OF COMMON MEANING

"Community," derived from the Latin word *communitas*, is made up of the preposition *cum* (with, together) and the noun *unitas* (unity). It means "a many turned into one without ceasing to be many." Lonergan links dialectic with community because the nature of community is ambivalent. It implies cooperation. Human community is a matter of a common field of experience, a common mode of understanding, a common measure of judgment, and a common consent. "Community is the possibility, the source, the ground of common meaning; and it is this common meaning that is the form and act that finds expression in family and polity, in the legal and economic system . . . , in literature, art and religion, philosophy, science and the writing of history. Still, community itself is not a necessity of nature but an achievement of man,"[44] based on the basic components of human consciousness—differentiated on the empirical, intellectual, and rational levels. Both in their personal and communal life, people rely on common sense.[45] They are subject to differentiations of meaning. Any community is composed of various individuals, each of whom is rooted in his/her own conscious intentionality. As conscious, each person intends goals. Presently we are considering what goals persons may have when they form a community, but it is also true that their goals may lead to sources of conflict among some individuals. To deal with such conflicts, a proper understanding of the meaning of meaning is needed. We cannot dichotomize community from a dialectic of meaning. A human community is involved, for example, in the practice of history and the sciences or of daily life. Various individuals form communities on the premise that diversity can be accommodated or reconciled. They hope that others want to pursue goals similar to theirs. Goals imply a set of values. Ideally, values, prior to being chosen, should be understood by a group of people with a common experience. For Lonergan,

---

44. Lonergan, "Natural Right," 170. Many Western communities today have failed to develop in young persons an awareness of their human intellectual-moral potential. This is a failure in education in that secularists and believers become alienated from one another as the former are cut off from the deeper insights found in religious practice.

45. "By common sense is meant a nucleus of habitual insights such that the addition of one or two more will bring one to the understanding of any of an open series of concrete situations. By that understanding one will grasp how to behave, what to say, how to say it, what to do, how to do it, in the currently emerging situation. Such a nucleus of insights is centered in the subject: it regards his world as related to him, as the field of his behavior, influence, action, as colored by his desires, hopes, fears, joys, sorrows" (Lonergan, *Method in Theology*, 71).

community is not just an aggregate of individuals, for that overlooks its formal constituent based on common meaning:

> Common meaning calls for a common field of experience and, when it is lacking, people get out of touch. It calls for common or complementary ways of understanding and, when they are lacking, people begin to misunderstand, to distrust, . . . to resort to violence. It calls for common judgments and, when they are lacking, people reside in different worlds. It calls for common values, goals, policies and, when they are lacking, people operate at cross-purposes.[46]

There are three kinds of human communities, all of which are achievements of common meaning. The first is primitive or intersubjective community. Being a "primitive community, its schemes of recurrence[47] are simple prolongations of pre-human attainment, too obvious to be discussed or criticized, too closely linked with more elementary processes to be distinguished sharply from them."[48] Its scope is to satisfy vital needs. "It precedes civilization and underpins it and remains when civilization disintegrates or decays. It corresponds to experience and desire. Its basis being spontaneous, it manifests itself as an elemental feeling of belonging together. Its nucleus is the family. Its expansion is the clan, the tribe, the nation."[49]

The second kind is civil community which arises when people begin to ask how conventions differ from nature. Practical intelligence develops structures such as economics and politics that would master men as well as nature. In primitive societies, one can identify the good simply with the object of desire; but in civil communities there arises a further component, which Lonergan names the good of order,[50] that is, a "complex product embracing and harmonizing material techniques, economic arrangements,

---

46. Lonergan, *Method in Theology*, 356. In *Violence*, Arcamore dialectically addresses key symbols of religiously motivated violence through Lonergan's insights. Too often, religion is viewed as causing violence rather than preventing it. We stress how Lonergan rediscovers some elusive links between religion and peacemaking. Religion must not be a tool of violence due to false beliefs. How can a common meaning of individuals and politicians prevent conflicts?

47. Mike Bretz writes: "Schemes of recurrence are conjoined dynamic activities where . . . each element generates the next action, which in turn generates the next, until the last dynamic regenerates the first one again, locking the whole scheme into long term stable equilibrium" ("Emergent Probability," 1).

48. Lonergan, *Insight*, 237.

49. Lonergan, "Role of a Catholic University," 115.

50. The three levels of the good correspond to the divisions in our knowing: experience, understanding, and judgment. The object of appetite is spontaneous, just as experience is given without any reason being supplied.

and political structures."[51] Civil community would satisfy vital needs by means of practical cooperation over the long term. While the discoveries of practical intelligence were at first an incidental addition to the spontaneous fabric of human living, they now tend to "penetrate and overwhelm its every aspect. For just as technology and capital formation interpose their schemes of recurrence between man and the rhythms of nature, so economics and politics are vast structures of interdependence invented by practical intelligence for the mastery not of nature but of man."[52]

The third kind is that of cultural community: "As the dialectic in the individual and in society reveals, man is a compound-in-tension of intelligence and intersubjectivity, and it is only through the parallel compound of a culture that his tendencies to aberration can be offset."[53] Culture is the set of meanings and values informing a way of life. "It may remain unchanged for ages. It may be in process of slow development or rapid dissolution."[54] A cultural community, based on a common set of meanings and values, "is the field of communication and the influence of artists, scientists, and philosophers. It is the bar of enlightened public opinion to which naked power can be driven to submit. It is the tribunal of history that may expose successful charlatans and may restore to honor the prophets stoned by their contemporaries."[55] Intersubjective community dialectically transitions into civil community which in turn dialectically passes over to cultural community. There is interdependence here because mere intersubjective spontaneity is not self-sufficient. There are practical imperatives that small communities cannot attend to. A family cannot build its own school, road, or supermarket. This points to the fact that man has practical needs

51. Lonergan, *Insight*, 238.

52. Lonergan, *Insight*, 238. Coulter writes that Reinhold Niebuhr's "Essay at Sixty Years" rests on the premise that "in theory democracy accounted for the spiritual and social nature of human existence. . . . Democracy could help realize our capacity for transcendence by unleashing the indeterminate variety of human creativity." This made it "potentially a permanently valid form of social and political organization." Niebuhr agreed with Maritain's view that our individualistic version of democracy "constructed by bourgeois civilization was . . . in the process of disintegration." Democracy must find a more adequate cultural basis that takes seriously the Christian doctrine of sin in the effort to balance the freedoms of individuals and of communities. "Human creativity and vitality will become destructive given human sinfulness." This is the background of Niebuhr's metaphors of children of darkness and children of light to two basic approaches to democratic life ("Children of Light," 1).

53. Lonergan, *Insight*, 261. He stresses that humans are quite conscious of underlying tensions: "Present desires and fears," present in all animals, can be intellectually integrated by us, but this involves much "tension" (497–98).

54. Lonergan, *Method in Theology*, xi.

55. Lonergan, "Role of a Catholic University," 109.

far beyond that of the intersubjective community. Whatever man makes of nature or of himself, it carries the mark of one's culture. Cultural community (cosmopolis) depends on civil community, for any culture has to be expressed one way or another through practical intelligence. All of these interactions (responding to persons' vital needs and promoting the good) are approached by Lonergan as a dynamic structure within our cognitional praxis.[56]

A Human Subject or Person as Conscious, Dynamic Structure

The notion and reality of community are linked to that of person. In *Insight*, Lonergan challenges his readers to come to know things as well as one's self. He has us ask what is happening when one comes to know? What constitutes one as a person? By person, he means a subject who in knowing is aware that he/she knows, wills, and chooses, who speaks and "in speaking is aware that he is speaking."[57] He focuses on the dynamic flow of consciousness in humans within the world—a flow which provides the horizon for one's knowing and being. A fundamental premise of his philosophy is that one should explore not only objects but also "consciousness itself"[58] as well as its energizing potential. Because our consciousness is intentional, we as persons are dynamic—never in a state of achieved perfection—but ever striving. Lonergan does not equate a subject with substance; he distinguishes them. The shift from substance to subject (or person) is pivotal to Lonergan's legacy.

---

56. Lonergan's method is that of a dynamic theory-praxis (knowing-doing) motivated by the pure desire to know. It is consonant with Inglehart's views in *The Silent Revolution*, which argues that beneath the frenzied activism of the 60s and the quiet of the 70s, a "silent revolution" occurred in the Western world which gradually but fundamentally changed political life. It led to two important changes: 1) a shift from an emphasis on material values and physical security toward a concern with the quality of life, and 2) an increase in the political skills of Western publics enabling them to play roles in making political decisions. In *Modernization*, Inglehart argues that economic development, cultural change, and political change go together in rather predictable patterns. Industrialization leads to related changes such as mass mobilization and diminishing differences in gender roles. Changes in worldviews reflect changes in the economic and political environment, but these take place with a generational time lag and lead to basic shifts in values, deemphasizing instrumental rationality.

57. Lonergan, "Consciousness and the Trinity," 125.

58. Finamore, "Centrality," 44. Authentic persons consciously develop their subjectivity as a unified striving.

A person is not a static substance; he/she is dynamically intelligent.[59] This realization was a turning point in Lonergan's life allowing him to explore "consciousness" and its relation to knowing.[60] For him, consciousness is a self-present flow; there is an awareness immanent in our cognitional acts. Lonergan distinguishes between act and content, "between seeing and color, hearing and sound, imagining and image, insight and idea. To affirm consciousness is to affirm that cognitional process is not merely a process of contents but also a succession of acts."[61] Lonergan rejects the classicist view of culture and its focus on substance rather than on concrete persons. Here we touch on a key point guiding this book: Lonergan renews our human ability to link our minds and hearts within communities. So often, in English, we speak of mind and heart. *Bringing Lonergan Down to Earth* seeks to ethically, communally, link the two and apply their complementarities to world problems, to interfaith challenges.

Lonergan stresses that "A man is a man whether he is awake or asleep, young or old, sane or crazy, sober or drunk, a genius or a moron, a saint or a sinner."[62] For those who view a person as being a "substance," those differences are merely "accidental." For them, human nature is something we "start with." On this view, "the man, the being, is just the substance, and the qualities are added on; they come to the substance."[63] But this is just half of the problem since a human being is a subject. By making the transition from substance to subject, Lonergan helps us understand why a change in

---

59. Lonergan, "Mathematical Logic," 137. Substance is "not what you see and feel, it is what you understand in what you see" and feel, that is, a concrete unity. "There is a concrete principle of unity-identity-wholeness that makes this set of phenomena one thing: the *causa essendi* of this being what it is, a man, or a horse, or a cat, or so on. Grasping that intelligible unity, not finding simply a term with respect to which my extroverted consciousness operates satisfactorily, is what is meant by substance." Lonergan concentrated on the subject, not substance.

60. Lonergan, *Verbum*, 3–11. Here one reads Lonergan's interpretations of the legacies of Augustine and Aquinas. He corrects a mistaken tradition within philosophy and theology which had spoken about our acts of human understanding in terms which largely derive from how we understand and speak about our acts of sensing. These acts possess an immediacy which tends not to belong to acts of understanding since our experience of self should tell us that acts of understanding do not usually occur with the immediacy of our acts of sensing. The introduction states: "In working out his concept of *verbum* Aquinas was engaged not merely in fitting an original Augustinian creation into an Aristotelian framework but also in attempting, however, remotely and implicitly, to fuse together what to us may seem so disparate: a phenomenology of the subject with a psychology of the soul" (vii).

61. Lonergan, *Insight*, 344–45.

62. Lonergan, "Existenz and Aggiornamento," 241.

63. Lonergan, "Existenz and Aggiornamento," 241.

accidents affects the whole man. The subject is a substance that *is present to itself as conscious*. Lonergan establishes a demarcation line between the study of substance or soul and the study of persons as *subjects*. The former involves notions such as essence and potencies: the latter involves the notion of consciousness and the operations of experiencing, understanding, judging, deciding-loving.

There is a world of difference between the two approaches.[64] For Lonergan, subjects as persons are intellectually open due to their desire to know. He focuses on persons as subjects because deep in our make-up, there is a dynamic openness, a desire to know. To explain his meaning, Lonergan speaks of three kinds of openness: "Openness as fact is the inner self, the self as ground of all higher aspiration. Openness as achievement is the self in its self-appropriation and self-affirmation. Openness as gift is the self-entering into personal relationship with God."[65] We all have an unrestricted drive to know, but this drive has to be developed both personally and communally. Development connotes achievement. One comes to know one's unrestricted drive to know through different activities. But because humans are prone to biases, a higher viewpoint on the level of being is needed to offset the negative effects of bias. This higher viewpoint on the level of being is a gift. We humans are dependent beings. "We do not know ourselves very well; we cannot chart the future; we cannot control our environment completely or the influences that work on us; we cannot explore our unconscious and preconscious mechanisms."[66] Since our control is only rough and approximate, we have to believe and trust, to risk and dare.

The notion of the subject is "foundational" in Lonergan's work—granted that it is an ambiguous, "difficult, recent, and primitive" topic.[67] For Lonergan, to speak "on being oneself, is to speak in public about what is private, intimate, more intimate perhaps than one has explicitly conceived. Such existential speaking cannot be tidily tucked away into a category: at once it is psychological, sociological, historical, philosophic, theological, religious, . . . for some, even mystical; but it is all of them because the person is all and involved in all."[68] The notion of the person as subject is, in fact, a very recent one. The turn to the subject as an explicit philosophical theme only began with the coming of modernity in the person of Descartes: "If one wishes to find out what a subject is, it is not enough to read ancient or medi-

---

64. Lonergan, "Subject," 73.
65. Lonergan, "Openness and Religious Experience," 201.
66. Lonergan, "Self-transcendence," 315.
67. Lonergan, "Christ as Subject," 173.
68. Lonergan, "Existenz and Aggiornamento," 240.

eval writers. They did not treat the matter explicitly. They did not work out systematically the notion of the subject."[69] While the notion of the subject is the invention of modern thinkers, it took Descartes (see Exploration 2) to treat it in earnest. Lonergan notes that there have been great philosophers from other epochs who treated the theme of human consciousness:

> Aristotle, St Augustine, St Thomas had an extraordinary grasp of the facts of consciousness. But I should not offer to prove this to people that have no grasp of the facts, no sense of history, and no inclination to transcend the merely verbal intelligence of computers.[70]

For Lonergan, the notion of the human subject is a radical one; it comes first in the order of reality. "It is primitive. It cannot be reached merely by combining other, better known concepts. It can be reached only by directing one's attention to the facts and to understanding them correctly."[71]

Positivists claim that theology and metaphysics are imperfect modes of knowledge that must be supplanted by knowledge based on natural phenomena as verified by the empirical sciences. They do not grant that there is a primitive rock on which everything else can be based.[72] But for Lonergan, there is such a rock: its precise character lies in the realization that any theory of our conscious and intentional operations is bound to be incomplete and needs further clarifications. The said rock is the subject in his/ her conscious, unobjectified attentiveness, intelligence, reasonableness, and responsibility manifested in the operations and in one's development. The expression of this awareness is modern. Lonergan subscribed to the Cartesian project to the extent that he asked Cartesian-like questions such as "Who is a man? Who is to be a man? The answer is 'I', 'we'. The first person supposes consciousness. "What has to be a man is not just any instance of rational animal. It is one that is awake. . . . Such awareness is consciousness, and that consciousness is not to be thought of as thinking about oneself.

---

69. Lonergan, "A Reply," 173. As to system-person relationships, one must insist, as have Lonergan and many writers on spirituality, that one needs a spiritual life to transform daily experience into revelatory moments.

70. Lonergan, "A Reply," 174.

71. Lonergan, "A Reply," 174.

72. Lonergan set out to correct many mistakes of philosophers thus bringing them down to the earth of their own empirically established experience—which is what self-appropriation is all about. A case can be made that the later Lonergan sublated his earlier notion of the mind by stressing that if one's heart does not influence the mind's workings then we run into problems. See Catherine King, *Finding the Mind*, 20, 35. We fully agree with her view.

One is conscious no matter what one is thinking about."[73] One is conscious when *doing* the thinking.

For Lonergan, the human subject and human consciousness are one and the same in that the human subject is "a substance that is present to itself, that is conscious."[74] Descartes had glimpsed this fact which Lonergan eventually spelled out at length by showing how the notions of the human subject and of consciousness point to the same reality. Descartes's glimpse is revealed in his *Meditations* where he stresses the fact that he is a thinking being who affirms, denies, wills, etc. "The fact that it is I who am doubting and understanding and willing is so evident that I see no way of making it any clearer."[75]

Lonergan grants this but specifies that it is one's consciousness that is the starting point. Our human consciousness involves the distinct activities of experiencing, understanding, judging, deciding, and loving. Lonergan categorizes these activities into two groups: our cognitive consciousness operating from below upwards and our affective consciousness operating from above downwards.[76] His entire opus develops various aspects of this *twin operational reality*, as summarized here in *Insight*:

> Man is in process. His existing lies in developing. His unrestricted desire to know heads him ever towards a known unknown. *His sensitivity matches the operator of his intellectual advance with a capacity and a need to respond to a further reality than meets the eye* and to grope his way towards it. Still, this basic, indeterminately directed dynamism has its ground in potency; it is without the settled assurance and efficacy of form; it tends to be shouldered out of the busy day, to make its force felt in the tranquility of darkness, in the solitude of loneliness, in the shattering upheavals of personal or social disaster.[77]

For Lonergan, our consciousness is constituted of different, interdependent operations:

---

73. Lonergan, *Topics in Education*, 81.
74. Lonergan, *Topics in Education*, 83.
75. Descartes, *Meditations on First Philosophy*, 28.
76. Lonergan, "Healing," 106. He approaches history focusing on possible ways of conversion. If ideologues distort historical-cultural processes, failing to understand that the infinite lurks within us, this book pivots between sensory content and the depths characterizing realist, converted persons. We rely on GEM's upper blade as a set of generalities demanding specific determination that comes from the lower blade of hypotheses and the revision of hypotheses (*Insight*, 600). The blades act as a heuristic feedback structure that can help transform our endeavors.
77. Lonergan, *Insight*, 648. Emphasis added.

As the many elementary objects are constructed into larger wholes, as the many operations are conjoined in a single compound knowing, so too the many levels of consciousness are just successive stages in the unfolding of a single thrust, the *eros* of the human spirit. To know the good, it must know the real; to know the real, it must know the true; to know the true, it must know the intelligible; to know the intelligible, it must attend to the data.[78]

The interdependent operations of our conscious intentionality ground *generalized* empirical method's structure.[79] Each operation is a vital component of the cognitional-volitional aspects of consciousness. In keeping with our general intent, we stress the intensity[80] with which Lonergan invites us to also wisely deal with the tensions that so often mar human living in an all-too-broken world.

The Cognitional-Volitional Levels of Human Consciousness in Generalized Empirical Method

Generalized empirical method (GEM) treats consciousness itself prior to addressing each of its individual activities. Consciousness is "an awareness of oneself or of some aspect of oneself. One is aware that the window is open, but conscious that one is about to sneeze."[81] The first three levels of consciousness constitute the cognitional aspect, while the fourth moral-religious level constitutes the volitional aspect. The cognitional levels pertain to knowledge and its operations of experiencing, understanding, judging. The first level refers to our attending to the data of experience in consciousness. On this empirical level, things are sensed, perceived, imagined, felt, spoken about. Consciousness is selective; when one talks about selection, a special interest is involved. "Things can be forced upon consciousness,

---

78. Lonergan, *Method in Theology*, 13. We call attention to the *"stretching" implied* in "tension" and one's intense response to tensions. For us, this stretching is to be related to persons' polyphonic stretching toward the intelligible, the good.

79. Lonergan, *Understanding and Being*, 348, defines structure as a set of entities related to one another. In knowing, the structured relations of empirical-intelligent-rational consciousness includes the intelligible and the unconditioned.

80. Such intensity is heightened in the fervent *eros* of the spirit as found in some mystics who stand outside self, in ecstasy. St. Paul opened himself to the indwelling of Christ. Charles Stang writes "Dionysius draws on the Platonic and Philonic taxonomies of madness and ecstasy," (*Apophasis and Pseudonymity in Dionysius*, 1) but corrects these views by appealing to St. Paul.

81. Lonergan, "Prolegomena to the Study," 55.

Meaning and the Human Good as Constitutive of Human Communities   45

and consciousness cannot run off in any direction whatever. But normally consciousness is a directed organization of selected data. And governing that direction and selection is what we care for, . . . aim at."[82] Not all impressions made upon our sense organs get into consciousness. "It is what you are interested in that gets into consciousness. Consciousness selects; it floats upon the series of demands for attention."[83] Our desire to know is not satisfied with experiencing alone: it takes us beyond experiencing to ask why, how, what for? On this second intellectual level, we inquire, come to understand, and express what we have understood, and we work out the implications of our expression. Our drive to understand is satisfied when understanding is reached but is dissatisfied "with every incomplete attainment and so it is the source of ever further questions."[84] Intelligence thus promotes us to the third, rational level which distinguishes truth from falsity by reflecting, marshalling the evidence, and passing judgment. Reasonableness "takes us beyond the answers of intelligence to ask whether the answers are true and whether what they mean really is so."[85] In knowing, there is a fuller

> unfolding of the same intention: for the desire to understand, once understanding is reached, becomes the desire to understand correctly. . . . The intention of intelligibility, once an intelligible is reached, becomes the intention of . . . the true and, through truth, of reality.[86]

In turn, one is led to a quest for self-transcending values. The call to self-transcendence is most important—a normative dictate of reason touching on human responsibility. "When being reasonable, we focus on knowing the truth, we put aside our feelings. We think with cool heads. But when, being responsible, we focus on action, our consciousness is flooded by feelings. We deliberate with warm hearts."[87] This involves the volitional aspect of consciousness. In Part I, we implicitly dwelled on this volitional aspect when we reflected on Jesus' call to follow him in establishing the kingdom of God.

Lonergan prods us to develop transformational structures in our lives; our book focuses on the intensity of genuine commitment to which Jesus calls us. In *Insight*, Lonergan explored our pure desire to know, but in

---

82. Lonergan, *Topics in Education*, 83.
83. Lonergan, *Topics in Education*, 84.
84. Lonergan, *Method in Theology*, 35.
85. Lonergan, *Method in Theology*, 11.
86. Lonergan, "Subject," 81.
87. Dunne, *Doing Better*, 51.

Method, he began to stress the role of the heart, of interiority expressed in genuine human feelings. If Lonergan's clarification of human knowing in *Insight* studies *cognitional interiority*, his later venture into the transformational aspects of our lives—rooted in a mystic[88] eye of love—emphasizes *spiritual interiority* that deepens GEM's cognitional aspect[89] (granted that cognitional interiority is closely linked to the affective-volitional aspect of one's consciousness). Our present venture into the nature of community (Part II) will be complemented in Part III with an examination of religious conversion, of interiority, and of loving hearts. We argue that GEM's volitional aspect can be channeled through an eye of love willing to surrender to God's love. For Lonergan, consciousness is "a polyphony with different intensities sung simultaneously.... The peace of a good conscience and the disquiet released by memory of words wrongly said or deeds wrongly done" form a "single stream"[90] involving the unconscious, conscious, cognitive, and volitional aspects of our knowing and doing.

Our "Desire to Know" as Reinforced by the Intensity of our Volitional Consciousness

William Mathews, Lonergan's biographer, writes[91] that our "restless desire for truth and value" are central to Lonergan's *generalized* empirical method. In our view, "volitional" is to be understood as related to feelings, passion,

---

88. For a mystical vision that prioritizes God's love, which is also our endeavor, see Martini, "Value of the Thought," 21–24. Cardinal Martini, in "At the Service," stresses and confirms Lonergan's own innate mystical bent.

89. One must not be erudite or have undergone intellectual conversion to live in the realm of spiritual interiority. Louis Roy sketches the parallel treatment that Lonergan developed in "Healing and Creating in History" and in the two mediating-mediated phases in *Method in Theology* (Roy, "Religious Experience," 12). For Roy, a subject experiences its psychical, cognitive, and affective intentionality. In addition to this first kind of interiority, Lonergan identifies a second kind of interiority—that of religion. Walter Conn, basing himself on William James and Lonergan, proposes "an understanding of the self as *a duplex, dialectical*, first-person reality constituted by consciousness and experienced as 'I' and 'me.'" Two focal points are involved here: "the drive to be a self, a center of strength; and the dynamism to move beyond the self in relationship. These two elements are inextricably connected and must always be understood together: namely, separation *and* attachment ... and autonomy *and* relationship" ("Understanding the Self," 3) Conn's duplex reality reinforces our cognitional-affective approach.

90. Lonergan "Religious Knowledge," 132. Scientists do have insights into systems but can hardly explain the foundational nuances of self-transcendence intimated in both the subconscious and the conscious aspects of life.

91. Mathews, *Lonergan's Quest*, vi.

Meaning and the Human Good as Constitutive of Human Communities 47

and commitment to values.[92] "Cognitional appropriation of the truth is solidary with volitional and sensitive appropriation."[93] Lonergan paraphrases Pascal's remark that "the heart has reasons which reason does not know."[94] Pascal was hearkening back to St. Augustine in whose thought the will predominates.[95] Augustine, for instance, tells the story of how, as a boy, he and his friends had stolen pears from a nearby tree laden with fruit:

> To shake the fruit off the tree and carry off the pears, I and a gang of naughty adolescents set off late at night . . . and carried off a huge load of pears. Even if we ate a few, nevertheless our pleasure lay in doing what was not allowed. . . . Such was my heart, O God, such was my heart. I stole something which I had in plenty and of much better quality.[96]

Augustine's story points to the importance of our heart's obscure motivations. Reason and heart do differ! For Lonergan, reason means the compound of the activities on the first three levels of cognitional activity, namely, of experiencing, of understanding, and of judging. Beyond these three levels, there is affective consciousness where the heart reigns supreme. The heart's reasons stem from feelings that are intentional responses to values. There are two aspects of such responses. The absolute aspect is a recognition of value; the relative aspect prefers one value over another. For Lonergan, the heart is the subject on the existential level of intentional consciousness in the dynamic state of love.[97] Besides the factual knowledge reached by experiencing, understanding, and verifying, there is another kind of knowledge reached through the judgments of value of a person in love. Feelings are instrumental, a way to help us authentically live true values. "Feelings reveal values to us. They dispose us to commitment. But they do not bring about commitment. For commitment is a personal act, a free and responsible act, a very open-eyed act in which we would settle what we are to become."[98] Here, a person is confronted with the issue of the good.

---

92. A major difference between early and late Lonergan is his notion of judgment of value which does away with a fatigued faculty of will. The pursuit of the good leads one to perform what is truly good, the valuable in our lives. The oft-quoted Romans 5:5, "God flooding our hearts with love," summarizes his new emphasis on love.

93. Lonergan, *Insight*, 584.

94. Lonergan, *Method in Theology*, 115.

95. Peters' *Logic* paves a middle road between the Enlightenment's "worship" of reason and postmodernism's emphasis on freedom. He takes on David Hume's skepticism, providing an alternative to postmodern atheism.

96. Augustine, *Confessions of St. Augustine*, II:4.9.

97. Lonergan, *Method in Theology*, 115.

98. Lonergan, "Natural Right and Historical Mindedness," 173.

Once one apprehends the good through feelings, one has to make a choice. The good is human insofar as it is realized through one's choices. "Without human apprehension and choice, we would not exist, . . . we would not have our cities and so on."[99]

One realizes oneself inasmuch as one freely choses the good. Lonergan's view resembles those of the existentialists; but for him, being and the good are coextensive: the subject moves to a further dimension of consciousness as his/her concerns shift from knowing being to actualizing the good.[100] Lonergan explores how freedom and responsibility are to be grounded. Subjects constitute themselves as they fashion their world—being personally responsible for their own lives, and collectively for the world in which they live. It is not by mere introspection, but by reflecting on our living with others, that we come to know ourselves. In so doing, we refine our apprehension of true values.

> The good that a person chooses is not the good by essence but rather the good by participation. There is a pregnant sense of the word "good" in which One alone is good. According to St. Thomas there is a strong sense of the Aristotelian . . . "What is it?" Here one is referring "to a full understanding of the object. When you ask, "What is the good?," you are asking, "What is good by its essence?" There is only one thing that is good by its essence, and that is God. Everything else is good by participation; just as there is only one thing that exists by essence, and everything else exists by participation.[101]

Our desire to know is linked to our implicit, sometimes hidden, search for ultimate truth:

> Man's transcendental subjectivity is mutilated or abolished, unless he is stretching forth towards the intelligible, the unconditioned, the good of value. The reach, not of his attainment, but

---

99. Lonergan, *Topics in Education*, 32.

100. Duffy, *Ethics*, 10, clarifies this further dimension: "What Lonergan does in a way unparalleled by other 'existential' thinkers is to give an account of what is normative in human action. He endorses a phenomenologically ostensible contemplation as part of a critically realist philosophy, but he cautions against simply taking existentialism and incorporating it within Scholastic philosophy. When objectivity is considered 'idealistic,' unattainable, or merely a hangover from hyperrationalist philosophy, then 'authentic subjectivity' tends to denote something other than the principle of objectivity. Like Kierkegaard, Lonergan contends that objectivity, as properly conceived, is the fruit of authentic subjectivity, and to denounce it is 'to induce, not a merely incidental blind spot in one's vision, but a radical undermining of authentic human existence.'"

101. Lonergan, *Topics in Education*, 30–31.

of his intending is unrestricted. There lies within his horizon a region for the divine, a shrine for ultimate holiness, which cannot be ignored.[102]

Consciousness, as a polyphony with different intensities, challenges us in our daily lives. Our unrestricted drive to know and to love originates in the mind's dynamism as rooted in God; otherwise one can hardly explain our restlessness. It is a radical dynamism of the mind toward being and its manifestation as the true and the good. Our hearts and minds seek meaning and the good in their fullness.[103] There must be a God-Being toward which the human subject intelligence leads.

> Being is whatever is grasped intelligently and affirmed reasonably. Being is proportionate or transcendent according as it lies within or without the domain of man's outer and inner experience. The possibility of transcendent knowledge, then, is the possibility of grasping intelligently and affirming reasonably a transcendent being. . . . As man, so God is a rational self-consciousness, for man was made in the image and likeness of God. But what man is through unrestricted desire and limited attainment, God is as unrestricted act. But an unrestricted act of rational self-consciousness, however objectively and impersonally it has been conceived, clearly satisfies all that is meant by the subject . . . with an intelligence and a reasonableness and a willing that is his own.[104]

Striving toward God requires intense commitment. If human existence is to be authentic it must be willing to love in unrestricted fashion: "Authenticity is realized when judgments of value are followed by decision and action, when knowing what truly is good leads to doing what truly is good."[105] With Lonergan we stress the dynamics of knowing and loving. A person exists authentically in the measure that he/she succeeds in being self-transcendent. This has its most enduring ground in holiness, in God's gift of his love to us. In this respect, too, the community has an indispensable role to play.

---

102. Lonergan, *Method in Theology*, 103. See Mombula, *Human Community and Dialectic*, 41.

103. This desire for meaning and the good supplies the framework and background for our overall investigation.

104 Lonergan, *Insight*, 663, 691. For a helpful summary of the *radical nature* of our four cognitional-volitional operations as treated in GEM, including its approach to morality, see Tad Dunne, "Lonergan."

105. Lonergan, "Theology and Man's Future," 152.

> As it is only within communities that men are conceived and born and reared, so too it is only with respect to the available common meanings that the individual . . . comes to find out for himself that he has to decide for himself what to make of himself. Such is the existential moment. It is momentous, for it can be authentic or inauthentic. . . . As Kierkegaard asked whether he was a Christian, so divers men can ask themselves whether they are authentically religious.[106]

The world provides contexts within which one can initiate the work of self-appropriation. In this respect, Lonergan was influenced by Husserl's *Lebenswelt* (lifeworld) as a framework for all his research: one's particular surrounding world "is the locus of all our cares and endeavors—this refers to a fact that occurs purely within the spiritual realms. Our surrounding world is a spiritual structure in us and in our historical life"[107] (See Exploration 5). In our own effort to bring Lonergan down to earth, we are faced with a dilemma: To what extent should we explore the complicated philosophical problems Lonergan delved into? Our solution is to touch on such issues in the text but refer detailed discussions to Part IV's twelve Explorations that go into how Lonergan approached such key thinkers as Aristotle, Aquinas, Descartes, Hegel, Marx, Husserl, and Wittgenstein.[108] Despite their vast differences, there are commonalities among them. For example, Aristotle, Hegel,[109] and Lonergan all insist on the centrality of human community. Lonergan's stress on "horizons" is also helpful in contextualizing great thinkers.

---

106. Lonergan, "Post-Hegelian Philosophy of Religion," 213.

107. Husserl, *Crisis*, 272. *Welt* (world) is derived from old German *Weralt*, "that which nourishes life." To stress this, Husserl spoke of *Lebenswelt* (life-world). See David Jousset, *Le vocabulaire allemand de la philosophie*, 123.

108. Paul Johnston, in *Contradictions of Modern Moral Philosophy*, argues that much recent moral philosophy is confused as to the source of correct moral judgements; many modern approaches to ethics cannot make much sense of traditional moral beliefs. Some would have us reject ethics as a set of outdated, misguided claims with the result that they are left with finding some ways of preserving moral beliefs. The result is a contradiction at the heart of ethics. It is often difficult to tell whether a contemporary philosopher ultimately rejects or endorses the idea of objective right and wrong. For Johnston, the central issues of ethics cannot be resolved by conceptual analysis. Lonergan and Charles Taylor both move beyond conceptual analyses as they highlight so as to resolve the contradictions of today's moral theorists.

109. Lonergan and Hegel both considered themselves as being in the Aristotelian tradition. Still, "There is always some risk in trying to draw parallels or contrasts between different thinkers who lived in different time periods and who were motivated by different philosophical and cultural concerns" (Baur, "Lonergan and Hegel," 535).

The Importance of Horizons and Dialectic in Lonergan's Lifework

For Lonergan, a horizon has two poles—objective and subjective—which condition one another. Dialectic is "a concrete unfolding of linked but opposed principles of change; it occurs if (1) there is an aggregate of events of a determinate character, (2) the events may be traced to either or both of two principles, (3) the principles are opposed yet bound together, and (4) they are modified by resulting changes. Dialectic is a unity of opposites, of which there are three types: complementarity, contradiction, and genetic. Let us consider each of the three in turn.

The dialectic of complementarity occurs when different viewpoints or horizons reinforce one another. Each part is what it is in virtue of its functional relations to other parts; there is no part that is not determined by the exigence of other parts. The whole possesses a certain inevitability in its unity, so that the removal of any part would destroy the whole. A university exemplifies this in that it has such different domains of interest as faculty, administrators, nonprofessional staff members, students, etc. Each is aware of and recognizes the need for the others. No single point-of-view or horizon is complete or self-sufficient. Together, they represent the motivations and knowledge required for the collective, collaborative effort required to run a university. One must coordinate complementary horizons.

In the dialectic of contradiction, the different horizons exclude one another. No common ground can be found: "What in one is found intelligible, in another is unintelligible. What for one is true, for another is false. What for one is good, for another is evil. Each may have some awareness of the other and so each in a manner may include the other. But such inclusion is also negation and rejection."[110] An illustration of this kind of dialectic is Hitler's Holocaust. In his novel, *Night*, Elie Wiesel alludes to his own experience in a Nazi concentration camp. He witnessed human cruelty close at hand but was powerless to stop the torture and execution of his father and other Jewish victims.[111]

A genetic dialectic considers the various stages in a process. It identifies how a process, despite differences, constitutes an organically whole entity. This can be illustrated in a dialectic of personhood. A child grows into adulthood only by "negating" childish traits. Given stages of the same person differ, yet they are organically united: later stages remain rooted in the earlier stage but in a transformed way.

---

110. Lonergan, *Method in Theology*, 236.

111. Such a traumatic experience, however, did eventually motivate Wiesel to show a heartfelt solidarity with all.

> What sublates goes beyond what is sublated, introduces something new and distinct, puts everything on a new basis, yet so far from interfering with the sublated or destroying it, on the contrary needs it, includes it, preserves all its proper features and properties, and carries them forward to a fuller realization within a richer context.[112]

The three types of dialectic are a fitting way to conclude this chapter on meaning and the good since, reinforcing one another, they can help overcome the ideologies haunting humanity. Our book's strategy includes the deeper dialectical-foundations Lonergan developed in *Method*. In *Method*, Lonergan argues that a community is not just a number of persons within a geographical frontier. Rather, it is an achievement of common meaning striving to foster the good.[113]

Any community depends on people's choices[114] as based on the intentional structure of human consciousness of persons intending meaning and value. Meaning and the good stand in an isomorphic relation: "As human knowing rises on three levels, so also the good that humans pursue contains the threefold components of the experiential, the intellectual and the reflective."[115] Concretely, it results in the particular good, the good of order, and the good of value. A human community stems from a common intentionality; being a matter of choices based on meaning on the part of many, it is an achievement collaboratively brought about despite the tensions and conflicts besetting the community.

---

112. Lonergan, *Method in Theology*, 241.

113. With Aristotle, Lonergan holds that the goods are many, but adds that the process of achieving is itself a good.

114. Logotherapy is based on an existential analysis focusing on Kierkegaard's will to meaning as opposed to Adler's Nietzschean doctrine of will to power or Freud's will to pleasure. Meaning, for Kierkegaard, is a lived experience, a quest to find one's values, beliefs, and purpose in a meaningless world. For Victor Frankl, logotherapy's founder, rather than power or pleasure, striving to find meaning is the most powerful motivating force in humans. His notions of a "super-meaning" which transcends man and of an existential act of commitment on man's part are ways to combat what he called the mass neurosis or despair affecting many today. See Tyrrell, "On the Possibility and Desirability."

115. Lonergan, "Role of a Catholic University," 108.

3

Further Tensions Affecting Meaning and the Human Good

CHAPTER 2 STUDIED THE good and communities as related to meaning amidst various tensions. We turn to examine this issue in more depth. For Lonergan, meaning and the good underpin any community whose members, be they near or far, attach the same meaning to their symbols and uphold the same good of value. This criterion tests whether people agree or disagree upon meaning or the good. "As common meaning constitutes community, so divergent meaning divides it."[1] Lonergan addresses such issues in his "dialectic of community."[2] Even though a community be divided, it is still a community intent on meaning and value, both of which are non-negotiable elements for any community. To eliminate meaning would be to eliminate "symbols, art, language, literature, religion, science, history, philosophy, theology."[3] Meaning underpins community; one has to go back to it when a community shows signs of weakness. However, changes of an his-

---

1. Lonergan, *Method in Theology*, 357.

2. Lonergan, *Method in Theology*, 242–44. Lonergan here is concerned with the dialectical elements characterizing groups in society and which affect community, and situations. This "affects community for, just as common meaning is constitutive of community, so dialectic divides community into radically opposed groups. It affects action for, just as conversion leads to intelligent, reasonable, responsible action, so dialectic adds division, conflict, oppression. It affects the situation, for situations are the cumulative product of previous actions and, when previous actions have been guided by the light and darkness of dialectic, the resulting situation is not some intelligible whole but rather a set of misshapen, poorly proportioned, and incoherent fragments." 358.

3. Lonergan, "Time and Meaning," 104.

torical nature are inevitable (even necessary) for the vitality of communities in their quest for meaning. Since families, laws, the state, and the economy are not fixed and immutable entities, they adapt to changing circumstances. "They can be reconceived in light of new ideas, they can be subjected to revolutionary change. All such change essentially is a change of meaning—a change of idea or concept, of judgment or evaluation, of order or request."[4]

The tensions affecting meaning and the good that arise in communities are also played out in persons. A person is a "unity-in-tension,"[5] caught in the two dialectical poles affecting the cognitional and volitional aspects of our consciousness. The cognitional aspect is the intellect's ability to know the truth; the volitional aspect indicates the intellect's desire to accomplish the good. The "unity-in-tension" within persons begs the question of how intellect and will are related. The empirically, intelligently, rationally conscious subject of self-affirmation becomes a morally self-conscious subject. Humans are not only knowers but also doers whose intelligent-rational consciousness grounds both the doing and the knowing. From that identity of consciousness there springs inevitably an exigence for self-consistency in knowing and doing. Still, moral living is difficult, *almost* "impossible."[6]

In principle, the relation between meaning and the good is an isomorphic one. For Lonergan, far from being a matter of mere resemblance between individual elements, the relation also applies to values. "Meaning in its full extent is what is understood in the concrete situation and actions of the person, from frowns to long speeches, and as such is the formal element in this process of the human good."[7] The good of order is an intel-

---

4. Lonergan, "World Mediated by Meaning," 109.

5. Lonergan expands on this idea of unity-in-tension, saying: "Indeed, consciousness is much more obviously of this unity in diverse acts than of the diverse acts, for it is within the unity that the acts are found and distinguished, and it is to the unity that we appeal when we talk about a single field of consciousness and draw a distinction between conscious acts occurring within the field and unconscious acts occurring outside it" (*Insight*, 349).

6. Lonergan, *Insight*, 622. The Greeks developed a basic meaning of knowing and doing in family and state. For Aristotle, man "is more of a political animal than bees or any other gregarious animal is evident. Nature, as we often say, makes nothing in vain, and man is the only animal who has the gift of speech. Whereas mere voice is but an indication of pleasure or pain, and is therefore found in other animals . . . , the power of speech is intended to set forth the expedient and inexpedient, and therefore likewise the just and the unjust" (*Politics*, 1253a 7–19).

7. Lonergan, *Early Works on Theological Method*, 41. In "Isomorphism," he writes: "Two sets of terms, say A, B, C and P, Q, R are said to be isomorphic if the relation of A to B is similar to the relations of P to Q, the relation of A to C is similar to the relation of P to R, the relation of B to C is similar to the relation of Q to R, etc." Isomorphism supposes "different sets of terms; it neither affirms nor denies similarity

ligible unification of an organizational type, though it may be much more spontaneous than any deliberately conceived organizing blueprint. Value is chosen in judgments of value in that it is a rational choice. Rational choice is required to judge correctly given the fact that there persists an inherent unity-in-tension among persons and the communities they establish.[8]

Meaning and the Structure of Conscious Intentionality as Grounded in Being

Trying to define the term "meaning" leads to the difficulty of begging the question as to the meaning of "meaning," whose etymology is related to German *Meinung* and its verb form, *meinen* (to mean). For Lonergan, meaning is crucial both on existential and cultural levels. It "is embodied or carried in human intersubjectivity, in art, in symbols, in language, and in the lives and deeds of persons."[9] If it is that pervasive, why bother talking about it? Because what is common is not always well understood; often, it is simply taken for granted. Lonergan approaches meaning by investigating the structure of our conscious intentionality. Meaning is intrinsically linked to the acts or operations of consciousness, that is the "awareness immanent in cognitional acts. But such acts differ in kind, and so the awareness differs in kind with the acts."[10] Still, these different acts constitute a unity.

> Besides cognitional contents there are cognitional acts; different kinds of acts have different kinds of awareness: empirical, intelligent, rational. But the contents cumulate into unities. What is perceived is what is inquired about; what is inquired about is what is understood; what is understood is what is formulated; what is formulated is what is reflected on; what is reflected on is

---

between the terms of one set and those of other sets; but it does assert that the network of relations in one set of terms is similar to the networks of relations in other sets" (133).

8. See Lonergan, *Insight*, 242–44, on the "Dialectic of Community." While it is true that a social component is naturally implanted in us, it is also true that it is not without tensions and conflicts. Not all tensions and conflicts are destructive; some are constructive. While the former is to be addressed in a dialectic of contradiction, the latter involves a dialectic of complementarity or a genetic dialectic. When Lonergan says that "community is primordial," he is not negating the interdependence of both terms. Something is primordial because another thing follows. Human subjects and community imply one another. One can link the two through the notion of obligation.

9. Lonergan, *Method in Theology*, 57.

10. Lonergan, *Insight*, 346.

what is grasped as unconditioned; what is grasped as unconditioned is what is affirmed.[11]

Stressing the Roles of Meaning as Constitutive Components of our Lives

For Lonergan, mankind is a concrete aggregate of persons developing over time,

> where the locus of development and the synthetic bond is the emergence, expansion, differentiation, dialectic of meaning and of meaningful performance. On this view, intentionality, meaning, is a constitutive component of human living; moreover, this component is not fixed, static, immutable, but shifting, developing, going astray capable of redemption; on this view, there is in the historicity, which results from nature . . . changing forms, structures, methods.[12]

Authentic forms of meaning can help liberate the lives of both individuals and communities. Different acts of meaning are isomorphic with different levels of the human good. Meaning is grounded in knowing; the good is grounded in acts of willingness. But this is only part of the story since it is being that grounds both knowing-meaning and the good as willed. Without the notion of being there is neither knowledge nor meaning:

> As the notion of being underpins all contents and permeates them and constitutes them as cognitional, so also it is the core of meaning. . . . Being is what is to be known through the totality of correct judgments. . . . It is whatever is to be known by intelligent grasp and reasonable affirmation. But being that is proportionate to human knowing not only is to be understood and affirmed but also is to be experienced.[13]

For Lonergan, the inquiring mind which intends everything, unfolds itself on the level of experience (using the data of sense and/or

---

11. Lonergan, *Insight*, 349.

12. Lonergan, "Transition from a Classicist World-view," 5–6. Redemption is the third differential of the human good. Lonergan also writes that "Christians find a redemptive role in suffering—not just in the negative sense suffering has in Buddhism" (*Topics in Education*, 63–69). Yet, for both Buddhists and Christians, conversion and community must counter egoism" (Grudzen and Raymaker, *Steps toward Vatican III*, 146).

13. Lonergan, *Insight*, 381, 416.

consciousness), on the levels of understanding and perception as well as of reflection and judgment. He explores the analogy of meaning to compare and integrate those three operational levels[14] and finds their grounding in the all-inclusive notion of being. Meaning, when fully developed, "intends something meant."[15] Is this not a circular definition? No, for it adequately summarizes how human consciousness is intrinsically linked to meaning, as something operative. It establishes a mutual relation between cognitional acts and the realms of meaning. Meaning is not restricted to the conceptual, as in Scotus or Frege.[16] Rather, basing himself on our conscious, intentional operations, Lonergan explains how we come to know through the reality of one's cognitional operations. Different modes of conscious and intentional operations "give rise to different realms of meaning."[17] Common sense, the first realm of meaning, "is that vague name given to the unknown source of a large floating population of elementary judgments which everyone makes, everyone relies on, and almost everyone regards as obvious and indisputable."[18] In theory, the second realm of meaning, things are conceived and known, "not in their relations to our sensory apparatus or to our needs and desires, but in the relations constituted by their uniform interactions with one another."[19]

Common sense and theory are related to one another through the systematic exigence as it effects the transition from the first to the second stage of meaning. The systematic exigence results in "the possibility of theoretically differentiated consciousness, one that is correlated with the level of understanding."[20] There is also a critical exigence since man desires

---

14. Lonergan, "Analogy of Meaning," 184. Analogy means proportion and implies a harmonious relationship. In philosophy, it refers to a cognitive process establishing a relation between two completely or mostly different objects. The past is a present that is no longer. And the future is the present that is not yet. Past and future are both like the present and unlike the present. "In general, the present and the past are said to be analogous when they are partly similar and partly dissimilar." Lonergan, *Method in Theology*, 225.

15. Lonergan, *Method in Theology*, 62.

16. Frege, the founder of analytic philosophy, wanted to reduce most of mathematics to logic. His distinction between *Sinn* (sense) and *Bedeutung* (reference) leaves out the transcendent. Involved is an oversight of what constitutes full acts of meaning, of reasonable judgments as referring to reality as known. See Beards, *Lonergan, Meaning and Method*, which sheds light on the aesthetic experience and concrete reality of human arts as transcendent.

17. Lonergan, *Method in Theology*, 81.

18. Lonergan, *Insight*, 314.

19. Lonergan, *Insight*, 258.

20. Dadosky, "Is there a Fourth Stage?," 770.

to understand fully. The critical exigence brings us to the third realm of meaning, which leads to interiority: "while the transition from common sense to theory introduces us to entities that we do not directly experience, the transition from common sense and theory to interiority promotes us from consciousness of self to knowledge of self."[21] Finally, the fourth realm of meaning is that of "transcendence in which the subject is related to the divinity in the language of prayer and of prayerful silence."[22] This fourth realm is mediated by a transcendental exigence of love.

Regarding meaning and the structure of our conscious intentionality, meaning is not secondary as naïve realists would want us to believe. Rather, for Lonergan, reality is both constituted and mediated by meaning. At the root of every human community there is meaning: common meaning constitutes community: meaning must be communicated. "The genesis of common meaning is an ongoing process of communication, of people coming to share the same cognitive, constitutive, and effective meanings."[23] People establish communities through communication, and conversely, community constitutes and perfects itself through people communicating. How does all this impact our project?

Correlating Time and Meaning in Kingdom-Oriented Communities

Today, underlying people's crises of faith, there is a crisis of culture provoked by a seeming inability to properly retrieve the past in meaningful ways. For Lonergan, "The study of literatures, of culture, of philosophy, of religion, can become simply an archipelago of islands with no relations between them."[24] The fact that all knowledge is concerned with the development of meaning implies time and history. Time *can be* approached as only a mechanical succession of events, but Lonergan, following St. Augustine, speaks of present and eternal time and correlates this with overall meaning:

> The time of meaning is not a succession of mathematical points such as is the time of mechanics. It is a now of a subject that is identical through time and of a subject that is not, in his

---

21. Lonergan, *Method in Theology*, 259.

22. Lonergan, *Method in Theology*, 257. In the Catholic tradition, there are three stages to a deep interior life. These include the traditional emphasis on the fourfold aspects of prayer as thanksgiving, reparation, adoration, and petition.

23. Lonergan, *Method in Theology*, 357.

24. Lonergan, "Time and Meaning," 94. Beards, *Lonergan, Meaning and Method*, favors a "deep grammar" to free analytical philosophy from its metalogical foundations.

> considerations, confined to meaning things that are present; he means equally well the things that are past and future.[25]

Words denote what is absent, what is present, what is near, what is far,

> but also the possible, the ideal, the ought-to-be for which we keep on striving though we never attain. So, we come to live, not as the infant in a world of immediate experience, but in a far vaster world that is brought to us through the memories of other men, . . . through the pages of literature, through the labors of scholars, through the investigations of scientists, through the experience of saints, through the meditations of philosophers and theologians.[26]

Lonergan is here echoing Augustine's view in two ways. First, the relation of meaning and time implies that meaning develops since meaning has something to do with human consciousness as self-corrective. Second, meaning can bring one to the past, to the present, and to the future; there is no past without reference to the present and to the future, nor a present without the past and the future, nor a future without the past and the present. Symbols play a role here. For Lonergan, a symbol is "an image of a real or imaginary object that evokes a feeling or is evoked by a feeling."[27] A country's flag, for example, is a symbol carrying meaning. When one sees the flag hanging in front of a building, one assumes that it is a governmental one. However, symbols can carry contradictory meanings.

During the Vietnam War, for example, "The flag meant one thing for a patriot and another to a war protester. . . . We might say that the dialectic of their conflict"[28] led to confusion. Symbols are not univocal, they open the door to multiple meanings. From intersubjective meaning one easily moves on to incarnate meaning. A man, "either in his totality or in his characteristic moment, his most significant deed, his outstanding achievement or sacrifice, is a meaning."[29] Incarnate meaning is not restricted to individual life but can be extended to the life of a community. The way of life of a community or civilization may be meaningful, or it may become meaningless. Art, too, has it role to play in how individuals or even a community interpret and respond to emerging problems, as Lonergan notes:

---

25. Lonergan, "Time and Meaning," 108.
26. Lonergan, "Dimensions of Meaning," 253.
27. Lonergan, *Method in Theology*, 64.
28. Sauer, *Commentary on Lonergan's Method*, 92.
29. Lonergan, "Analogy of Meaning," 188.

> Art can be viewing this world and looking for the something more that this world reveals, and reveals, so to speak, in silent speech, reveals by a presence that cannot be defined. . . . There is to art an interpretative significance as a possibility. Not all art has it, but when art is without ulterior significance, which is not formulated but lived . . . it is separating objects from the ready-made world by way of exuberance, like the exuberance of a child, or by way of a distraction.[30]

The various forms of meaning interpenetrate. Common sense differs from technical and literary meaning.[31] Through concepts and propositions people explore literary, "intersubjective, incarnate, symbolic, and artistic meaning."[32] People live in two worlds. From infancy, they live in a world of immediacy, a world revealed by sense and alive with feeling. Gradually, through the analogy of meaning grounded in being, they move into a world mediated by meaning and motivated by values.

> In this adult world, the raw materials are indeed the world of immediacy. But by speech one asks when and where, what and why, . . . how often? Answers cumulatively extrapolate from what is near to what is ever further away, from the present to one's own and to others' memories of the past and anticipations of the future, from what is or was actual to the possible, . . . the ideal, the normative.[33]

The analogy of meaning also affects the ways communities function. Intersubjective relations, civil and cultural communities, are not univocal. They are similar inasmuch as they are all constituted by meaning and value. The cultural is "a set of meanings and values informing a common way of life. There are as many cultures as there are distinct sets of such meanings and values."[34] Intersubjective community underpins both civil and cultural communities. The difference lies in the fact that the former constitutes social aspects whereas the latter constitutes cultural aspects. For Lonergan, the social is

---

30. Lonergan, *Topics in Education*, 222. The point that Lonergan wishes to make here is the importance of meaning

31. "Technical," derived from the Greek *techne* (skill), was used to point to their moving from *mythos* to *logos*. It now also means sets of meanings applied to fields such as computer languages where meaning is not constitutive but "a noise source." If it is distorted in transmission, the receiver reverses distortion. Soni and Goodman, *Mind at Play*, 139.

32. Lonergan, "Analogy of Meaning," 192.

33. Lonergan, *Lonergan Reader*, 522.

34. Lonergan, *Method in Theology*, 301.

> A way of life, a way in which men live together in some orderly, predictable fashion. Such orderliness is to be observed in the family . . . in society with its classes and elites, in education, in the state and its laws, in the economy . . . in the Churches and sects.[35]

Meaning within a community stems from a cumulative process. "Human reality, the very stuff of human living, is . . . in large measure constituted through acts of meaning."[36] Coupled with this is that the differentiation between the stages of history leads to pressing existential quests for more freedom:

> The classical mediation of meaning has broken down. It is being replaced by a modern mediation of meaning that interprets our dreams and our symbols, that thematizes our wan smiles and limp gestures, that analyzes our minds and charts our souls, that takes the whole of human history for its kingdom to compare and relate languages and customary morals, political, legal, educational, economic systems, sciences, philosophies, theologies, and histories.[37]

The common sense of Greek mythology has given way to *logos*, to the realm of theory, which had started with the pre-Socratics and continued throughout subsequent epochs. Many modern crises are in large part due to misunderstood carryovers of classical culture into modern culture.[38]

The Invariant Structure of the Good

The good has an invariant, but open, structure, whose interlocking elements are present in any place and time. These interlocking elements are those of the particular good, the good of order, and values.[39] Following Aristotle, Lonergan defines the good as that at which everything aims, but he adds: "As human knowing rises on three levels, so also the good that men pursue

---

35. Lonergan, "Absence of God," 102.
36. Lonergan, "Dimensions of Meaning," 252.
37. Lonergan, "Dimensions of Meaning," 265.
38. This book asks how kingdom-oriented communities can help overcome the loss of meaning in today's societies. It seeks to recover and live the silent language of love that permeates any genuine striving after authenticity.
39. Lonergan, *Topics in Education*, 33, 39. "A sense of belonging together provides the dynamic premise for common enterprise, for mutual aid and succor, for the sympathy that augments joys and divides sorrows" (*Insight*, 237).

contains a threefold aspect"[40] characterized by three ends, namely 1) the life of nature (in the restricted sense of vital, sensitive spontaneity); 2) the good life (based on reason or rational appetite); and 3) the life of divine grace.[41] When pursuing the good, people communicate so that the three levels of community may correspond to those of both knowing and the good. We turn to consider each of these three levels in turn so as to better link them in Part III as one of the *foundational structures* of kingdom-oriented communities in their efforts to promote the good. This is important because promoting the good hinges on a search for the *key* to spiritual interiority. Finding and using that key is crucial for reconciling the inner- and outer-oriented dimensions[42] of life in general. Regrettably, for all too many Christians, the kingdom remains a mere ideal. What is needed today is to truly live the Christian life so as to actively and effectively promote the ideals of the particular good, of the good of order, and of values in daily life.

One may illustrate the particular good with eating. "The object of appetite is the good on an elementary level. When attained, it is experienced as pleasant. . . . But we experience aversions no less than desire, pain no less than pleasure."[43] On the elementary level, the good is coupled with its opposite, the bad. A particular good such as eating is by definition recurrent.

The good of order is concerned with satisfying recurrent needs. Governments must take appropriate measures to maintain the good of order by devising means that ensure that particular goods are provided. The good of order "stands to single desires as system to systematized, as universal condition to particulars that are conditioned, as a scheme of recurrence that supervenes upon the materials of desires and the efforts to meet them."[44] It enables us to enjoy particular goods over the long run. The desire for peace, for example, is to be met by governments. As to an economy[45] as a good of

---

40. Lonergan, "Role of a Catholic University," 108.

41. Lonergan, "Finality, Love, Marriage," 38.

42. In his Nobel lecture of 1964, Martin Luther King noted that every person "lives in two realms, the internal and the external. The internal is that realm of spiritual ends expressed in art, literature, morals and religions. The external is that complex of devices, techniques, mechanisms . . . by means of which we live. We have allowed the means by which we live to outdistance the ends for which we live" ("Quest for Peace and Justice," para. 4).

43. Lonergan, *Understanding and Being*, 225.

44. Lonergan, *Insight*, 619–20. Calls are made for an elusive peace. While "religious loving is without conditions" (Lonergan, *Method in Theology*, 242), the catch is that governments care more about aggressive forms of "self-defense."

45. The word "economy" is derived from two Greek terms: *oikos* (house, dwelling place) and *nomos* (law). Literally, economics means the law of the household management. Lonergan defines it as "a shifting network of exchanges in which firms supply

order, it ensures the proper distribution of needed resources. Systems are devised to ensure that needs are met. The family is an institutional good of order whereby a man and a woman live together and assume rights and obligations. A polity (such as a government), an economy, and a family all use what Lonergan calls schemes of recurrence in their various endeavors:

> As we understand the unities that are things and the systematic correlations that explain their operations, so also men grasp and formulate . . . , economic arrangements, political structures. These too are instances of the good, but they stand as higher syntheses that harmonize . . . the satisfactions of individual desires. Intellectually, the good is the good of order.[46]

The good of order is subject to change depending on the call of the moment. New insights may demand a different type of the good of order. This should come as no surprise since humans have an unrestricted drive for both the truth and the good. The drives are endless, necessitating constant change. The good of order is dynamic both in the sense that it orders the dynamic unfolding of desires and aversions, and in the sense that it itself is a system on the move. The good of order

> possesses its own normative line of development, inasmuch as elements of the idea of order are grasped by insight into concrete situations, are formulated in proposals, are accepted by explicit or tacit agreements, and are put into execution only to change the situation and give rise to still further insights. Still, this normative line provides no more than a first approximation to the actual course of social development.[47]

The third element in the invariant structure of the human good "is value. Not only are there setups, but people ask, 'Is the setup good?' They say, 'There is nothing wrong with him, it's the setup.' Children fight about particular goods, but men fight about the value of a good of order."[48]

---

households with goods and services while members of households seek work and receive income from firms" (Lonergan, *Macroeconomic Dynamics*, 12).

46. Lonergan, "Role of a Catholic University," 115. The good of order is intrinsically linked with the notion of the recurrence of the particular good. It has four aspects: "a regular recurrence of particular goods, coordinated human operations, the triple condition of these coordinated human operations—habits, institutions, and material equipment—and finally, the personal status which results from the relations constituted by cooperation" (Lonergan, *Topics in Education*, 36).

47. Lonergan, *Insight*, 620.

48. Lonergan, *Topics in Education*, 36.

Most persons seek a life free from evil and biases but laden with value. Derived from the Latin *valere* (to be of worth), the notion of value was an implicit element in the studies of Plato[49] and Aristotle on the truth, being, and the good. "Just as the notion of being intends but, of itself, does not know being, so too the notion of value intends but, of itself, does not know value. Again, as the notion of being is a dynamic principle that keeps us moving toward ever fuller flowering of the same dynamic principle," value keeps us "moving toward ever fuller realization of the good, of what is worthwhile."[50]

Value goes beyond concepts of time, space, culture, and language. As a universal, immanent- transcendental notion[51] (as are being and meaning), value moves us toward the truly worthwhile. Asking whether something is worthwhile is a fundamental question that recalls Aristotle's definition

---

49. Plato's view of knowing as an intellectual gazing on ideas is incomplete. It has caused untold confusion across the centuries. It may be that it is not Plato who has caused the confusion; rather, it is those who have misread the issue. The critical question that arises regarding the Platonic view of knowing touches on the importance of particular things. Hence it has been called the problem of abstract universals and concrete particulars. This way of asking the question is based on a false presupposition. For Lonergan, one must rely on an inverse insight to avoid the confusion. Instead of asking how the universal idea relates to the particular, one must ask: "What am I doing when I am knowing?" In medieval philosophy, the answer to Platonism was Aquinas's version of Aristotle. This version included both Plato's intelligible essence through ideas that refer abstractly to an object (e. g. tree), and to an "actual existence" that needed to be verified empirically (this tree). For Aristotle and Aquinas, full human knowing requires both idea (insight-intelligible form) and experience of a sensible individual. Aquinas's distinction between "essence and existence" is at the heart of his writings. It influenced Lonergan's cognitive theory and distinction between being intelligent and being reasonable. An insight understands an "essence," but "existence" is affirmed in a judgment. Aristotle recorded the different types of questions we ask in his *Posterior Analytics*. When we ask, "What is X?," we want to understand the essence of "X," and when we ask, "Is it so?," we want to know if "X" is actually real. Aquinas called the "essence" component the *quidditas* = whatness = Aristotle's "*to ti en einai*" (Lonergan, *Verbum*, 15, 177). The "existence" component for Aquinas is the *veritas* = truth, affirmed in reasonable judgment. Augustine rejected his early Neo-Platonist view when he grasped that for Christians *veritas* is existential. This helped him grasp the reality of what John's Gospel (1:14) meant by "and the Word was made flesh."

50. Lonergan, "Subject," 82. For Lonergan, the transcendental notions "promote the subject from lower to higher levels of consciousness, from the experiential to the intellectual, from the intellectual to the rational, from the rational to the existential." Not only do the notions promote the subject to full consciousness and direct him to his goals, "they also provide the criteria that reveal whether the goals are being reached" (Lonergan, *Method in Theology*, 34–35).

51. Although transcendence is defined as the opposite of immanence, the two are not mutually exclusive. For example, pantheists argue that God is both within and beyond the universe; "in it, but not of it."

of nature "as an immanent principle of movement and of rest."[52] In man, such a principle "is the human spirit as raising and answering questions. As raising questions, it is an immanent principle of movement. As answering questions satisfactorily, it is an immanent principle of rest."[53] We pose questions for intelligence, for reflection, and for deliberation. The question "Is it really worthwhile?" implies value. It demarcates the line between feelings which regard one's self and those which are disinterested. Any question leads to an answer which should satisfy the inquiring mind to some extent, but the question for deliberation points to value which satisfies the inquiring mind to the highest degree:

> The drive to understand is satisfied when understanding is reached but it is dissatisfied with every incomplete attainment.... The drive to truth compels rationality to assent when evidence is sufficient but refuses to assent and demands doubt whenever evidence is insufficient. The drive to value rewards success in self-transcendence with a happy conscience and saddens failures with an unhappy conscience.[54]

For Lonergan, there is value in improving the actual order, in avoiding what might destroy an actually functioning order. The good of value presupposes both the particular good and the good of order.[55] So as to help remedy the tensions that have marked the histories of mankind and that of the churches, we have focused on the kingdom of God. Today, many of Jesus' followers in the West live in a nihilist culture that marginalizes or negates *beliefs*. But we rely primarily on *faith*. Before examining, in Part III, how Lonergan's method offers individuals, and mankind in general, the possibility of living two forms of interiority, we turn to study in more detail Lonergan's insights into the human heart. While Islamist terrorists rebuke, attack Western "unbelievers," Lonergan prescribes foundations of the heart which can help the faithful address secularist, atheist views.[56] Chapter 4 ex-

---

52. Aristotle, *Physics II*, 1, 195b.

53. Lonergan, "Natural Right and Historical Mindedness," 173.

54. Lonergan, *Method in Theology*, 35. "Particular objects of appetite are values insofar as they lie within a good of order; it is not sheer appetite but intelligently ordered appetite. A good of order is a value ... because that is the order that happens to exist at any given time" (Lonergan, *Understanding and Being*, 226).

55. The actual good of value presupposes the formal good of order which itself "presupposes the potential good of a manifold to be ordered." Lonergan, *Insight*, 629.

56. Giles Fraser argues that "France's much vaunted secularism is not the neutral space it claims to be. The triumph of atheistic rationality over the dangerous totalitarian obscurantism of the Catholic Church is one of the great foundation myths of republican France" ("France's Much Vaunted Secularism," 2). Coded within this mythology is the

plores how authentic living can, in principle, help us and kingdom-oriented communities pursue goals that, by *transcending* this world, can potentially help save and unite a divided humanity in our actual "real" world.

---

idea that "liberty, equality, fraternity can flourish only when religion is suppressed from the public sphere" ("France's Much Vaunted Secularism," 2).

4

The Importance of Insights, Common Sense in Human Experience

VARIOUS IMPLICATIONS OF OUR DRIVE TO KNOW

LONERGAN WRITES THAT "DEEP within us all, emergent when the noise of other appetites is stilled, there is a drive to know, to understand, to see why . . . to explain."[1] This drive to know unfolds in various ways such as in science or in the common sense of everyday life. "The occurrence of insight is not restricted to the minds of mathematicians, when doing mathematics, and to the minds of physicists, when engaged in that department of science. On the contrary, one meets intelligence in every walk of life."[2] Lonergan's account of common sense touches on many issues.[3] His main interest is in the fact and nature of insight. An act of insight is an intellectual, cumulative event; it is subject to emergent probability[4] and prone to biases. As to

---

1. Lonergan, *Insight*, 28.
2. Lonergan, *Insight*, 198.
3. Lonerga*n* notes that "If you draw a map of a city, you are expressing a relation of things to one another; and when one looks at a map in a strange city, one can ask, 'Where am I? How do I relate my 'here' with this map?" (*Topics in Education*, 140). Similarly, "when you ask, 'What time is it?' you want to correlate your 'now' with the public references obtained from a clock. The scientific procedure of relating things to one another builds up maps and clocks that leave the whole commonsense approach to things out of the picture" (140).
4. Emergent probability implies the development of schemes of recurrence relative also to events characterized by such variables as time, place, and the concrete

the cumulative nature of insight, Lonergan insists that our minds are not "a factory with a set of fixed processes." Rather, they are a universal tool which

> erects all kinds of factories, keeps adjusting and improving them, and eventually scraps them in favor of radically new designs.... There is not some fixed set of a priori syntheses. Every insight is an a priori synthesis; insight follows on insight to complement and correct its predecessor; earlier accumulations form viewpoints to give place to higher viewpoints.[5]

As a development of the subject, common sense helps transform the world. Still this is subject to aberration. Besides the progressive accumulation of related insights, one can cumulatively refuse insights. The insights that occur in common sense and that are practical by nature are integral to needed transformations of the world. Such insights occur "not for the sake of the pleasure of contemplation, but to use knowledge in making and doing. This leads to the transformation[6] of man and his environment. An authentic common sense can help persons transcend their biases, which in turn provides the contexts for persons to change situations or create new worlds around them.

1a Common Sense Affects Persons in Creative Ways: Patterns of Experience

In *Insight*, Lonergan explores the relations between common sense and science. First, in chapters 1–5, he illustrates how understanding occurs in various areas of knowledge; in chapters 6–7, he then explains what common sense is. As to scientists, he writes: "The scientist seeks intelligible systems that cover the data of his field."[7] But he adds that common sense also generates insights:

> By common sense is meant a nucleus of habitual insights such that the addition of one or two more will bring one to the understanding of any of an open series of concrete situations. By that

---

conditions of actual functioning. This book does not address in depth Lonergan's treatment of development in genetic method. See Lonergan, *Insight*, 484–92.

5. Lonergan, *Insight*, 430.

6. On sustainable human development in an African context, see Ogbonnaya, *Lonergan, Social Transformation*, which addresses vulnerable economic areas on our planet and appeals to the principle of solidarity which should bind all humans.

7. Lonergan, *Insight*, 208. "Let the term, science, be reserved for knowledge that is contained in principles and laws and either is verified universally or else is revised" (Lonergan, *Method in Theology*, 233).

understanding one will grasp how to behave, what to say, what to do ... in the currently emerging situation. Such a nucleus of insights is centered in the subject: it regards his world as related to him, as the field of his behavior, influence, action, as colored by his desires, hopes, fears, joys.[8]

Common sense effects a change in a person. Since he/she is a changing, dynamic entity, it follows that there are different contexts in which the insights occur. Such contexts are "patterns of experience." A pattern is a context or "set of intelligible relations that link together sequences of sensations, memories, images, conations, emotions, and bodily movements."[9] Richard Liddy notes that "Lonergan emphasizes the changes that commonsense understanding introduces into a person by detailing the various 'patterns' in which human consciousness can flow: biological, aesthetic, intellectual.... A common dimension of all these patterns of experience is that they change us: they open us up to new dimensions of our own being and new dimensions of reality."[10]

In the biological pattern of experience, a person directs senses, memory, and imagination toward the activities of nourishment, reproduction, and self-preservation. Extroversion is a basic characteristic of the biological pattern of experience functioning in and through persons' sense organs.

> The bodily basis of the senses in sense organs, the functional correlation of sensations with the positions and movements of the organs, the imaginative, conative, emotive consequences of sensible presentations ... all indicate that elementary experience is concerned, not with the immanent aspects of living, but with the external conditions and opportunities. Within the full pattern of living, there is a partial, intermittent, extroverted pattern of conscious living. It is this extroversion of function that underpins the confrontational element of consciousness itself.[11]

In the aesthetic pattern of experience, one experiences conscious living as a joy in itself: "One is led to acknowledge that experience can occur for the sake of experiencing, that it can slip beyond the conflicts of serious-minded biological purpose, and that this very liberation is a spontaneous, self-justifying joy."[12] To limit oneself to the biological pattern of experience

---

8. Lonergan, *Method in Theology*, 72.
9. Lonergan, *Insight*, 206.
10. Liddy, *Startling Strangeness*, 105.
11. Lonergan, *Insight*, 207.
12. Lonergan, *Insight*, 207–8.

would involve a narrowing down of the range of the human consciousness. The aesthetic field expands this range. "The artist establishes his insights, not by proof or verification, but by skillfully embodying them in colors and shapes, in sounds and movements, in unfolding situations."[13]

The intellectual pattern of experience is reflected in the fact that the Greeks defined man as a knower, seeking to understand everything, neither confusing the trees with the forest nor content to merely contemplate the forest. When "Newton was working out his theory of universal gravitation, he lived in his room for weeks on end. . . . He slept only when necessary, but as soon as that was over he was back to work. He was totally absorbed in the enucleation, the unfolding, of his idea. Insofar as it is possible for a man, he was living totally in the intellectual pattern of experience."[14]

The dramatic pattern of experience affects ordinary human living: "Man is capable of aesthetic liberation and artistic creativity, but his first work of art is his own living. The fair, the beautiful, the admirable is embodied by man in his own body and actions before it is given a still freer realization in painting . . . and poetry. Style is the man before it appears in the artistic product."[15]

1b Common Sense, Theory, and the Blindness Our Biases Provoke

For Lonergan, common sense is affected by the patterns of experience—but human biases often interfere. We come to know through both common sense and correct theories, but common sense has inbuilt limitations, it makes mistakes.[16] Science "is a development of intelligence that is complementary to the development named common sense. Rational choice is not a choice between science and common sense; it is a choice of both, of science to master the universal, and of common sense to deal with the particular."[17]

---

13. Lonergan, *Insight*, 208.

14. Lonergan, *Topics in Education*, 86. As to the pattern of experience, Lonergan writes: "To learn thoroughly is a vast undertaking that calls for relentless perseverance. To strike out on a new line and become more than a week-end celebrity calls for years in which one's living is more or less constantly absorbed in the effort to understand, in which one's understanding gradually works round and up a spiral of viewpoints with each complementing its predecessors and only the last embracing the whole field to be mastered" (*Insight*, 210).

15. Lonergan, *Insight*, 210–11.

16. Common sense is unable to realize that it is a specialized development "of human knowledge, incapable of coming to grasp that its peculiar danger is to extend its legitimate concern for the concrete and the immediately practical into disregard of larger issues and indifference to long-terms results" (*Insight*, 251).

17. Lonergan, *Insight*, 203.

Both are accumulations of insights from experience, both are the product of human collaboration. Both can be compared to a self-correcting circuit:

> Just as the mathematician advances from images through insights and formulations to symbols that stimulate further insights, just as the scientist advances from data through insights... so too, the spontaneous and self-correcting process of learning is a circuit in which insights reveal their shortcomings by putting forth deeds or words or thoughts, and through that revelation prompt the further questions that lead to complementary insights.[18]

Common sense and theory both help develop human intelligence through accumulations of insights. Still, both are prone to biases as well as to radical oversights. Common sense is

> subject to a dramatic bias, an egoistic bias, a group bias, and a general bias that disregards the complex theoretical issues... and their long-term consequences from which it blindly suffers. Scientists are not just scientists but also men of common sense; they share its bias insofar as their specialty does not correct it; and insofar as their specialty runs counter to the bias of common sense, they find themselves divided and at a loss for a coherent view of the world.[19]

Biases are oversights due to human failure to observe the transcendental precepts: be attentive, be intelligent, be reasonable, be responsible. As to their intelligibility, common sense and science are indirectly related. Science grasps the intelligibility of the concrete with which common sense deals in practical ways. The two are partners in applied science, in technology, and in inventions. "It is their successful cooperation that "supplements inventions with organizations, knowhow, and specialized skills."[20] We do not have to choose between common sense and science since they complement one another. You can have both. Scientists use the scientific method "because their inquiry moves off from the familiar to the unfamiliar, from the obvious to the recondite."[21] But they do have to attend to things as related to us to be able to explain how things are related to one another. "When they reach the universal relations of things to one another, they are straining beyond the native range of insight into sensible presentations, and they need the

---

18. Lonergan, *Insight*, 197.
19. Lonergan, *Insight*, 415.
20. Lonergan, *Insight*, 323.
21. Lonergan, *Insight*, 202.

crutches of method to fix their gaze on things as neither sensibly given nor concrete nor particular."[22] The world of theory and the world of common sense do speak different languages. Common sense uses ordinary language. Theory develops technical languages. This gives rise to vast differences. The sciences would speak with universal validity; common sense speaks only about the particular. The sciences need methods to reach their abstract and universal objects.[23] But scientists need common sense to apply methods properly in executing the concrete tasks of particular investigations, just as logicians need common sense if they are to grasp what is meant in each concrete act of human utterance. Still, the differences between common sense and science must not be overemphasized. Because language and common sense originate within human communities, it is hard to draw the exact line of demarcation between science and common sense. For many sociologists, the self is socially constructed through language. The question then arises: How do we derive the technical languages used in science? Yes, they develop within communities, but the more profound differences between the worlds of common sense and of theory are located in the structure of consciousness. This structure is the same in common sense and in theory, but it functions differently. Consciousness takes a different orientation according to the patterns of experience in which one is engaged, for it is a stream immersed in the temporal succession of different contents. However, the direction of the stream varies. Lonergan illustrates this with the example of Thales and a milkmaid. Being so intent upon the stars, Thales did not see the well into which he tumbled. "The milkmaid was so indifferent to the stars that she could not overlook the well. Still, Thales could have seen the well, for he was not blind . . . the milkmaid could have been interested in the stars, for she was human."[24]

Hegel's dialectic of master and slave in *The Phenomenology of Spirit* sheds light on this issue. Hegel illustrates how one's self-consciousness functions with his example of the master who wants to lord it over the slave. By extension, man wants to lord it over the universe. If Lonergan's account of

---

22. Lonergan, *Insight*, 208.

23. Lonergan, *Verbum*, 139, modernizes the Aristotelian-Thomistic view of abstraction in science, mathematics, philosophy, etc. One's insights enrich and illuminate a sensible image and make it intelligible, thus linking the *concrete* level of presentations via direct and reflective insights with the *abstractive, universalized* world of concepts. The *illuminating role of an insight is pivotal* for it anticipates intelligibility, and then erects heuristic structures in its grasp of significant ideas. The abstractive procedures of classical method are complemented by the inverse insights that yield statistical methods. Further practical and speculative insights yield the heuristic structures of dialectic and genetic methods. See Lonergan, *Insight*, 30, 38–40, 87, 111, 133, 484–527.

24. Lonergan, *Insight*, 205.

Thales's experience illustrates the intellectual pattern of experience guiding science, Hegel's account of the master-slave relationship describes an initial situation "where you have a master who is really master and the slave who is really slave. But time goes on, and the master becomes more and more dependent upon the slave, and the roles become reversed."[25] Lonergan accepts Hegel's account of role reversals in that it can help us relate the four functions of meaning (the cognitive, efficient, constitutive and communicative functions) to one another. In his post-*Insight* work, Lonergan stresses that meaning is *not a merely secondary* affair, so that what counts is the reality that is meant and *not* the "mere" meaning that refers to it.[26] For an infant, the world is no bigger than the nursery. As a child learns to talk, his little world of immediacy comes first. But as he/she grows up, the world of immediacy shrinks into a less important corner of the real world which we come to know only through the mediation of meaning.[27] In adult life, one is in a position to transform one's self as well as the environment. This is

> effected through the intentional acts that envisage ends, select means, secure collaborators, direct operations. . . . Besides the transformation of nature, there is man's transformation of man himself; and in this second transformation the role of meaning is not merely directive but also constitutive.[28]

Common sense, in its dialectical tensions with theory and in the various patterns of experience, changes persons in creative ways. It effects its own type of changes in the world we inhabit.

2 Common Sense as Effecting Changes in Objects and in the World around Us

For Lonergan, meaning is ubiquitous. In the drama of human living, "human intelligence is not only artistic but also practical. At first, there appears to be little to differentiate man from the beasts, for in primitive fruit-gathering cultures, hunger is linked to eating by a simple sequence of bodily movements. But primitive hunters take time out from hunting to make spears, and primitive fishers take time out from fishing to make nets.[29]

---

25. Lonergan, "Philosophy of History," 76. Marx stressed man's desire to transform nature.
26. Lonergan, "Dimensions of Meaning," 252.
27. Lonergan, *Method in Theology*, 76.
28. Lonergan, "Dimensions of Meaning," 255.
29. Lonergan, *Insight*, 232–33.

Primitive tools eventually led to modern technologies. Modern technology did not spring out of nowhere. Rather, since antiquity, common sense, community, tradition, and science have been interrelated. As products of human ingenuity, spears and nets illustrate both the idea of the old mechanical arts and the more refined achievements of modern technology. The primitive fruit-gathering cultures were confronted with new problems which led them to invent. "As inventions accumulate, they set problems calling for more inventions. The new inventions complement the old only to suggest further improvements."[30] This eventually leads to successions of mechanical and technological higher viewpoints marking epochs in humanity's material progress.

Common sense knows it needs various forms of cooperation. For Lonergan, cooperation down the ages is to be supplemented by the cooperation occurring "at any given place and time. Without cooperation down the ages human life today would not differ from that of the most primitive tribe."[31] A group can do much more than scattered individuals. A group of groups is much more efficient than an isolated group. Grouping of groups can be reapplied again and again. Cooperation that occurs across disciplines demands a division of labor. Persons specialize in the skillful use of particular tools and in the expeditious performance of particular tasks. The concrete realization of new practical ideas

> calls forth some economic system, some procedure that sets the balance between the production of consumer goods and new capital formation, some method that settles what quantities of what goods and services are to be supplied, some device for assigning tasks to individuals and for distributing among them the common product. . . . As technology evokes the economy, so the economy evokes the polity. Most men get ideas, but the ideas reside in different minds, and the different minds do not quite agree. Of itself, communication only reveals the disparity. What is wanted is persuasion, and the most effective persuader becomes a leader. . . . The problem of effective agreement is recurrent. Each step in the process of technological and economic development is an occasion on which minds differ, new insights have to be communicated, enthusiasm has to be roused, and common decision must be reached.[32]

---

30. Lonergan, *Insight*, 233.
31. Lonergan, "Dialectic of Authority," 5.
32. Lonergan, *Insight*, 234.

The Importance of Insights, Common Sense in Human Experience

For Lonergan, "Community means people with a common field of experience, with a common or at least complementary way of understanding people and things, with common judgments and common aims."[33] To the three levels of cognitional activity and the human good, there correspond the three levels of human community: intersubjective community, civil community, and cultural community. The latter two are involved in dialectic. Communities, too, must be willing to tackle our human biases.

3 How Human Biases Hinder the Transformative Potential of Common Sense

Four biases inhibit human development.[34] Unlike the patterns of experience that foster insights and human development, biases impede insights, or if insights do occur, they are mutilated in decisions made by both individual persons and communities. "As individuals, so societies fail to reach the universal willingness that reflects and sustains the detachment and disinterestedness of the unrestricted desire to know."[35] Lonergan traces such failures to our four human biases. Biases occur both in individual subjects and in communities. Let us consider each of the four biases in turn.

First, there is a dramatic bias of unconscious motivation which results from the trauma of a psychological wound and prevents one from being attentive to relevant data that would arouse feelings associated with the wound. It has to do with a feeling of being threatened by others and includes "the challenges to intersubjective relations."[36] This bias exposes one to many conflicts in community. Lacking a fuller view of reality results in forms of behavior that generate misunderstanding both in ourselves and in others. In this area, Lonergan is influenced by Freud's view that "consciousness is the surface of the mental apparatus," and that "it is essential to abandon the

---

33. Lonergan, "Dialectic of Authority," 5.

34. "All men are subject to bias, for bias is a block or distortion of intellectual development, and such blocks occur in four principal manners" (Lonergan, *Method in Theology*, 231). Bias has many ramifications: "Devaluation, distortion, corruption may occur only in scattered individuals. But it may occur on a more massive scale, and then the words are repeated, but the meaning is gone.... The unauthenticity of individuals becomes the unauthenticity of tradition" (80). In that case, a person can do not more than "authentically" realize unauthenticity.

35. Lonergan, *Insight*, 651. In *Insight*, Lonergan speaks of three biases, and in *Method*, of four. When referring to three kinds, he associates the dramatic bias (unconscious motivation) with individual egoism. Group bias and the general bias of common sense occur in a plurality of different human subjects (Snell and Cone, *Authentic Cosmopolitanism*, 103).

36. Dadosky, "Desire, Bias, and Love," 247.

overvaluation of the property of being conscious.... The unconscious is the true psychical reality."[37]

Second, aside from tensions and conflicts driven by hidden forces, a bias of individual egoism leads one to violate precepts and to disregard of others. Egoists do not turn into altruists overnight. They find loopholes in social arrangements which they exploit to enlarge their own share and diminish the shares of others in current instances of the particular good.[38]

Third, group bias (group egoism) also provokes conflict if it leads "to mistaken evaluations due to a loyalty to one's own group matched by hostility to other groups.... Hostile groups do not easily forget their grievances, drop their resentments, overcome their fears and suspicions."[39] Group egoism is as damaging as individual egoism. It cannot be justified even when it seeks to defend the group.

Fourth, general bias results from people being guided only by common sense, immersed in the particular and concrete. "They have little grasp of large movements or of long-term trends. They are anything but ready to sacrifice immediate advantage for the enormously greater good of society."[40] General bias induces persons to remain prisoners of habits, making opportunistic choices for immediate gain. As a result, one concentrates on short-term rather than on long-term benefits.

The biases have negative consequences on individuals, on communities, and on civilizations. Not only do individuals develop and suffer breakdowns, so, too, do societies.

---

37. Sigmund Freud, as cited by Berthold-Bond in "Hegel, Nietzsche, and Freud," 195. "Freud adopts as the motto for his *Interpretation of Dreams* Virgil's dictum that 'if I cannot bend the higher powers, I will move the infernal regions'—the higher powers being the sphere of consciousness and rationality, whose structures cannot be fully understood without tracing them back to the 'infernal regions' of the unconscious" (Berthold-Bond, "Hegel," 194).

38. Lonergan, *Method in Theology*, 53. Lonergan is not a prophet of doom. He is opening commendable paths for us to follow.

39. Lonergan, *Method in Theology*, 53. For John Dadosky, "Group bias refers to the privileging of one group over another and can lead from milder forms, such as stereotyping, to more dramatic forms, such as racism" ("Bias," 248). When group bias and dramatic bias blend, it can result in persistent conflicts and war between groups.

40. Lonergan, *Method in Theology*, 360. Seeking to build on Lonergan, Dadosky adds an "intellectualist bias," when he writes: "If general bias is the bias of common sense . . . the adamant preference for common sense over theory," then there might "be an opposite bias that prefers the world of theory over the world of common sense. . . . An excess of theory could cut off the human subject from the concrete experience of the world" ("Bias," 248).

Beyond the Biases and the Tensions of Community: Pathways to Human Freedom

For Lonergan, science and logic are a development of intelligence that complements the development of common sense. "Rational choice is not between science and common sense; it is a choice of both, of science to master the universal, and of common sense to deal with the particular."[41] The mutual concerns uniting common sense and theory are that both deal with the world mediated by meaning as opposed to the world of immediacy as that of an infant. This is so because when one begins to talk, one enters into the world mediated by meaning. Both common sense and the fields of theory are rational; each has their own privileged domain. What we know day in, day out as we go about life constitutes the realm of common sense. It is the domain of human living which aims at the successful performance of daily tasks and at discovering immediate solutions to daily problems. By its very nature, common sense is particular and practical. It varies from one place to another, from one period of time to another. What is familiar in one place may or may not be familiar in another. What works in one setting may not work in another. Spontaneous common sense remains in the world of things related to us. In the theoretical mode of scientific knowing, one deals with the world of things related to themselves. It is methodical. This can lead to tensions in the intersubjective domains affecting persons and communities. Lonergan helps us resolve some of these tensions while opening pathways to freedom. He does so by surveying the scientific facts and noting how they apply to daily experience:

> In the history of human societies there are halcyon periods of easy peace and tranquility that alternate with times of crisis and trouble. In the periods of relaxed tension, the good of order has come to terms with the intersubjective groups. It commands their esteem by its palpable benefits; it has explained its intricate demands in some approximate yet sufficient fashion; it has adapted to its own requirements the play of imagination, the resonance of sentiment, the strength of agreement and consent. Then a man's interest is in happy coincidence with his work; his country is also his homeland; its ways are the obviously right ways; its glory and peril are his own.[42]

---

41. Lonergan, *Insight*, 203.

42. Lonergan, *Insight*, 241. The rule of law is a must, but it must be just—which is often not the case. The cataclysms that followed the "Arab Spring" of 2010 are another instance of events in need of moral-ethical underpinnings.

Despite this serenity, there are moments when members of a community collide, when things fall apart. "This is human community at its worst."[43] Here one needs to invoke the dialectic of contradiction so as to deal with the tensions and conflicts arising within human communities. This dialectic is to be applied in times of crisis and to all their existential connotations:

> The time of crisis can be prolonged, and in the midst of the suffering it entails and of the aimless questioning it engenders, the intersubjective groups within a society tend to fall apart in bickering, insinuations, recriminations, while unhappy individuals begin to long for the idyllic simplicity of primitive living in which large accumulations of insights would be superfluous and human fellow-feeling would have a more dominant role.[44]

For Lonergan, humans can be redeemed from evils by charity modeled on Christ's love. "As alienation and ideology destroy community, so the self-sacrificing love that is Christian charity reconciles alienated man to his true being, and undoes the mischief initiated by alienation and consolidated by ideology."[45] Inasmuch as one is inauthentic, there is needed a reversal which is made possible by 1) an *intellectual conversion* through which one enters the world mediated by meaning; 2) a *moral conversion* by which one comes to live in a world motivated by values; and 3) a *religious conversion* "when one accepts God's gift of his love bestowed through the Holy Spirit."[46] Intellectual conversion solves conflicts on the level of meaning, moral conversion solves conflicts on the level of the human good, and religious conversion solves conflicts on the level of the relationship with the absolute or God.[47] Let us examine some such conflicts more closely, keeping in mind our "logic-of-the-heart-conversion" goals.

43. Shea, "Horizons on Bernard Lonergan," 83–84.

44. Lonergan, *Insight*, 242.

45. Lonergan, *Method in Theology*, 364. "While society does not survive without a large measure of community, it remains that community is imperfect" (360). To ignorance and incompetence there are added alienation and ideology. We seek to develop a logic of the heart so that a spirit of global solidarity may reinforce self-transcending initiatives.

46. Lonergan, "Reality, Myth, Symbol," 389.

47. "There are fundamental conflicts stemming from an explicit or implicit cognitional theory, an ethical stance, a religious outlook. They profoundly modify one's mentality. They are to be overcome only through an intellectual, moral, religious conversion" (Lonergan, *Method in Theology*, 235). Lonergan relates these to Joseph de Finance's vertical exercise of freedom which consists in a set of judgments and decisions enabling one to pass from one horizon to another in such a way that the new horizon represents not just a broadening or a deepening of the preceding one, but rather its

Meaning and the Human Good as Adversely Affected by Conflicts

Conflicts do not arise from occult forces or some mysterious influences; they arise from the way persons think and live, from attaching different meanings to given cases. Meaning affects the process of one's knowing-doing operations' dynamic structure. This structure is a moving system, subject to nonsystematic elements which can bring about conflicts due to the distortions of counterpositions and, in the limit, of mythic consciousness. "It is here that the interpreter has to deal with the dialectical, with the intrusion of the nonsystematic into moving system, with the ambivalent tendency of the counter-position and the mythical either to bring about its own reversal or to attempt to save itself by . . . shifting its ground."[48] Ideally, meaning and communication are at the heart of any community. In communicating, we assume that people understand; but misunderstandings do occur. Words can motivate people, but they can also lead to community breakdowns. Differences in meaning can create islands of opposed values. "Without a common field of experience people get out of touch. Without a common mode of understanding, there arise . . . fear, hostility. Without a common measure of judgment people live in different worlds."[49] Common consent is needed lest people act at cross purposes. A cohesion that once seemed automatic has to be bolstered by the . . . threats that secure a passing semblance of unity but may prepare a lasting resentment,"[50] or even rebellion.

The human good can also be affected by conflicts arising from differentiations in consciousness. Hegel illustrates this reality in his comments on Sophocles's *Antigone* when discussing the ethical consciousness of the early Greeks. Antigone comes into conflict with Creon (her father and the ruler of Thebes) by insisting on burying her brother Polynices. Creon does not want him buried for having betrayed Thebes. "Two laws tragically conflict."[51] Antigone and Creon both respect state laws, but does allegiance to the state override familial obligations? As to this, Creon opposes Antigone. Their opposite stands anticipate the fact that today also conflicting views on important issues do occur. Both within and among groups, different interpretations of the good or of the meaning of a law can lead to conflict. Lonergan aptly highlights the destructive effects of conflicting

---

overturning: a radically new beginning (40). The conversions occur in man's *conscious* life. We address the complexities of *moral-religions* conversions in Parts I, II, III; and of *intellectual* conversion in Part IV.

48. Lonergan, *Insight*, 614.
49. Lonergan, "Natural Right and Historical Mindedness," 170.
50. Lonergan, "Natural Right and Historical Mindedness," 171.
51. Mudde, "Risky Subjectivity," 183.

priorities among social classes. He notes that what is good for some groups "is mistakenly thought to be good for the country or for mankind, while what is good for the country or for mankind is postponed or mutilated. There emerge the richer classes and the poorer classes, the rich become ever richer, while the poorer sink into misery."[52]

In 1848, Marx and Engels, in their *Communist Manifesto*, wrote that history is one "of class struggles. Freeman and slave, patrician and plebeian . . . in a word, oppressor and oppressed, stood in constant opposition to one another, carried on an uninterrupted, now hidden, now open fight, that each time ended, either in a revolutionary reconstitution of society at large, or in the common ruin of the contending classes."[53] Indeed, some groups indulge in false superiority complexes. For Lonergan, the opposition between social classes is a distortion of the social process—one is no longer oriented toward sharing the good: "Groups exaggerate the magnitude and importance of their contribution to society. They provide a market for the ideological facade that would justify their ways before the bar of public opinion. If they succeed in their deception, the social process is distorted."[54] In situations where individuals as well as groups are divided, there is a lack of cooperation—of the very ingredient needed to promote the good of order. As a result, various conflicts flare up with dire consequences:

> The cooperation . . . required for the good of order, can break down in friction and conflict, strikes and lockouts, sedition and revolution: a complete breakdown of the good order. Again, the good of order can be sapped on the level of the conditions of cooperation. There can be mistaken or vicious habits; people can acquire skill to do not only what is good but also what is evil. There can be unsuitable, intractable institutions, excellent in a different age but now antiquated. There can be institutionalized evils, setups based on error, structures geared to war. . . . There can be the destruction of personal relations and status through hatred, envy, jealousy, lust, resentment, grievance. People with grievances, nations with grievances, very easily can become warped in their entire outlook.[55]

---

52. Lonergan, *Method in Theology*, 360.
53. Marx and Engels, *Communist Manifesto of 1848*, 79.
54. Lonergan, *Method in Theology*, 360.
55. Lonergan, *Topics in Education*, 34.

Toward Preventing or "Minimizing" Decline in the Face of Evil

If the needed cooperation for bringing about the good of order is lacking, then disorder, even evils, will afflict institutions. Human communities are imperfect. Both on the individual and group levels, what is good for one may or may not be good for others.[56] Good and evil get endlessly intertwined due to conflicting interests. As opposed to the positive aspects of the good, negative elements such as privations, harm, destruction, and even evils can intrude.

Eric Cassel describes how suffering can threaten a person's integrity within the complex social and psychological realities constituting a medical setting. Persons suffer when they perceive their impending destruction. This continues until "the threat of disintegration has passed or until the integrity of the person can be restored."[57] Suffering often involves "acute pain, shortness of breath, or other bodily symptoms," but it also extends "beyond the physical. It involves a state of severe distress 'associated with events that threaten the intactness of the person.'" It can occur "in relation to any aspect of the person, whether it is in the realm of social roles, the relation with self, body, or family, or the relation with a transpersonal, transcendent source of meaning."[58] Just as the good of order is a system providing particular goods over a period of time, so, too, there exist organized, chronic forms of evil. A scheme of recurrence means that something occurs and recurs. A crime wave, a depression, a war, for example, all need organized structures that keep "evils recurring."[59] People are inventive not only in honoring the human good, but also in doing evil. For Lonergan, totalitarian states possess

> not merely every technique of indoctrination and propaganda, every tactic of economic and diplomatic pressure, every device for breaking down the moral conscience . . . , but also the terrorism of a political police, of prisons and torture, of concentration camps, of transported or extirpated minorities, and of total war.[60]

---

56. Lonergan notes that "Kierkegaard distinguishes three types of existential subjectivity: the aesthetic, the ethical, and the religious. The aesthetic is connected with the particular good, the ethical with order, with what is right and wrong, and the religious with the relations between man and God" (*Topics in Education*, 42).
57. Cassel, "Nature of Suffering," 131.
58. Cassel, "Nature of Suffering," 131.
59. Lonergan, *Topics in Education*, 43.
60. Lonergan, *Insight*, 247. "An economy can falter, though resources and capital equipment abound, . . . though labor asks for work and industry is eager to employ it." One can prime the pumps and make x occur, but if the schemes are not functioning

Sadly, this is still the case today as manifested in three ways of *negating values*:

> First, the order can exist yet not be transparent. It can be too complex, too intricate for people to apprehend. This is a great danger and difficulty in modern society. The destruction of the significance of smaller groups makes the social system something that the average man cannot understand.
>
> Second, one can negate value by becoming alienated: one just drifts, makes no choices, not wanting to be a center of intelligent, rational, free, responsible choice. Insofar as he makes a choice at all, it is a choice to be like everybody else, to be one of the crowd, to conform.[61]

Third, negations of religious values occur in secular states that cannot come to terms with the reality of sin. People become estranged, as if all were components in a machine. "Man's acceptance of this world ceases to be an acceptance of God's will. We find it hard to see that this world is good."[62]

Religious communities should help reorient people toward authentic values in the midst of rampant value denials.[63] In chapter 6, we shall touch on how mystics of various faiths have helped their religious communities deal with such dilemmas. An orientation toward the divine on a *basis of values* is crucial. God is not a human invention[64] as Freud and Marx claim:

> As the question of God is implicit in all our questioning, so being in love with God is the basic fulfilment of our conscious intentionality. That fulfilment brings a deep-set joy that can remain despite humiliation, failure, privation, pain, betrayal, desertion. That fulfilment brings a radical peace, the peace that the world cannot give. That fulfilment bears fruit in a love of

---

properly, x fails to occur. Both the economy and the polity can fall apart. In a revolution, violence goes unchecked; "laws lose their meaning; . . . until from sheer weariness with disorder men are ready to accept" any effective authority. Yet "a revolution is merely a passing stroke of paralysis in the state. There are deeper ills" that appear "in the limit in the disintegration and decay of whole civilizations" (235).

61. Lonergan, *Topics in Education*, 44–46.

62. Lonergan, *Topics in Education*, 47.

63. There is much movement toward renewal within the church. When the Vatican does not allow controversial issues such as women's ordination to be discussed within its precincts, organizers find a venue outside the Vatican. Visionaries such as Lonergan have been rethinking and developing multifarious possibilities for our new age.

64. One of Lonergan's short philosophical proofs of God's existence is as follows: "If all reality is completely intelligible, then God exists. But all reality is completely intelligible. Therefore, God exists" (Lonergan, *Insight*, 695).

one's neighbor that strives mightily to bring about the kingdom of God on the earth.[65]

Religious experience is manifested differently in various historical epochs and their cultures. Humans are inventive. They may come up with alien elements that obscure or distort the question; the obscurity and the distortion are amplified when people want to expand their own power. However much religious answers differ, there is a common transcendental tendency of the human spirit that questions the significance of its own questioning, and so comes to the question of God. Unfortunately, differences in religious expression have been unending causes of tension and conflicts. Some members of the various religions are now trying to put aside their differences so as to jointly counter violence and terrorism. Lonergan uses Wilfred Cantwell Smith's faith-belief distinction to mediate between religions. Faith transcends but does not negate beliefs expressed in dogmas. As an archetypal ground of human consciousness, faith enters in one's life as a realm of mystery. In this realm, love precedes knowledge. Faith, as an inner eye of love,[66] can embolden persons to heroism in difficult times. This mystical "eye" penetrates beneath the surface of life's sordid aspects so that one may act courageously and justly. *Bringing Lonergan Down to Earth* focuses on both Christian and non-Christian beliefs with a view to overcome tensions and build transformative faith bridges[67] among religions.

Community, Moral Obligation, and Cognitive/Spiritual Interiority

Etymologically, community implies a common burden. The word's second half, *munitas*, is derived from the Latin *munus* (communal gift), which is associated with such notions as *officium* (office) and *donum* (gift). Implied here are 1) an exchange among community members who share a common experiencing, understanding, and judging; and 2) continuously reciprocating a gift. This touches on a community's moral aspects and the mutual

---

65. Lonergan, *Method in Theology*, 105. "Theological categories will be transcultural only in so far as they refer to that inner core (i.e., the dynamism of human consciousness in its knowing, choosing, and loving). In their actual formulation, they will be historically conditioned and so subject to correction, modification, and complementation" (284).

66. Rusembuka notes that "a metaphor from above downwards may at once refer to God's affectivity and grace. It is then, in both cases, a call to be in love—a fourth level that sublates other levels" (*Two Ways of Human Development*, 98).

67. Pivotal to building bridges is Lonergan's notion of *encounter*. See Lonergan, *Method in Theology*, 136, 247–50. On how mystics can or might help build spirituality-based bridges, see Raymaker and Durrani, *Empowering Climate Change Strategies*, 67.

obligations incurred by its members. This may give rise to tensions and conflicts. For Lonergan, failing to "be attentive, intelligent, reasonable, responsible" provokes tension and conflicts in a community. Communities and their members should ideally be rooted in both cognitive and spiritual interiority. The questions "What am I doing when I am knowing? Why is doing that knowing? What do I know when I do it?" all have an impact on cognitive-spiritual interiority:

> With these questions one turns from the outer realms of common sense and theory to the appreciation of one's own interiority, one's subjectivity, one's operations, their structure, their norms, their potentialities . . . and into the realm where God is known and loved.[68]

In Part III, we shall further pursue the implications of persons' *interior life*[69] reciprocally linked with other selves in communal relationships. "As the world of common sense and its language provide the scaffolding for entering into the world of theory, so both the worlds of common sense and of theory and their languages provide the scaffolding for entering into the world of interiority."[70] Interiority implies the notions of free will on the fourth level of consciousness which complements empirical, intellectual, and rational consciousness. On this fourth level, there arises the question: What am I to do? This calls for exploring the moral aspects of being related to others.

Adequately Reflecting on Ethical Theory, the Levels of the Human Good, and Cosmopolis

Lonergan defines the good in Aristotle's terms as that which everything seeks or runs after:

> It is not only what is sought or desired that is good; the capacity to desire is also good, and the desiring itself is good; and having the concrete situation in which the desiring can go on to

---

68. Lonergan, *Method in Theology*, 83–84.

69. For McCarthy, the key to religious renewal for Lonergan was the "critical investigation of human interiority" that reveals the structures of consciousness, the primordial desires for knowledge and goodness, and the impact upon them by the unconditional gift of God's love (*Authenticity as Self-Transcendence*, 292). At issue here are the conscious dynamics that underlie both the growth of Christian faith, and the achievements of modern culture. Deviations from such dynamics underlie the various forms of inauthenticity that weaken both culture and the churches.

70. Lonergan, *Insight*, 259.

operations through which one obtains the good is also good; having the cooperation necessary to get there is also good. This means that both the good that is sought and the seeking itself are good, as well as the skills that go into the process of fulfilment. What everyone seeks is certainly good, but there is a whole set of other elements that are related to it, and they are good too.[71]

Among such other elements are the three levels of the good, as well as the good of value. Unless one is given to ideology, one cannot avoid asking the question of value. "A life of pure intellect or pure reason without the control of deliberation, evaluation, responsible choice is something less than the life of a psychopath."[72] Questions of value arise on the fourth level, when one asks oneself whether something is worthwhile; they go beyond questions for intelligence—What? Why? How? What for? They also go beyond questions for reflection when they ask, "Is that really so?" Questions on the fourth level of deliberation normally lead to a decision which ends one's process of reflection.

As long as I am reflecting, I have not decided yet. Until I have decided, the reflection can be prolonged by further questions. But once I have decided and as long as I remain decided, the reflection is over and done with. The proposed course of action has ceased to be a mere possibility; it has begun to be an actuality.[73]

This is so because humans are both knowers *and* doers. The same intelligent and rational consciousness grounds doing as well as knowing. One must act on the basis of what he/she has experienced, understood, and judged: the identity of consciousness inevitably gives rise to an exigence for self-consistency in knowing, doing, and in acting ethically. For Kant, the root of ethics lies in the categorical imperative which his wished-for universal moral law (See Exploration 4). For Lonergan, the root of ethics lies in the dynamic structure of rational self-consciousness:

I am empirically conscious inasmuch as I am experiencing, intellectually conscious inasmuch as I am inquiring or formulating intelligently, rationally conscious inasmuch as I am seeking to grasp the virtually unconditioned or judging on the basis of such a grasp. But I become rationally self-conscious inasmuch as I am concerned with reasons for my own acts, and this occurs

---

71. Lonergan, *Topics in Education*, 28.
72. Lonergan, *Method in Theology*, 122.
73. Lonergan, *Insight*, 635.

when I scrutinize the object and investigate the motives of a possible course of action.[74]

An act is moral insofar as it fulfills these conditions. One is effectively rational and ethical only if one acts consistently with one's knowing. Even if there are different codes of ethics, authenticity requires an ethical coherence between knowing and doing. Wanting to go beyond the vague "aloofness" of a Kantian *a priori* in ethics,[75] Lonergan contextualizes the horizons within which we make judgments of value. Inasmuch as one is raised within a community, it is only with respect to the available common meanings that one grows in experience, understanding, judgment, and responsibility, and so comes to decide for one's self what to make of one's self. "Such is the existential moment."[76] The act of freedom "is an orientation in life and in one's existential being."[77] For Lonergan, redemption and the cultural factors of cosmopolis are fostered by grace and values: "Corresponding to judgments of value, there is cultural community. It transcends the frontiers of states

---

74. Lonergan, *Insight*, 634. "Still one's own rational consciousness is an accomplished fact in the field of knowing, and it demands in the name of its own consistency its extension into the field of doing" (*Insight*, 625). Insight and judgment constitute the acts which when rightly exercised are isomorphic with being. Lonergan's explorations of insight provide a deeper understanding of the harmonious unity of intelligence and reason. The later Lonergan's shift to interiority analysis reinforces the isomorphism between meaning and one's actions.

75. Baumgartner, in "Foundation of Value Theory," notes why Brentano rejected Kant's *a priori* concepts, that is, he saw the views of Descartes and Locke on the acquisition of knowledge as having pointed in the right direction, but regarded Kant's epistemology as obscurantist and reactionary. Husserl, a student of Brentano, later transformed Brentano's descriptive phenomenology into transcendental phenomenology, which Lonergan then adapted to develop GEM.

76. Lonergan, "Post-Hegelian Philosophy of Religion," 213. He rejects mechanist determinism because it undermines the spontaneity of human consciousness. It conceives all things as of a single kind. It posits things as instances of the "already out there now real"; it makes every event completely determined by laws of the classical type. The "combination of the two views leaves no room for a succession of ever higher systems, for the mechanism would require the higher component to be a 'body,' and determinism would exclude the possibility of the higher component modifying lower activities" (*Insight*, 280). In contrast, Lonergan's moral theory treats the human good and freedom as non-negotiable moral elements. Morality is a dialectical joining between reflection and action. Reflection has to do with intellect and human meaning whereas action has to do with will and the human good. Indeed, there is distinction but there is also relation between the two. For Lonergan, there is correspondence between that which one judges and how one should behave. Judgments are not only inward but must also be executed in our outward behaviors.

77. Lonergan, "Human Good, Meaning, and Differentiations," 35.

and the epochs of history. It is cosmopolis, not as an unrealized political ideal, but as a longstanding, nonpolitical, cultural fact."[78]

Cosmopolis would offset the effects of biases and community tensions inasmuch as it is open to supernatural solution. The supernatural "not only meets a human need but also goes beyond it to transform it into the point of insertion into human life of truths and . . . of an alliance"[79] of love that brings God to humans. Cosmopolis and kingdom-oriented communities are needed to credibly live out the genuine commitments that should characterize Christian life. For Lonergan, "There will result a heightening of the tension . . . whenever the limitations of lower levels are transcended. . . . When the higher integration is emergent in consciousness, not only is the tension itself conscious as an inner opposition and struggle but also it is objectified socially and culturally."[80] This book strives to help reprioritize Lonergan studies in pursuit of such a higher integration. It is an effort to retrieve interiority as an effective player in human affairs, as a needed dynamic viably informing an effective cosmopolis.

---

78. Lonergan, "Role of a Catholic University," 109. We explore GEM-points of insertion in interdisciplinary, interreligious, transformative efforts. The paradigm shift that occurred in Vatican II has opened doors among religions, giving us ways to act upon the forward-looking vision initiated in the Vatican II Council.

79. Lonergan, Insight, 747.

80. Lonergan, Lonergan Reader, 329. Human intentionality works from lower to higher levels as well as from higher to lower. In the latter case, one starts at the fourth level of values, of committed love (Lonergan, "Healing and Creating in History," 106). Here one lives within a horizon of a particularly sensitive area of one's life, which enables one to more easily accept, at the third level, truths that agree with what we value at the fourth level. As we progressively accept these truths, we gain a deeper understanding of their significance at the second level. Our horizon also influences the first level, making us more attentive to more important data and experiences. See Roy, "Religious Experience," 7–12.

5

Kingdom-Oriented Communities Called to Self-Transcendent Deeds

A SPECIAL WAY OF READING AND APPLYING LONERGAN'S METHOD

WE ARE PROPOSING A special way of reading Lonergan that stresses *living* the conversions both personally and communally. Having noted the roles of cosmopolis and higher viewpoints, we continue to prepare for Part III, chapter 6, where we shall focus on ways to restructure theology as informed by a dialectic of history. Lonergan's dialectic of history is best read within the context of the crises of the first half of the twentieth century and its consequences in the second half of that century. Lonergan once noted that for Bertrand Russell, the root cause of our problems lies in the fact that "our intellectual development has outrun our moral development,"[1] but, for Karl Popper, it lies in the quandary that "we are good, perhaps a little too good, but we are also a little stupid."[2] In his *The Poverty of Historicism*,[3] Popper blames the "historicists" Hegel and Marx for having provoked much

---

1. Lonergan, "Healing and Creating in History," 100.
2. Lonergan, "Healing and Creating in History," 101.
3. For Popper, historicism is the view that history is "governed by historical laws that make historical prediction possible" (Weinstein and Zakai, "Exile and Interpretation," 190). In the preface to his *Poverty of Historicism*, Popper argues that we cannot predict by way of rational or scientific methods the future developments of scientific knowledge.

of the evils that have afflicted humans such as Nazism. Far from being a historicist, Lonergan sketches his own historical contexts. He agrees with Marx that humans are protagonists of history but rejects Marx's claim that history has been altogether perverted by rationalism. Rather, he views history as guided by human knowledge and will—which, sadly, are both prone to the various biases, and even to evil.

Lonergan "had witnessed the devastating impact on human history of deeply flawed accounts both of economics itself and the relationships between economics, politics, and cultures."[4] He began to link economics and history. Like Marx, he recognizes that an economy is the stuff of which history is made, but he adds that the human good is historical and that the economy is a component of the good of order. For him, a depression comes about, not for lack of raw materials, nor for lack of factories and railways, nor for lack of capital—money is going begging. Nor is it for lack of people willing to work or invest. "It is just that the whole setup has gone awry. . . . That is a case of the evil in the depression. You can see the absence of the good of order."[5] This is why Lonergan also developed his own notions of the good and of meaning.[6] Something had gone wrong in people's views on meaning. The culprit was classicism. Today, our disengagement from classicism "must be open-eyed, critical, coherent, sure-footed."[7] As opposed to classicism, Lonergan defines culture as "the set of meanings and values that informs a way of life. It may remain unchanged for ages. It may be in process of slow development or rapid dissolution."[8] On classicist assumptions,

> there is just one culture. That one culture is *not* attained by the simple faithful . . . or the barbarians. Nonetheless, career is always open to talent. One enters upon such a career by diligent study of the ancient . . . authors. One pursues such a career by learning Scholastic philosophy and theology. . . . One succeeds by winning the . . . favor of the right personages.[9]

For Lonergan, the crisis of the good of order manifested in the Great Depression was partly due to a crisis in meaning and to a static classicist

---

4. Ormerod et al., "Development of Catholic Social Teaching," 395.
5. Lonergan, *Topics in Education*, 34.
6. "History and meaning are closely related in the thought of Bernard Lonergan. For him, history is an expression of meaning that is open to growth in authentic living or to decline into unauthenticity" (Teevan, "Praxis," 150).
7. Lonergan, "Belief," 98.
8. Lonergan, *Method in Theology*, 11.
9. Lonergan, *Method in Theology*, 326.

mentality.[10] This is what led him to study history. For the rest of his life, he sought ways to help heal history in creative ways: "History has to be understood in the twofold sense of history that is written and history that is written about. The latter has to do with historical process, the totality of . . . human actions, and historicity."[11] Two common threads running through such thinkers as Hegel, Marx, Husserl and Wittgenstein are their study of the various social processes to which humans are subject and their rejection of a mind-world dualism.[12] But, unlike these and many other philosophers, Lonergan grounds his views in the drive to know. Here we want to emphasize that for Lonergan man is a historical subject: "I am simply attempting to portray the significance of the past in the present, and, thereby, to communicate what is meant by saying that man is a historical being."[13] History fashions persons; each person is molded by his/her past. It is on that basis that one has to live or else begin afresh. Groups are historical entities living the consequences of their past. Lonergan assesses the possibility of all members of a group suffering total amnesia. Then there would be a total collapse of all group functioning because groups, too, live on their past, and their past, so to speak, lives on in them. The present functioning of the good of order is what it is mostly because of past functioning and only slightly because of the minor efforts now needed to keep things going and/or improving them. "To start completely afresh would be to revert to a very distant age."[14]

10. For Lonergan, "to confine the Catholic Church to a classicist mentality is to keep the Catholic Church out of the modern world and to prolong the already prolonged crisis within the Church" (Lonergan, "Doctrinal Pluralism," 75).

11. Lonergan, "Philosophy of History" 69. McPartland cites 1) history as a constitutive element of humans as an ontology of history); 2) the nature and scope of historical method yielding an epistemology of history; 3) general patterns or grand-scale ideal-types" as broad speculative sweeps of historical events (Lonergan, "of History," 69).

12. According to Husserl's diagnosis, the roots of the twentieth century's crises "lay in the failure to provide an adequate philosophical treatment of human subjectivity." He referred to this failure as a "crisis of psychology." For Husserl, the crisis in Europe was at heart a crisis of rationality. He identified Descartes's distinction between the rational subject and the physical world as the starting point of modern rationalism but argued that "early modern philosophy had failed to adequately conceptualize the notion of subjectivity" (Feest, "Husserl's Crisis," 44).

13. Lonergan, *Method in Theology*, 182. The historicity of human thought and action are (1) that theories, affirmations, courses of actions are expressions of human understanding, (2) that understanding develops over time and, as it develops theories, affirmations, courses of action change, (3) that such change is cumulative, and (4) that the cumulative changes in one place or time are not to be expected to coincide with those in another" (325). "Each of us lives in a world mediated by meaning, a world constructed over the years by the sum total" of our activities (221).

14. Lonergan, *Method in Theology*, 181.

For Lonergan, just as history makes us, so, too, we create history. Political regimes, schools, hospitals, and roads all stem from persons developing their potentialities. "They augment knowledge by science and perpetuate intuitions through art; they . . . protect and hasten health by medicine; and generation succeeds generation in this heritage of culture through the testament of education. All of this is a rhythmic transformation of natural potentialities by human effort."[15] Lonergan also writes that history is constituted by individuals within communities. "What a man says, what he works for are a function of his experience, . . . what he approves of and disapproves of, what he wants and does not want. His mental activities include an interpretation, an idea, of what he himself is,[16] as well as of what stands for, his nature and destiny. This is true of the individual, as well as of a group. Lonergan assesses such realities through his notions of the dynamics of history. Any healing of history affects both individuals and communities since the two are intrinsically linked. All communities have their own time-bound history and development. Dialectic implies development within the flow of history: "What goes on in the subject, what goes on in the dialogue, what goes on in the development of opinions on a single question, that also has relevance to the total field of human development; and that is history."[17]

Meaning and the human good also have their historical lineages. For Lonergan, the "notion of the human good is interchangeable with his notion "of the structure of history"[18] as it influences freedom or the roles of an economy. Being part and parcel of the good of order, an economy is historical inasmuch as it helps fashion history. Tensions do arise between essential freedom (a native capacity), and effective freedom (the deployment of this capacity). Briefly said, Lonergan's concern for history is very much related to his study of our unrestricted drive to know, as well as to his cognitional theory based on that unrestricted drive.

The structure of our knowing and doing does not function in a vacuum. Rather the four basic precepts of being attentive, intelligent, reasonable, and responsible challenge all humans. But since the actuation of the structure arises under social conditions and within cultural traditions, one must acknowledge one's historicity: "A contemporary ontology would distinguish two components in concrete human reality: on the one hand, a constant,

---

15. Lonergan, *For a New Political Economy*, 12.
16. Lonergan, "Philosophy of History," 73.
17. Lonergan, "Philosophy of History," 75.
18. Lonergan, *Topics in Education*, 24. One can best approach transcendence and immanence in the world religions, and even in atheism by adverting to the subjective side of acts of meaning and to how such acts can be "objective."

human nature; on the other hand, a variable, human historicity."[19] One acquires nature at birth, but historicity is what a person makes of one's self.

The state of being situated in history implies three dialectically-moving vectors. The first vector is progress taken as the outcome of experiencing, understanding, judging, and deciding; this must be performed in optimal fashion. The second is that of decline, which is also an outcome of these four types of operations when deformed by various malfunctions, such as the biases. The third vector is redemption, including its anthropological, historical, and religious dimensions. It is an outcome of God reaching out to humanity in order to correct human failure.[20] Recall St. Augustine's definition of time as a stretching of the soul with its double meaning of present and eternal time. Time and history are interrelated, but time has to do with minds whereas history affects communities. History involves, as it were, a stretching of communities. When these are stretched over long periods of time, a civilization ensues. Implied in the idea of an "Augustinian-GEM stretching" is the notion of creative development.[21]

What Hinders Creative Human Development and Civilizational Progress

For Lonergan, nature creates, but so do humans when initiating a development. Development is an otherwise coincidental manifold of data or images integrated by insights:

> The effort to systematically formulate what is grasped by insight, or alternatively the effort to act upon it, gives rise to further questions, directs attention to further data, leads to the emergence of further insights, and so the cycle of development begins another turn. For if one gives free rein to the detached and disinterested desire to know, further questions keep arising. Insights accumulate into viewpoints, and lower viewpoints yield to higher viewpoints.[22]

---

19. Lonergan, "Natural Right and Historical Mindedness," 170.

20. Lonergan, "Insight Revisited," 272.

21. Here, one may recall the dynamism of conscious intentionality since history reflects this intentionality. There is no history without conscious intentionality and the two transcendentals of truth and the good, both of which are "comprehensive in connotation unrestricted in denotation, invariant over cultural change" (Lonergan, *Method in Theology*, 11).

22. Lonergan, *Insight*, 483.

Kingdom-Oriented Communities Called to Self-Transcendent Deeds

Our drive to know is cumulative in structure; it involves development, that is, "a flexible, linked sequence of dynamic and increasingly differentiated higher integrations that meet the tension of successively transformed underlying manifolds through successive applications of the principles of correspondence and emergence."[23] Any development builds upon previous stages, while integrating new forms which it then transforms. The process of knowing is continuous as one moves endlessly within two spheres of variable content:

> Pragmatically, there is the sphere of reality that is domesticated, familiar, common; on the other hand, there is the sphere of the ulterior unknown, of the unexplored and strange. . . . The first expands with every advance in knowledge of proportionate being. Again, the two spheres may be as separate as Sundays and weekdays, or they may interpenetrate. . . . Finally, while everyone by the dynamic structure of his being is orientated into the second sphere, it seems reserved to the outer accident of circumstance and the inner experiences that leave one now aghast, now amazed.[24]

Human development occurs from below upwards and from above downwards. This means that "achievement builds on what is inherited. It begins from experience, is enriched by understanding, is accepted by sound judgment, is directed not to satisfactions but to values."[25] Inversely, the way of heritage works from above downwards:

> It begins in the affectivity of the infant, the child, the son, the pupil, the follower. On affectivity rests the apprehension of values. On the apprehension of values rests belief. On belief follows the growth in understanding of one who has found a genuine teacher and has been initiated into the study of the masters of the past. Then to confirm one's growth in understanding comes

---

23. Lonergan, *Insight*, 479.

24. Lonergan, *Insight*, 556. "Symbols help us . . . affectively unify what logical discourse abhors." *Method*, 66.

25. Lonergan, "Natural Right," 180. Schepers comments that the way of achievement is a creative human striving from below upwards ("Human Development," 141). An appropriate image is the gradual ascent of a mountain, on which the arrival at each succeeding plateau provides a broader, farther-reaching vista. Such an effort begins with elemental experience and rises through our levels of consciousness. This is to be complemented by striving after the ideals of a faith as a mustard seed that moves mountains (Matt 17:20), of Lonergan's cosmopolis or of Ibn Arabi's W*ujud*—all of which incorporate realist ideals motivating reformers. *Wujud*, a synonym for mercy, is *the standard way* to denote the stuff of reality normally translated as existence or being (Chittick, "Compassion," 2).

experience made mature and perceptive by one's developed understanding.[26]

The creative process works within civilizations which develop both from below upwards and from above downwards. But besides development, there is decline and disintegration because it is hard to maintain sustained development. Just as man falls short due to a lack of being attentive, intelligent, reasonable, and responsible, so historically, civilizations disintegrate. "A civilization breaks down and disintegrates when the creative minority fails to exercise its creative power, leading to a withdrawal of the allegiance of the majority, a loss of social unity, and a failure of self-determination"[27] (see Exploration 10 on Toynbee). History is fragile because man is fragile.[28] Humans often fail to address their personal and communal shortcomings, and their biases. One needs to act on judgments of fact, but

> the facts are ambivalent. The objective situation is all fact, but partly it is the product of intelligence and reasonableness, and partly it is the product of aberration from them. The whole of man is all fact, but it also is malleable, polymorphic fact. No doubt, a subtle and protracted analysis can bring to light the components in that polymorphic fact and proceed to a dialectical criticism of any proposal or program.[29]

Lonergan wants to help us overcome the biases that impede progress. The commonalities of biases are basically simple in that a person's intelligence, reasonableness, and willingness

> (1) proceed from one's detached, disinterested, unrestricted desire to know, (2) are potentialities in process of development toward a full effective freedom, (3) supply the higher integration

---

26. Lonergan, "Natural Right and Historical Mindedness," 181.
27. Cargas, "Arnold Toynbee," 217.
28. Fragility manifests itself in many ways, but this does not hinder development. Greek philosophers had already understood this but without having the concept of liberation. Aristotle, in *De Anima*, describes how the vegetative, sensitive, and intellective "parts" are integrated in humans. The sensitive part is the seat of irascible appetites which may negatively influence one's freedom for development; this part must not be rejected wholesale. In his *Nicomachean Ethics*, Aristotle writes "Fear and confidence and appetite and anger and pity and in general pleasure and pain may be felt both too much and too little, and in both cases not well; but to feel them at the right times, with reference to the right objects, towards the right people, with the right motive . . . is a characteristic of virtue" (6, 1106 b 20–23). In Greek, virtue (*arete*) implies excellence based on one's sensitivity which promotes creative development. Human disintegration is due to the inappropriate use of one's sensitivity.
29. Lonergan, *Lonergan Reader*, 286.

for otherwise coincidental manifolds on successively underlying psychic, organic, chemical, and physical levels, (4) stand in tension with sensitive and intersubjective attachment, interest, and exclusiveness, and (5) suffer from that tension a cumulative bias that increasingly distorts immanent development . . . and the outer conditions under which the immanent development occurs.[30]

The said tensions divide and disorientate cognitional activity. This leads to contrary views of the good, which in turn can make the good seem to be misdirected and vice versa. "The only adequate correction is the emergence of further insights."[31] The human incapacity for sustained development is closely linked with decline: There is progress, its principle being liberty, but there also is decline and its principle of bias. There is progress when the drive to know develops normally or smoothly. Decline, on the other hand, happens when one's drive to know is disrupted. For Lonergan "the wheel of progress not only turns but also rolls along. But the wheel of decline has a similar but opposite momentum . . . until things just fall apart."[32] Each person potentially has an unrestricted drive to know, but he/she can also fall short of this natural desire and its many demands:

> Just as sustained attentiveness, insight, reasonableness, and responsibility create a situation ever more in consonance with intelligent advance . . . so too every bias away from human authenticity brings about a situation ever more inhuman. . . . It is up to man to be intelligent, act intelligently. . . . But oversights, the blindness of passion, the flimsy excuse, the plausible fallacy, the distortion of compromise, the waywardness of indulgence, all create a human world made in their own image and likeness. Such is the dialectic of decline.[33]

Blinded by biases, people often fail to follow the demands of the drive to know to its proper conclusion. Freud discovered that we are subject to hidden motivations in our actions. Lonergan notes, "There is the latent bias of unconscious motivation. There is the conspicuous bias of individual egoism that endeavors to circumvent public purpose for private gain. There are the shared delusions of groups bias"[34] which prompt people to seek only the interests of their own group. They are deluded into thinking that group

30. Lonergan, *Lonergan Reader*, 287.
31. Lonergan, *Insight*, 259.
32. Lonergan, "Post-Hegelian Philosophy of Religion," 215.
33. Lonergan, *Macroeconomic Dynamics*, 94.
34. Lonergan, "Moral Theology," 305.

interests are a contribution to the well-being of mankind.[35] Due to the general bias of common sense, one seeks only short-term goals. Common sense "includes the common nonsense of its omnicompetence, and so it insists on palpable short-term benefits at the cost of long-term evils."[36] It is due to such shortsightedness that both individuals and societies "fail to reach the universal willingness that . . . sustains the detachment of the unrestricted desire to know."[37] This affects social situations:

> The social situation is the cumulative product of individual and group decisions, and as these decisions depart from the demands of intelligence and reasonableness, so the social situation becomes, like the complex number, a compound of the rational and irrational. . . . There results the social surd. Then to understand his concrete situation, man has to invoke not only the direct insights that grasp intelligibility, but also the inverse insights that acknowledge the absence of intelligibility. The social surd which should be discounted as mere proof of aberration is regarded as evidence in favor of error. . . . Intelligence and reasonableness are found irrelevant to concrete living.[38]

Just as individuals can ignore reason's dictates, so can communities and civilizations when they begin to block intelligence. A civilization progresses when blessed with creative persons; failing that, disintegration ensues. Referring to Toynbee, *A Study of History*, which argues that as long as creativity is in charge, situations become increasingly intelligible, Lonergan comments:

> The implementation of insights in a situation not only modifies the situation but also suggests still further insights and so still further complementary changes. In contrast, when intelligent proposals are mangled by compromise, their implementation results in an objective surd. It does not make sense. It calls not for further insights but for further compromises. Only with great difficulty can that call be resisted by a leadership that already has preferred dominance to creativity.[39]

---

35. A human science must honor the empirical principle: there are no true factual judgments without a foundation in relevant data (both those of sense and of consciousness). GEM avoids reductionisms since it does not confine human knowledge to the world of experience, nor confuse factual judgments with normative judgments of value.

36. Lonergan, "Moral Theology," 305.

37. Lonergan, *Insight*, 651.

38. Lonergan, *Lonergan Reader*, 285, 312.

39. Lonergan, "Post-Hegelian Philosophy of Religion," 214. Patrick Brown writes that "implementation," although a key Lonerganian theme, has tended to be ignored by

Civilizations disintegrate when the status quo and compromise begin to prevail and

> responsible decisions fail to win acceptance. The creative minority wishes to remain in the saddle; it can choose to become a merely dominant minority; to go along with the apologists that praise such practical wisdom; to be lulled into the easy security of philosophies that stand on the unreasoning and so irrefutable basis of animal faith. The shift may occur gradually enough to pass unnoticed, but once it has occurred, consistency becomes a force working for its perpetuity.[40]

To new challenges there must correspond new responses, or else decline ensues. With Toynbee, Lonergan argued that using old social institutions as the vehicles for new social practices or idolizing formerly creative but presently outmoded ideas, institutions, or techniques[41] results in decline. After *Insight*, Lonergan began to focus on our consciousness's affective side where love is as important as the intellectual aspect. In his 1959 lectures on education, for example, he argues that the structure of history is a triadic process of progress, decline, and redemption. We must break with "the dead hand of the past, its institutions . . . the resentments and hatred it accounted for."[42] Recovery is also to be linked to the economy and to an updated knowledge of economic theory.[43]

As to economics, Lonergan partially agrees with Marx, but insists that it is not to be divorced from morality. Experts in morality and economics can and must reconcile the two.[44] An economy takes care of vital values; morality addresses our deeper values. Citizens with a common concern for values should seek to undo any organizing of human living on the basis of competing egoisms. This calls for conversion, a new understanding "of oneself because, more fundamentally, it brings a new self to be understood.

---

many of his followers (www.philipmcshane.org/forum/forums/reply/1115/).

40. Lonergan, "Post-Hegelian Philosophy of Religion," 214; this is due to subjects' minor inauthenticity, to traditions' major inauthenticity.

41. Luke 9:16 attests to this: "No one sews a piece of unshrunk cloth on an old cloak, for the patch pulls away from the cloak, and a worse tear is made. Neither is new wine poured into old wineskins, lest the skins burst, and the wine is spilled. One must pour new wine into fresh wineskins, so that both be preserved."

42. Lonergan, *Topics in Education*, 65. In "Dialectic of Authority" he notes that Christ's suffering is a "model of self-sacrificing love" (10). We stress Lonergan's relevance by integrating beliefs within an encompassing faith open to secularist views.

43. Lonergan, "Questionnaire on Philosophy," 370.

44. Lonergan, "Healing and Creating in History," 108.

It is putting off the old man and putting on the new."[45] This calls for authenticity. Our human biases show how vulnerable and sinful we are. Still, we can recover from sin. A sinful life is inauthentic. Were humans always authentic, the vector of creativity would consistently ensue. Unfortunately, this is not the case:

> Human authenticity is not some pure quality, some serene freedom from all oversights, all misunderstanding, all mistakes, all sins. Rather it consists in a withdrawal from unauthenticity, and the withdrawal is never a permanent achievement.[46]

Healing is not merely a matter of method which would permit everything to flow smoothly. In this area, one has to go mere "method." One must not forget that at the heart of Lonergan's method, change and conversion are central, indispensable elements that require change(s) in both persons and communities. Warning us of delusions in this area, Lonergan notes that there can lurk beliefs "that there is an island of safety called 'method,' that if you follow the method, you will be all right: in the sense that there is some algorithm, some set of rules, some objective solution, independent of each man's personal authenticity, honesty . . . That is not the case. The only solution lies in 'the good man.'"[47] A good man abides by the unrestricted drive to know. "If man's will matched the detachment and the unrestricted devotion beyond of the pure desire to know, the problem of evil would not arise."[48] Solutions call for people to live up to the dictates of the unrestricted drive to know so as to make the truth their own. "Our reasonableness demands consistency between what we know and what we do; and so, there is a volitional appropriation of truth that consists in our willingness to live up to it, and a sensitive appropriation of truth that consists in an adaptation of our sensibility to the requirements of our knowledge and our decisions."[49] Intellectual conversion "draws a sharp distinction between the world of immediacy and the world mediated by meaning, between the criteria appropriate to operations in the latter."[50] Moral conversion occurs when a person "acknowledges a distinction between satisfactions and values and is committed to values even where they conflict with satisfactions."[51] Reli-

---

45. Lonergan, "Doctrinal Pluralism," 86.
46. Lonergan, *Method in Theology*, 252.
47. Lonergan, "Human Good, Meaning, and Differentiations," 345.
48. Lonergan, *Insight*, 739.
49. Lonergan, *Insight*, 581–82.
50. Lonergan, "Natural Right and Historical Mindedness," 179.
51. Lonergan, *Insight*, 582.

gious conversion, as affective, is commitment to love in the home, to loyalty in the community, to faith in the destiny of humans.

Human Biases, Religious Conversion, Cosmopolis, and the Kingdom of God

Lonergan helps us explore the roles of redemptive communities within cosmopolis. It is an illusion to think that history is nothing but progress. Decline also occurs: "The dramatic subject, as practical... develops capital and technology, the economy and the state. By his intelligence he progresses, and by his bias he declines"[52] leading to both a shorter and a longer cycle of decline. The shorter cycle is due to group bias; the longer cycle originates in the general bias of common sense. Through laws, a society can partially correct the effects of both individual and group biases, but laws alone do not suffice. "While society can be counted on to combat individual bias and one group will contest the bias of another, some further element is needed to resist the rationalizations, screening memories and myths that affirm the perfections of the in-group ... and a narrow practicality."[53]

Since general bias is more resistant, Lonergan offers a twofold, higher-viewpoint solution[54] on the levels of mind and being. The longer cycle of decline "is to be met, not by any idea or set of ideas on the level of technology, economics, or politics, but only by the attainment of a higher viewpoint,"[55] that of cosmopolis which transcends mere practical thought. Cosmopolis cuts class and state down to size. Founded on the native disinterestedness of every intelligence, it "is too universal to be bribed, too effective to be ignored."[56] It rejects the rationalizations of group and class egoists. It transcends any particular loyalty to state, class, or group since it is the community of those seeking to rally a disordered society to the cause of the same disinterestedness and truth which unites them. It withdraws "from

---

52. Lonergan, *Insight*, 261.

53. Nordquest, "Cosmopolis," 38.

54. In *Insight*, Lonergan speaks of a succession of higher viewpoints characterizing the development of mathematics and of empirical science (41). But there is also the inverse phenomenon in which each successive viewpoint is less comprehensive than its predecessor.

55. Lonergan, *Lonergan Reader*, 143.

56. Lonergan, *Lonergan Reader*, 148. Nordquest, "Cosmopolis," 38, points to analogies between Aristotle's *polis*, Hegel's state, and Lonergan's cultural community. Cosmopolis as a cultural framework ranks above society and state and is *not* to be equated with *polis* or Hegel's state.

practicality to save practicality. It is a dimension of consciousness, a heightened grasp of historical origins, a discovery of historical responsibility."[57]

Religious Experience, the Polymorphism of Consciousness: Their Impact on Community Life

Intimately related to religious experience is the question of God's existence which lies on man's horizon. Intentionality implies our ability to inquire in unrestricted fashion. Lonergan calls this the inner self or "openness as fact, the ground of all higher aspiration" which is complemented by openness as achievement, namely "the self in its self-appropriation and self-realization."[58] One's unrestricted drive to know occurs through activities such as experiencing, understanding, judging. "Self-appropriation is first and foremost a process of taking possession of oneself as a knower and a doer."[59] Openness as gift is the self "entering into personal relationship with God."[60] Religion acknowledges man as a historical, embedded subject since it is concerned with man's relations to God and other humans

> So that any deepening or enriching of our apprehension of man possesses religious significance and relevance. But the new conceptual apparatus does make available such a deepening and enriching. Without denying human nature, it adds the quite distinctive categories of man as an historical being. Without

---

57. Lonergan, *Insight*, 266. Kant, *Perpetual Peace*, 121 had alluded to something similar. Because a type of "community prevails among the Earth's peoples, a transgression of rights in one place in the world is felt everywhere. . . . The cosmopolitan is an amendment to the unwritten code of national and international rights." He advises men to "act only according to that maxim whereby you can at the same time will that it should become a universal law." Kant's cosmopolitan ideal partly anticipated Lonergan's notion of cosmopolis.

58. Lonergan, "Openness and Religious Experience," 201.

59. Lonergan, *Lonergan Reader*, 18. In principle, the appropriation of heuristic procedures should enable one to solve problems and confront evil. Lonergan notes that the terms "empirical presentations," "inquiry," "insight," and "conception" "have a fixed element—their mutual relations—and a variable element that increases with self-appropriation. They are analogous—something fixed and something variable—and consequently they are open. We are not tying ourselves down to some sense of 'inquiry' that can be strictly formulated. Inquiry is what stands in certain relations to insight and conception, and that matrix of relations is the matrix that expresses one's own self-appropriation" (*Understanding and Being*, 478).

60. Lonergan, "Openness and Religious Experience," 201.

repudiating the analysis of man into body and soul, it adds the richer apprehension of man as incarnate subject.[61]

History involves both progress and decline, but people can recover from decline. Cosmopolis as higher viewpoint redeems history from decline: "Besides higher viewpoints in the mind, there are higher integrations in the realm of being,"[62] but only God can help us recover from evil. This is so because although there are ways to solve the problems of nature through accumulated insights, such an accumulation takes time, but humans are time-bound so accumulating the insight is restricted to a person's lifetime. Moreover, the understanding that man acquires in this fashion, the judgments that he forms, and the willingness that he obtains, all suffer from human biases. People have the tendency to speculate and to defend counterpositions.[63] For Lonergan, recovery is possible through religious conversion. Conversion "is intensely personal, utterly intimate, but it is not solitary. It can happen to many and they can form a community to sustain one another in their self-transformation, and to help one another . . . in fulfilling the promise of their new life."[64] What can become communal can also become historical—passing from generation to generation. It can spread from one cultural milieu to another, adapt to changing circumstances, "survive into a different age."[65]

Sadly, religion has often been a catalyst of division. Yet, for Scheler, despite the fact that men have waged war over the holy, the holy itself should be a source of unity. All divisions are based on arbitrariness, not on the holy itself.[66] For his part, Lonergan appeals to human communities,[67] each of which must come to terms with its history. Each person within a community has a mixed personal and historical stamp. History, as do communities, has a dynamic structure marked by progress, decline, redemption. As to progress, Lonergan insists that we must be attentive, intelligent, reasonable, and

61. Lonergan, "Theology in its New Context," 60–61.

62. Lonergan, *Insight*, 656.

63. Lonergan, *Insight*, 719.

64. Lonergan, "New Context," 67. The explicit formulation of GEM is historically "conditioned and can be expected to be corrected, modified. . . . What is transcultural is the reality to which such formulation refers, and that reality is transcultural because it is not the product of any culture but rather the principle that begets and develops cultures that flourish, as it also is the principle that is violated when cultures crumble and decay" (*Method in Theology*, 282).

65. Lonergan, "Theology in its New Context," 66.

66. Scheler, *Formalism in Ethics*, 86–94.

67. For Lonergan, all things human are under the dialectic "of righteousness and aberration" ("Sacralization," 242).

responsible. When we, individually or communally, fail to do so, the result is decline, a turn for the worse. But since we potentially have the ability to live by our innate drive to know and act rightly, chances are that some persons, having realized the dire state of affairs, will work to improve it. People living in a community are bound by obligation, while being responsible for their own becoming:

> There is a critical point in the increasing autonomy of the subject. It is reached when the subject finds out for himself that is up to himself to decide what he is to make of himself. In a first period, the self makes itself. But in a second period this making oneself is open-eyed, deliberate. Autonomy decides what autonomy is to be. The opposite to this open-eyed, deliberate self-control is drifting. The drifter has not yet found himself; he has not yet discovered his own deed, and so is content to do what everyone else is doing; he has not yet discovered his own will, and so is content to choose what everyone else is choosing; he has not yet discovered a mind of his own, and so he is content to think and say what everyone else is thinking and saying.[68]

In the face of today's exaggerated views on human autonomy, Lonergan refers us to the notion of the polymorphism of human consciousness which generates dramatic, egoistic, group biases as well as a general bias in common sense. It "intrudes into science confused notions of reality, on objectivity, and on knowledge."[69] For Lonergan, "being responsible" does not suffice to offset human decline because people and communities are prone to biases. God is the main protagonist of history: "I speak of redemption from within the Christian tradition, in which Christ suffering, dying and rising again is at once the motive and the model of self-sacrificing love."[70] History will be redeemed by self-sacrificing love. In the face of the limitations of our knowledge, the higher viewpoints of cosmopolis, faith, hope, love, and *interiority* are needed to complement our knowledge and to offset our biases.

---

68. Lonergan, "Existenz and Aggiornamento," 242.
69. Lonergan, *Insight*, 424.
70. Lonergan, "Dialectic of Authority," 10.

PART III

Spiritually Enriching Humanity by Living the Two Forms of Interiority—as Explored and Experienced, for Example, by Buddhist, Christian, and Muslim Mystics

IN PART III, WE continue our attempt to lay "heartfelt transformative bridges" that would complement the bridges which Pope Francis has been building among people of good will.[1] Lonergan, like the pope, spent his career doing just that; his overall work reinforces this book's kingdom-oriented theme.

A stress on communities, on bridge-building, on the heart, and on mercy implies that theology today must be reoriented. As we suggested earlier, communities should foster the good. They are complementary realities whereby Lonergan can help us overcome some of the dualisms haunting humanity. An examination of what mystics in the major world religions have written can also help us develop our transformative-bridges strategy.

---

1. In *Faith, Reason Give Harmonious Witness*, Pope Francis acknowledges the changed social-cultural context worldwide—marked by an epochal shift and anthropological-environmental crises. He calls for the presentation of a spiritual, intellectual and existential introduction to the heart of the gospel—which we seek to do on communal and personal levels.

6

Restructuring Theology to Focus on Kingdom-of-God and Cosmopolis Priorities[1]

LONERGAN'S METHOD AS A SELF-TRANSCENDENT PRAXIS

SELF-TRANSCENDENCE IS AT THE heart of community-building. Greed undermines community.[2] Psychic, intellectual, moral, and religious conversions can help people effectively integrate themselves in authentic communities. This book's exploration of the dynamics of such integrations is based on a socioethical praxis. Praxis is central[3] to liberation theologians' efforts to *restructure* theologies so as to make praxis "the very foundation

---

1. Philip Jenkins opines that by 2025 half of the Christian population will be in Africa and Latin America, with 17 percent in Asia ("Believing in the Global South," para. 3). Often, Christians in the south are more conservative than those in the North.

2. Rather than mixing the common good with crony capitalism, greed or unjust excess profit, Lonergan sets the economy in a social context aiming for the good of order. See De Neeve, "Lonergan's Economic Ideas Today," 4–10.

3. Lonergan closely links theory and praxis. Part I of *Insight* is "Insight as Activity." The second part, "Insight as Knowledge" begins with "Self-affirmation of the Knower" where he turns "from theory to practice." The same dynamic occurs in his *Method in Theology*, which moves from the mediated phase, from system to the mediating phase.

of theologizing."[4] Lonergan's interest in the praxis of self-transcendence is evident in *Method*'s stress on conversion. The models he uses are not intended to be "a hypothesis about reality; they are sets of interlocking terms and relations"[5] that describe reality and/or form hypotheses so as to help us devise ways to promote the greater good. The greater good is to be fostered by repentant[6] souls striving to live the two forms of GEM interiority. Part III will now explore a GEM praxis that radically rethinks[7] Lonergan's achievement by urging communities not to forget interfaith endeavors. Gerard Manley Hopkins's poetic insight that "the world is charged with the grandeur of God" is reflected in this book's exploration of the breadth of Lonergan's vision of interiority as an eye of love.[8] In our globalized, multi-religious world, we argue that mysticism (lived and expressed by mystics of the three major religions) can be interpreted as an "interfaith mysticism"[9] that can help unite religious, ethical persons as they individually and communally reach out to those in need and try to build a better, safer world society.

---

4. Lamb, "Praxis," 784. *Praxis*, a transliterated Greek word, indicates a rather complex set of meanings. It "does not mean simply action or activism in opposition to theory." Rather, it calls for "a transposition of the traditional" views between faith and reason. Lonergan "provides a context in which to transpose" the issues.

5. Lonergan, *Method in Theology*, xii.

6. Lonergan speaks of repentance not as merely feeling guilt but as being "an act of good will" (*Insight*, 722). We have related early ideals of Christian community and monastic communal ideals to contemporary ideals of social justice. Historically, a presumed compatibility between Buddhist monasticism and Communism failed due to the latter's materialist presuppositions. Our hope is that readers might decide to read Lonergan in more depth.

7. For Lamb, "The relationship of theory and praxis goes right to the core of the entire philosophical enterprise; it involves the relations of consciousness to being, of subject to object, of idea to reality, of word to deed, of meaning to history. Similarly, in theology, this relationship goes beyond a discussion of contemplative or active ways of life to raise such fundamental issues as the relations of faith to love, of church to world . . . of salvation to liberation, of historical and systematic to moral theology" ("Theory-Praxis Relationship," 149).

8. Our effort to develop an interfaith mysticism is based on the experiences of renowned mystics in the three world religions, as well as on the "eye of love," of interiority, and/or "ordinary mysticism."

9. For Dennis Tamburello, in his book *Ordinary Mysticism*, mystics were inspired by their creeds but reached deeper into the sources of love.

1 Some Christian Thinkers Who Reinforce Lonergan's Integration of Faith-Reason

Lonergan's *Method in Theology* charts ways to reconcile while deepening the ethics of secular and religious thinkers—a theme that underlies our attempt to "bring Lonergan down to earth" while confronting the sources and effects of violence.[10] Focusing on mercy and faith, Part III seeks to lay heartfelt transformative bridges among people of good will. An intensity such as that of Jesus or Lonergan is needed to impel further Christian efforts to achieve kingdom ideals. For Lonergan, forsaking the openness of our drives to know and to seek values is not an option. At the heart of Lonergan's attempt to reform the world is his notion of horizon whereby both the subjective and objective poles of lived human reality condition one another both symbolically and factually. Let us touch on the visions and praxis of Samuel Taylor Coleridge, Lonergan, Daniel Berrigan, C. S. Lewis, and Karen Armstrong, whose restructurings of theology and religious and secular thought have not thrown out the baby of an applied spiritual development with the bath water of an outdated classicism.

In his introduction to *The Rime of the Ancient Mariner*, Malcolm Guite writes that the more he read Coleridge, the more he saw that his poetry, his theology, revealed a deep "faith in a creator God who had made us in his own image, kindled our imaginations, and then entered his own creation to redeem us."[11] Like his mariner, Coleridge endured the agony of loneliness, and despair, but also like him he survived the ordeal, and "was rewarded with a visionary experience of transfigured beauty."[12] Lonergan, too, was a visionary who integrated the operational principles of heart and mind. In ways less obvious than Daniel Berrigan, he had a radical, intense streak. His early study of history informs his later work as reflected in the

---

10. Mary Gerhart detects the intensity informing Lonergan's Law of the Cross when she writes, "the perpetuity of violence suggests that a humanist or post-humanist response is not enough" ("Bernard Lonergan's 'Law,'" 79). To be "just a human being" is "to forsake the openness of pure desire" (*Insight*, 750). This can also lead to violence. Violence gives rise to an avalanche of "whys" that "push the boundaries of beginning and end, of cause and effect" into hard-to-overcome vicious circles.

11. Guite, "Mariner," para. 1. His "book was written in the conviction that Coleridge is not only one of the great romantic poets, but also a prophet for our time, that his rejection of a meaningless 'mechanistic/material' view of the world, and his return to a rich Trinitarian faith, combined with his capacity to share that vision and work out its implications for the way we live our lives, made him a writer with as much" to say to the twenty-first century as he had to say to his own age. See also Harter, *Faith*, 35, on symbols in Lonergan, Ricoeur, and Coleridge.

12. Adams, "Review of *The Rime*," 1.

way his economics attempts to provide a viable alternative to capitalism and socialism. His radical vision "complements Berrigan's prophetic politics and resistance, and vice versa."[13] As did Coleridge and Berrigan, Lonergan dedicated his life to helping redeem a fallen world.

In Part I, we focused on how Christians might help foster kingdom-oriented communities. Part II explored how Lonergan can help communities rooted in personal conversion. Part III now searches for ways whereby deeply-caring humans can cooperate in establishing the kingdom.[14] Human communities cannot be considered in static ways because the world keeps changing. As Lonergan notes, "In all its stages, world process is the probable realization of possibilities."[15] Ideally, in this world of emergent probability, persons and communities would orient themselves toward the good. For Lonergan, self-transcendence is the possibility of horizon. Horizons differ from one another, from one subject to another, from one community to another, but a horizon can potentially go beyond itself to reach another horizon. This book's horizon is guided by the "possibility of willing what is truly good and doing it, of collaboration and true love, of swinging completely out of the habitat of an animal and of becoming a genuine person in human society."[16] Lonergan's view on interiority and on differentiated consciousness plays a pivotal role here. He holds that only a highly differentiated consciousness can distinguish between the realms of meaning and effectively relate these realms to one another.[17] Undifferentiated consciousness indiscriminately uses the procedures of common sense, so that its explanations, self-knowledge, and religion are all rudimentary. Differentiated consciousness occurs when the critical exigence begins to focus on interiority, when "self-appropriation is achieved, when the subject relates his several procedures to the several realms, relates the several realms to one another by consciously changing his procedures."[18] Consistent with our kingdom-of-God orientation, we argue that communities should focus on Jesus' priorities such as we read in his Sermon on the Mount: "Blessed are the pure of heart for they shall see God" (Matt 5:8) and in one of his parables

---

13. Patrick Brown, "Lonergan and Berrigan," 185.

14. One may, for example, link Jesus' teaching that "the Kingdom is among you" to the International Raiffeisen Union, a worldwide Christian voluntary association of national cooperative organizations fostering the principles of Friedrich Wilhelm Raiffeisen (1818–1888) on self-help, self-responsibility, and self-administration.

15. Lonergan, *Insight*, 149.

16. Lonergan, "Horizons," 12.

17. Lonergan, *Method in Theology*, 84.

18. Lonergan, *Lonergan Reader*, 469. On getting beyond undifferentiated consciousness, see Lonergan, *Method in Theology*, 85.

"The stone which the builder rejected has become the cornerstone."[19] The atheist Sigmund Freud stressed the "divided self"[20] aspect of persons, but Jesus and Lonergan help us reintegrate ourselves not merely psychologically but on moral, social, and spiritual levels as well.

C. S. Lewis praises Christians who are "pure of heart." Many today hesitate to even mention heaven lest they be jeered about a "pie in the sky," that is, as if they were trying to escape from

> The duty of making a happy world here and now (and turning it) into dreams of a happy world elsewhere. But either there is 'pie in the sky' or there is not. If there is not, then Christianity is false, for this doctrine is woven into its whole fabric. If there is, then this truth, like any other, must be faced, whether it is useful at political meetings or not.[21]

Lewis subtly notes that

> We are afraid that heaven is a bribe, and that if we make it our goal we shall no longer be disinterested. It is not so. Heaven offers nothing that a mercenary soul can desire. It is safe to tell the pure in heart that they shall see God, for only the pure in heart want to. There are rewards that do not sully motives. A man's love for a woman is not mercenary because he wants to marry her, nor his love for poetry mercenary because he wants to read it, nor his love of exercise less disinterested because he wants to run and leap and walk. Love, by definition, seeks to enjoy its object.[22]

This book takes its stand on analyses such as that of C. S. Lewis. One must be more realistic than "Christians" who appease their conscience by downplaying Jesus' message to help others.[23]

Karen Armstrong's compassionate mediation of faith and reason reflects the faith-belief position of William Cantwell Smith and Lonergan.[24] It

---

19. Matt 21:42.

20. Laing explores this Freudian theme focusing on "schizoid," that is, "an individual the totality of whose experience is split in two main ways: in the first place, there is a rent in his relation with his world and, in the second, there is a disruption of his relation with himself" (*Divided Self*, 1).

21. Lewis, *Joyful Christian*, 257.

22. Lewis, *Joyful Christian*, 257.

23. For a critique of those who risk diluting the Christian message, see Maspero, *Rethinking*, 257.

24. In her document posted on the Internet, *Charter for Compassion*, Armstrong acknowledges Wilfred Cantwell Smith and Lonergan as guides in her approach.

helps rebut Ayn Rand's view on a selfish "objectivism." Whereas Armstrong advocates compassion, Rand lacks compassion—except when one can profit from it. Rand writes that throughout history, man has been offered the alternative of being moral through a life of sacrifice to others, or being "selfish" through a life of sacrificing others to oneself. She rejects this as a false alternative, holding that a selfish, non-sacrificial way of life is "both possible and necessary for man."[25] She adds that "objectivism" rejects belief in anything alleged to transcend existence. This claim is false inasmuch as the transcendent transcends earthly existence. She assumes that only "existence exists."[26] Lonergan has shown that the way we can verify existence and derive metaphysics is rooted in our cognitional process and the pivotal role of virtually unconditioned judgments[27] in that process. This underpins and complements GEM foundations for faith and religious commitments. But Ayn Rand opines that

> Existence is a primary: it is uncreated, indestructible, eternal. So, if you are to postulate something beyond existence—some supernatural realm—you must do it by openly denying reason, dispensing with definitions, proofs, arguments, and saying flatly, "To Hell with argument, I have faith." That, of course, is a willful rejection of reason.[28]

Rand's objectivism is naïve, a biased view that leads to an ideological atheism, one that is diametrically opposed to Lonergan's realist approaches to metaphysics, to existence, and to our hearts.

2.1 Thomas Merton Reinforces Lonergan's Integration of Faith-Reason through Buddhism

In negative theology, an experience of the divine cannot be expressed in words. Humans cannot define the infinite-yet-unified complexity of the divine. Any attempted description of the divine is mistaken. Lonergan avoids this dilemma[29] by emphasizing interiority and reintegrating the spiritual and communal dimensions of life. Prayer transforms persons. The Loner-

---

25. Rand, *Virtue of Selfishness*, 31.
26. Rand, "Existence," para. 1.
27. Lonergan, *Insight*, 349.
28. Rand, "Atheism," para. 2.

29. Paradoxically, this dilemma helps relate the three world religions in that all of their mystics acknowledge the limitation of words as to the Ultimate. But since humans need words to communicate, the experience of God is paraphrased in "beliefs" which help unite the believers of a given religion but separate them from other religions.

gan scholar Joe Martos notes in a personal email message that whenever someone tells him they do not believe in God, "I tell them that I probably do not believe in the type of God they are imagining."[30] If Lonergan, following tradition, is correct in saying that God is totally Other, then when people talk about God they are in fact talking about their private idea or image of God. It is virtually impossible to talk directly about God who is "in heaven" as we pray in the Lord's Prayer. Some argue that when people say they experience God or his power, what they are referring to is a conscious feeling or image through which they experience something beyond themselves. Whether one meditates silently as do Zen practitioners, or whether one dances communally as in Africa, or whether one bows in prayer as do Muslims, believers do pray—but in their various traditions. For Joe Martos, practically speaking, this is not unusual since

> When you look at a person, all you literally see are skin and clothes, all you hear are sounds. In Zen meditation, one only experiences silence. But, as in other experiences of a beyond adumbrated in prayer, the sense data point to real persons who are not reducible to sense data. Likewise, when you listen to what a person is saying, your ears are hearing physical sounds, but your mind is perceiving ideas not reducible to the physical.[31]

When someone rejects the existence of God, what they are saying is that nothing they have experienced can be identified with or as God. Still a spiritual experience may have been had.

Thomas Merton is an outstanding example of one who was both imbued in and developed an interfaith mysticism. John Coleman has traced Merton's interest in the religions of Asia to his student days. A strong admirer of Gandhi, he had reflected on "how Gandhi, a Hindu, had found a congenial 'second home' of sorts in the Christian Sermon on the Mount."[32] In

---

30. Martos, in an email communication from April 24, 2018, adds that "one can remember religious experiences one has had in prayer; one can name them abstractly as experiences of God's presence or as experiences of closeness to Christ. But I can only remember them concretely, that is, I can only remember the experiences themselves in some of their emotional intensity. Similarly, I have concrete memories of falling in love, meaning that I can remember them concretely, but I can only name or refer to them using abstractions such as falling in love or having my heart go out from me."

31. Martos, in a personal message from April 27, 2008, commenting on Maguire's stance from a Lonerganian perspective.

32. Coleman, "Merton," 5. Education means bringing students "out of their darkness." Both in Catholicism and in Buddhism there is a middle way to enlighten a person. The European Enlightenment greatly weakened the Catholic Church. With respect to comparing Buddhist-Christian enlightenment, Peter Kreeft writes: "Like Jesus, Buddha taught a very shocking message. And, like Jesus, Buddha was believed

the 1950s, "Merton began exploring Buddhism, especially Zen Buddhism. He thought he found some resonance between Zen and the Desert Fathers. Like Zen *roshis*,[33] the Desert Fathers practiced a loss of the self so as to merge it into a larger reality which transcends both self and object. They often enough gave the equivalent of Zen *koans* (unsolvable and puzzling riddles) for apprentice desert monks to meditate on. Their meditations on the *kenosis* (emptying of Christ) and the monk's similar emptying in poverty and acceptance of suffering struck Merton as akin to the Buddhist notion of emptiness.[34] When Merton sent a copy of his study of the Desert Fathers to D. J. Suzuki, the two began a long correspondence in the late 1950s.

> Merton refers to the doctrine of analogy in Aquinas by which it was just as legitimate to say of God that he is non-being as to affirm God is being, since God so transcends being as we know it that any attribution of being as we know it would mislead. Merton was quite taken by the mystical tradition of a kind of un-knowing in our contemplation of God. . . . Speaking as a monk and not a writer, I am happier with "emptiness" when I do not have to talk about it.[35]

For both Christianity and Buddhism, suffering is not a problem that one should stand outside of, as it were, so as to control it.[36] Buddhism and

---

only because of his personality. 'Holy to his fingertips' is how he is described. If you or I said what Buddha or Jesus said, we would be laughed at. There was something deep and moving there that made the incredible credible." The dramatic events of Buddha's life "offer a clue to this 'something.'" It is not Buddha's life or his personality that are central to Buddhism. "there could be a Buddhism without Buddha. There could not . . . be a Christianity without Christ. "Buddha" is a title, not a given name—like 'Christ.' It means 'the enlightened one', 'the one who woke up.' Buddha argued that we are all spiritually asleep until the experience of Enlightenment or Awakening" ("Comparing Christianity & Buddhism," 1–2).

33. *Roshi* is the Japanese honorific title used for a highly venerated senior teacher in Zen Buddhism.

34. Buddhism teaches that all is a vast, interconnected web of internally related networks, a teaching that we approach from a faith-mystic perspective, allowing us to apply Lonergan's "polyphony" to life and philosophy. Raymaker, *Buddhist-Christian Logic* explores this perspective, one that is hard to reconcile with Cartesian dualism.

35. Coleman, "Thomas Merton," 5.

36. In *Zen Masters*, Merton writes that Zen is "a lived ontology which explains itself not" theoretically, but "in acts emerging out of a certain quality of consciousness and awareness. Only by these acts and by this quality of consciousness can Zen be judged" (ix). For him, Zen and Christianity are compatible. In its essence, Buddhism is about suffering, its causes, and the paths to live with and yet beyond it. It is about emptiness (the delusion of a subject-object distinction and the nonsubstantiality and transient nature of all existence). It is also about universal compassion. Merton

Christianity, each in its own way, sees suffering as part of our very ego-identity and empirical existence. "The only thing to do about it is to plunge right into the middle of contradiction and confusion in order to be transformed by what Zen calls 'the great death' and Christianity calls 'dying and rising with Christ.'"[37]

Merton had anticipated and pioneered Lonergan's openness to interfaith dialogue as well as Paul Knitter's claim that without Buddha he could not be a Christian. Merton died in Bangkok after having visited India and Sri Lanka. He had spent three successive days conversing with the Dalai Lama who observed that "he had met for the first time a Christian spiritual man who opened his own eyes to what could be learned also by Buddhism from the west."[38] Both men agreed that a Buddhist-Christian dialogue, far from being based on a facile syncretism, must scrupulously respect important differences. It was during this final trip to Asia that Merton asserted that Karl Marx's main principle of "From each according to his ability, to each according to his need"[39] forms the very basis of monastic living.

Almost twenty years after Merton's death, a group of fifty Buddhist and Catholic monks met at Merton's monastery—under the Dalai Lama's tutelage—to discuss prayer and communal life, the stages in the process of spiritual development, and the spiritual goals of personal and social transformation.[40] Our stress on spirituality and on mercy or compassion parallels

---

approves of Suzuki's comment that the most important thing is love. Merton saw Christian mystics as approaching God apophatically (without words or images) as the void, as emptiness, the transcendence of subject and object, in pure darkness (the dark night of the soul and of the senses of John of the Cross). The pure void and pure light come together. Merton cites some enigmatic remarks by: 1) John of the Cross on *todo y nada* (everything and nothing at once!); 2) the mystic Jacob Boehme: "God is called the seeing and finding of the Nothing and, therefore, is called a nothing (though it is God himself) because it is inconceivable and inexpressible"; and 3) Meister Eckhart in which he found affinities to Zen: "To be a proper abode for God and fit for God to act in, a man should also be free from all things and actions, both inwardly and outwardly" (Coleman, "Thomas Merton," 5).

37. Coleman, "Thomas Merton," 5.

38. Coleman, "Thomas Merton," 5.

39. Marx, "Critique of the Gotha Program," 16. A phrase which Marx borrowed from Louis Blanc.

40. Mitchell, *Gethsemani Encounter*, vii. A Buddhist monk endorsed Merton's remark: "At the center of our being is a point of nothingness which is untouched by sin and by illusion, a point of pure truth, a point or spark which belongs entirely to God, which is never at our disposal, from which God disposes of our lives, which is inaccessible to the fantasies of our own mind or the brutalities of our own world." See Coleman, "Thomas Merton," 5.

Merton's call for a world peace that deemphasizes predatory egos.[41] Like Lonergan, Merton stressed experience as being the starting point in one's life of prayer. Thankfully, comparable ideals are presently being stressed, sought even by some teens and young adults.[42]

2.2 Reinforcing Lonergan's Integration of Faith-Reason with Insights into Silence

Silence has been a key ingredient, a foundation, of East-West spirituality—one that should impact on societal reformations in our age of constant noise. Romano Guardini expressed it well:

> By banishing silence, our society also exiled the meaningful word. A silence that is not a rejection of the language, but rather a reappraisal of the word. Those who love silence also love the essential word. Those who do not know a long and luminous silence will never be able to enlighten with the word. Only men and women who have meaningful silence have meaningful words. A silence, which is a secret place, a safe harbor to restore a deranged, worn . . . language.[43]

Both Lonergan and William Johnston[44] sought to help those who had banished silence from their lives. In his *Silent Music*, Johnston notes

---

41. Buddhists speak of mindful living, of mindfulness. Such a mindfulness—developed in East Asia—can serve as a modern bridge for contemporary interfaith encounters. Mindfulness is the energy of being aware and awake to the present moment. It is the continuous practice of touching life deeply in every moment of daily life. To be mindful is to be truly alive, present, and at one with those around you and with what you are doing. We bring our body and mind into harmony, integrating the needs of daily life and spirituality. We argue that mindfulness can complement Christian centering prayer. The latter has revived the contemplative teachings of early Christianity, presenting these in updated formats. It draws from the ancient contemplative practices of early Christians, on the practices described in the anonymous fourteenth-century classic, *The Cloud of Unknowing*, and in the writings of Christian mystics such as John Cassian, Francis de Sales, Teresa of Avila, John of the Cross, and Thomas Merton. It is based on such sayings of Jesus as in the Sermon on the Mount: "When you pray, go to your inner room, close the door and pray to your Father in secret. Your Father, who sees in secret, will repay you" (Matt 6:6).

42. See https://www.taize.fr/en on the many young people who trek every year to Taize for spiritual renewal.

43. Guardini, "Power of Silence," 15.

44. John Carmody notes that Johnston relied on Lonergan's writings and was aware of the cognitional problems and breakthroughs that can arise when mysticism is addressed from interfaith perspectives. In such cases, participants must deepen their meaning of consciousness. They must transform their feelings. Johnston rounds out

that "In the meditation of the great religions one makes progress by going beyond thought, beyond concepts, beyond images" so as to enter into "a deeper state of consciousness, or enhanced awareness . . . characterized by profound silence."[45] Lonergan evolved after writing *Insight*. He began to see the need to address the existential gaps in people's lives by stressing an affective interiority and a benevolent love-in-action. Our book seeks to "fathom"silent meditation to reach some of its apophatic-faith-based sources. In the "language of apophatic discourse," Buddhists and Muslims have analogous ideals and goals based in their own faith-apophatic[46] experiences. In *Silent Music*, Johnston documents the deeper faith experiences that can be experienced in Zen meditation and manifested in the alpha-theta rhythms of a meditator's brain.[47] Generalized empirical method (GEM) provides an integrative-ecumenical-polyphonic potential which radically, transcendentally, integrates different cultural-religious traditions so as to foster the common good.[48]

Lonergan's views on authenticating one's consciousness and purifying the affections. One should let "the divine darkness or cloud draw off one's poisonous memories so as to guide one's life-cycle passage, purify one's soul of its deep disorder . . . to regard them in transformed ways" ("Review of *Mirror Mind*," 90). Throughout *Mirror Mind*, Johnston speaks of sensitivity to such natural phenomena as the sound of water.

45. Johnston, *Silent*, 55. Mystics realize that God is beyond words (apophatic): a realism permitting lived ideals.

46. The kataphatic deals with what can be asserted about ultimate reality or God. In the history of Christian theology, beginning with the Neo-Platonists, "God" became increasingly abstract and less personal. An apophatic theology which asserts what God is not began to arise early in the history of the church. Apophatic thinkers assume that God's perfection means being unlike anything created. God is totally beyond human understanding and language. "Apophatic" includes such mystical approaches as a negative way (Turner, *Darkness of God*, 20, 33).

47. Johnston relies on the research of Elmer Green who "associates the alpha-theta train with what he calls 'reverie', a drowsy state found when the mind moves towards sleep or unconsciousness. . . . His subjects assert that this imagery is more vivid than that of dreams in that it is much more realistic" (*Silent Music*, 15). He adds that "the mind is full of unconscious imagery of which we are ordinarily unaware" but can be made conscious (*Silent Music*, 41).

48. GEM's radically integrative potential, its ability to reconcile traditions is reflected in its reliance on implicit definition within the sciences. In *Understanding and Being*, 47, Lonergan writes: "Insofar as you have no self-appropriation whatever, experience, understanding, judgment, decisions stand as do Hilbert's points and lines in their implicit definition. There is a purely relational structure; the four terms are defined by their relations to one another, the way 'point' and 'line' are defined by Hilbert, and there is no material realization that is relevant. Thus, the four terms—empirical presentations, inquiry, insight, and conception—could have a whole series of quite different meanings so long as the definitions remain merely implicit, and the definitions have to remain merely implicit if you have no self-appropriation at all. But in the measure that

3 Christian-Islamic Forms of Mystic Love-in-Action for the Good of All

GEM helps us bridge the faith and beliefs of the various religions by its focus on the crucial notion of interiority informed by an eye love—a path of spiritual attainment inspired by the renowned founders of the three major world religions. For Lonergan, our ability to question in unrestricted ways underlies our capacity for self-transcendence, while being in love in an unrestricted fashion is the proper fulfilment of that capacity. That fulfillment stems neither from our knowledge nor our choice. No! Love dismantles and abolishes the horizon "in which our knowing and choosing went on and it sets up a new horizon in which the love of God will transvalue our values and the eyes of that love will transform our knowing."[49] One is transported into a new conscious dynamic state of love, joy, and peace. Let us explore how some Muslim-Sufi mystics have lived their religious ideals faithful to their own tradition,[50] and on how such ideals are helpful in establishing "love-faith bridges" which are able to transvalue values. For William Chittick, God has no choice because mercy is integral to his creation. "God cannot give priority to wrath over mercy, to severity over gentleness, because that would be to give priority to unreality over reality . . . to others rather than to himself. It would contradict the . . . truth upon which the universe is built, the fact that there is no reality but God, there is no true existence but God's existence."[51] True faith, as an eye of love, is a horizon helping one reach out to all in our secularized world.[52] Horizons of true faith are

---

you have some degree of self-appropriation, the four terms take on a meaning from your experience of yourself; and the greater the degree of self-appropriation you have, the more meaning the terms take on, and the fuller, the richer are the implications."

49. Lonergan, *Method in Theology*, 106. It is not an either/or question as to integrating Muslims in the West, but rather one of both/and or when-and-if Christians, secularists, and Muslims can meet at a level of respectful, tolerant values.

50. The term *Sufi* generally refers to believers who have embarked upon the mystical path. It demonstrates how the individual worshipper can become increasingly close to God through continued devotion and love.

51. Chittick, "Anthropology of Compassion," 3. Classical Sufi scholars define *Tasawwuf* as "a science whose objective is the reparation of the heart and turning it away from all else but God. It refers to the inner or esoteric dimension of Islam—as integral to Islam as is Sharia and is complemented by outward practices." Such Sufis as Al-Ghazali and Rumi considered Sufism as based upon the tenets of Islam and Muhammad's teachings; we consider it to be a practice of the heart—a relevant dialogue partner with Lonergan and with the mystics of other religions.

52. For Brague, the term "secular society" is tautological, because "the ideal of secularity is latent with the modern use of the term society. Whatever comes after secularism won't be a 'society' any longer but rather another way for us to think about and

needed to reinforce efforts to help transform the world and build communities. We now turn to summarizing the interiority-based horizons of three great Sufi mystics:[53] Abu Hamid al-Ghazali (1058–1111 CE), Ibn al-Arabi (1165–1240), and Rumi (1207–1271).

Al-Ghazali on Interpreting the Divine Reality

Al-Ghazali was dissatisfied with the science and philosophy of his day, rooted as they were in observable phenomena. The divine reality transcends all such phenomena. As did Kant seven centuries later, Al-Ghazali realized that the methods of science and philosophy could not help a believer find certitude in his/her belief. During his period of clinical depression, Al-Ghazali resigned his teaching post; he went into a period of a mystical dark night of the soul. Having affiliated himself with a Sufi community, he traveled throughout the Middle East. During this period of reflection, he completed his masterwork, *The Revival of Religious Sciences*, which deals extensively with human and divine knowledge.[54] Al-Ghazali is misunderstood due to his other master work, *The Incoherence of the Philosophers*, which does not attack reason as such but uses Muslim philosophers' methods to show that their demonstrations do not meet their own logical standards of demonstration. This has contributed to the erroneous assumption that he opposed Aristotelianism and rejected its teachings.[55] His response to philosophers is quite complex; he adopted many of their teachings. He complains at the beginning of *The Incoherence* that philosophers are convinced that their way of knowing by "demonstrative proof"[56] is superior to theological knowl-

---

give political form to the being-together of human beings" ("Impossibility of Secular Society," para. 2). Brague then traces and faults the use of the term "secularism" by Holyoake (1817–1906) and John Stuart Mill (para. 3).

53. Mystic commonalities promote understanding among religions, whereas conceptualized beliefs tend to divide. To move beyond such impasses, Lonergan, Archives, 9993ADTE080, speaks of a need for a new "conceptuality."

54. *Revival* is a very profound treatment of *ilm* (secular knowledge) and *ma'rifa* (mystical knowledge) in the Islamic tradition. In his short, important *The Niche of Lights*, Al-Ghazali explains the Sufi experience of *fana* and *fana al fana* (self-annihilation and the annihilation of self-annihilation). *Fana* involves the experience of losing oneself completely and being one with divine truth; *fana al fana* expresses a further experience of annihilating the "self" in the experience of identity with the one divine truth. As with the enlightened Buddhist Oxherd, a mystic eventually returns to the market place and to ordinary life; he silently blesses others due to his enlightenment.

55. Averroes later wrote *The Incoherence of the Incoherence* which was his way to reconcile faith and philosophy.

56. Griffel, "Al-Ghazali," 99.

edge drawn from revelation and its rational interpretation. He asserts that this has caused some Muslim philosophers to neglect Islam, its ritual duties and religious law (*sharî'a*).

Al-Ghazali wrote *The Incoherence* because the Sufi mystic Mansur al Hallaj had been publicly crucified (922 CE) in Baghdad for seeming to claim identity with the divine by saying "I am the Truth" (*ana al Haqq*). His claim was interpreted as his being one with the divine, hence he was crucified like Jesus by legalist, literal-minded Muslims who thought he had committed blasphemy. Al-Ghazali's distinction between the real oneness of the divine and an experiential felt oneness with the divine helped stop the kind of reaction meted out to al Hallaj. The distinction helped save Sufism from attacks by the legalist authorities. After Al-Ghazali's work, Sufism flourished during the Middle Ages. Al-Ghazali did not reject the legalist interpretations of the *Qur'an*, but he forged a path for Sufism which had been part of Islamic religious life since the time of Muhammad. Sufis tend to understand the sayings of the *Qur'an* in ways based on their mystical experiences. Al-Ghazali wanted to preserve both tendencies in Islam. He built bridges of understanding between the two. The rise of Wahhabism in past centuries has led to a return of a domineering literal-minded legalism amongst some politically motivated Muslims.[57]

Ibn al-Arabi: Divine and Human Love

The great scholar-mystic Ibn al-Arabi explained the implications of the Islamic worldview. Basically, wrath has no sway with God. This is a recurrent theme in Ibn Arabi's writings who sees it expressed clearly in the Qur'an, where Allah says: "My mercy embraces everything" (7:56). Ibn al-Arabi

---

57. Griffel, "Al-Ghazali," 100, notes that *Incoherence* discusses twenty *falâsifa* (philosophy) teachings, denying that they are proven. For Al-Ghazali, none of the arguments upholding the teachings fulfills the epistemological standard of demonstration the philosophers set for themselves; rather, the arguments supporting the teachings are based not upon reason, but on unproven premises accepted only by *falâsifa*. By showing that these positions are supported by mere dialectical arguments, al-Ghazâlî sought to demolish what he deemed to be philosophers' hubris. He himself taught that all persons have a natural affinity for knowledge of God—active within a person's heart center. Ahmet Karamustafa writes that Al-Ghazali invokes *surah* 33:72 of the Koran: "'We did offer the trust to the heavens and Earth and the mountains, but they declined to bear it, for they feared it, but the human being undertook it.' This indicates that human beings possess a unique characteristic that distinguishes them from the heaven and Earth and the mountains, that renders them capable of undertaking the trust of God. This trust is experiential knowledge . . . the acknowledgement of the Divine transcendent unity, and the heart of every human being is prepared for undertaking the trust and inherently capable of it" (*Knowledge of God*, 394).

often reminds us that the *Qur'an* never says anything remotely similar about wrath or severity or vengeance. He tells us over and over that everything will find its final resting place with mercy (*rahma*) because mercy is real and all else is unreal. In a typical passage, for example, al-Arabi writes:

> The final issue will be mercy, because the actual situation inscribes a circle. The end of the circle curves back to its beginning and joins with it. The end has the property of the beginning. And that is nothing but Being. Mercy takes precedence over wrath. Because the beginning was through mercy. Wrath is an accident and accidents disappear.[58]

By al-Arabi's time, mercy (*Wujud*) was in general use among scholars and Sufis. Often it can be adequately translated as Being or Existence.[59] Al-Arabi realized that loving a creature was compatible with his Islamic faith. For him, loving a being for its beauty meant that you love none other than God. He notes in his *Futubat al-Makkiyah* (*Meccan Revelation*) that in all its aspects, the object of love is God alone.[60] His collection of love poems, *The Interpreter of Desires*, expressing his monotheist ideal, is often compared to *The Song of Songs*. He held that each mystic has a unique experience of God; it follows that no one religion can express the whole divine mystery; there is no objective truth about God to which all need to subscribe; since God transcends categories of personality, predictions about God's behavior or inclinations are impossible. Ibn al-Arabi developed positive attitudes toward other religions as these can be found in the *Qur'an*. He is very tolerant as shown in some of his verses. His tolerance is a point of reference for today's movement toward interfaith understanding and dialogue. He coun-

---

58. One way to bring out the implications of *Tawhid* (the oneness of God) is to place any Quranic name of God into the formula. For example, God is creator, and it follows that there is no creator but God. God is knowing. It follows that there is none knowing but God. "God is merciful. None is merciful but God." *Tawhid* asserts that "all real qualities belong exclusively to the Ultimate Reality; all qualities of created things are essentially unreal" (Ibn al-Arabi as noted in Chittick, "Anthropology of Compassion," 2).

59. For Sufis, *wujud* has more to do with finding God "than the existence of God. Although commonly translated as 'existence,' its original meaning is 'being found,' . . . the final stage of *fana* in which one is immersed in . . . finding God while all else is annihilated" (Chittick, "Compassion," 14). This profound view of *wuju-fana* is to be contrasted to western nihilism, popularly associated with both existentialism and postmodernism. While existentialism sought a critical response to nihilism, postmodernism is a diseased symptom of nihilism, GEM as an integral, critical method which helps us find God and spread the good news to nihilist and/or multicultural worlds.

60. See http://ibnarabisociety.org/ "The experience and doctrine of love in Ibn 'Arabi."

sels: "Do not attach yourself to any particular creed exclusively, so that you may disbelieve all the rest; otherwise you will lose much, nay, you will fail to recognize the real truth of the matter."[61]

Experiencing God's Grandeur with such Mystics as Rumi

The thirteenth century witnessed the institutionalization of mysticism within both Islamic Sufism and Christian religious orders (such as in the Franciscan and Dominican orders). Rumi symbolizes a meeting of East-West aspirations. He represents the generation that after Ibn al-Arabi helped Islam turn its face from east to west. He frequently traveled throughout central Asia and the Middle East. His most famous residence was in Konya (Turkey) where he is buried. Konya has now become a modern-day pilgrimage site for Sufis and others attracted to his life and writings. For Rumi, the names of God expressed the theophany of God in nature. The type of mystical union that Al-Ghazali, Ibn al-Arabi, and Rumi experienced parallels what mystics in the other religions have described.[62] The silent experiences of East-West mystics reveal religious commonalities that can help us find bridges of heart and mind,[63] based on universal ways of knowing and doing that transcend cultures, but not the depths of spirituality.

Sufism seeks to clarify the nature of the final state of perfection, "when it has settled down slowly to its ultimate Stillness. It is not something that belongs to any one religion. It is the Essence which has been filtered out from all four religions by Wisdom. It is the Essence which has analyzed and sifted right from wrong."[64] Sufists hope to discern the divine power

61. Quoted in Nicholson, *Mystics of Islam*, 105. Miguel Asin Palacios has studied Sufism's influence upon the Spanish Christian mystics such as St. Teresa of Avila (1515–1582) and St. John of the Cross (1542–1591). He concludes that the mystical writings of the latter parallel those of the Shazali order of Sufis, "still widely present and active in North Africa, Syria, and Arabia" (Schwartz, *Other Islam*, 74).

62. We are exploring how GEM-faith-centered horizons can help us find in sound religious-philosophical traditions wise ways that can help us reorient postmodernity's often vain strivings. Rumi's famous saying "When you do things from your soul, you feel a river moving in you, a joy" might very well be applied to Lonergan's life quest.

63. A noted exponent of Sufism is Fethullah Gulen, who began his teaching mission in Turkey and now lives in the US. Having taught a mysticism of heart and mind, he has been the inspiration for the global *Hizmet* ("Service") renewal movement. During the past thirty years, *Hizmet* has spread to over 100 countries. Gulen promotes "a tolerant Islam which emphasizes altruism, hard work and education." His movement is now persecuted in Turkey. Quoted in many internet sources including www.bbc.com/news/world-13503361.

64. Bawa Muhaiyaddeen Fellowship, "Sufi" para. 3. As to some difficulties in Christian-Muslim dialogue, see Schlorff, "Muslim Ideology and Christian Apologetics."

that resides within all created lives. Relying on God, Sufis seek to bestow love and mercy on all. We use Sufi-mystic insights among others to help build transformative bridges that might help adapt religious teachings today to an ever-more-secularized world. Possible ways of adapting the teachings of Christianity and Islam differ greatly. This is due to Christianity's critical investigation of its Scriptures and Islam's difficulty in reinterpreting itself.

For Islam, the *hadiths* (sayings of the prophet Muhammad) and even *fatwas* (rulings on a point of Islamic law given by a legitimate interpreter) are given authority that go much beyond the role of tradition and church councils in determining the authenticity and roles of Christianity's sacred texts. Such differences are not easy to bridge. It is not only in Europe but also in such places as Nigeria, Iraq, and Syria that Muslim extremists have terrorized populations. Al Qaeda's involvement in the destruction of the Word Trade Center Towers in 2001 and its ties to the Taliban in Afghanistan are cases in point. Due to an increase of fundamentalist-terrorist groups such as Boko Haram and Isis, pervasive feelings of insecurity exist among many Westerners. Still, GEM's ability to build bridges of understanding among humans and religions has been implicitly lived by such Catholic mystics as Thomas Merton, Bede Griffiths, Jacques Dupuis,[65] and by such spiritual East-West bridge-builders as Al-Ghazali, Averroes, and Rumi. This book argues that the kingdom of God complemented by cosmopolis can also help bridge religious-secularist differences. Do the ideals of the kingdom of God complement Islamic ideals so as to possibly offer a comprehensive response[66] to Muslim extremists? Groups such as Isis embody what is beyond bridging possibilities, but all should be open to possibilities of bridging misunderstandings confronting us today. We argue that mystics and spirituality offer mankind effective ways of bridging religious differences that avoid diluting the depths of genuine religious experience based on love.

---

65. The Belgian Jesuit Dupuis' *Toward a Christian Theology*, that advocates rapprochement with Hinduism, led to his being investigated for unorthodoxy; he was vindicated in 2001.

66. Nicholls, *Theology*, 156. The kingdom establishes "a common ground with Muslims in recognizing the importance of submission to God, but it also helps to focus the discussion on basic assumptions and provides an excellent basis for expounding the biblical message." The differences in interpreting biblical data on the kingdom and understanding the nature of the kingdom should not affect basic truths, nor their sociopolitical implications.

A Reductionist Failure to Experience God's Grandeur: Diluting Christian Symbolic Truths

Let us briefly examine a book by a Catholic who seems to specialize in abolishing horizons of self-transcendence. In *Christianity without God*, Daniel Maguire seems unaware as to why Christianity thrives in the developing world while losing influence in rich nations. He reduces Catholic teaching to symbolic forms devoid of real meaning. He sees Christianity's supernatural aspects as being comforting, but increasingly questionable. For him, a century of "scholarly research" has called into question the church's dogmatic "triad of a personal deity; an incarnate divine Jesus, who existed before his birth; continued living after death."[67] He does retain a form of symbolic power in the Bible exemplified in the Exodus liberation movement as a conscious vision of an egalitarian, communal society based on distributive justice. For Maguire, the prophets irked Israel when it found "implementing that vision too demanding."[68] In turn, Jesus followed the example of the earlier prophets. Maguire's quasi-burial of Christianity misuses Ricoeur's wise counsel that symbols must be interpreted. Maguire simply claims that Christians effectively killed Jesus' dream by projecting a version of Christianity that is out of sync with its roots.[69] We grant that popular Christianity today fails to give enough prophetic witness to the extent that some remain focused on personal needs and anxieties, and on nationalism rather than social inequalities. But Maguire's view is a far cry from Lonergan's realistic idealism grounded in the demands of true love. Our book appeals to the heart, to Christian values which resonate in believers—not to a mere would-be theology that fails to respect and integrate mystery within interdisciplinary concerns.

For Lonergan, all love is self-surrender. Being in love with God is being in love without limits or conditions. Just as unrestricted questioning enables us to transcend self, so being in love in an unrestricted fashion enables us to properly do so. It is not due to our knowledge that unrestricted

---

67. Maguire, *Christianity without God*, 2. Maguire may still have been within the pale in his earlier *Whose Church*, reviewed at www.scouserquinn.com/?p=4318. We stress the role of mystical faith that transcends beliefs; Maguire focuses on beliefs, not faith. Lonergan's distinctions between theology as deductive and as an ongoing process, and between myth and mystery offer viable ways to radically interpret Scripture and tradition as needed today. Lonergan, *Method in Theology*, 363.

68. Maguire, *Christianity without God*, 4.

69. As does Hugo Meynell in *An Introduction to the Philosophy of Bernard Lonergan*, we argue that while Nietzsche emphasized the role of the will in acquiring power, Lonergan focuses on God, authenticity, and community, as well as on the biases afflicting mankind.

love takes hold of a person. On the contrary, love dismantles the horizon in which knowing and choosing occurs. It sets up a new horizon in which the love of God can transvalue our values. One is transported into a new, dynamic state of love, joy, and peace that manifests itself in acts of kindness, fidelity, and self-control. This new dynamic state is conscious, but this does not mean that it is known. "Consciousness is just experience, but knowledge is a compound of experience, understanding, and judging. Because the dynamic state is conscious without being known, it is an experience of mystery."[70] It remains for those taken up by ultimate concern to join efforts to build loving communities in a world of many crises.

We accept Karen Armstrong's point that *mythos* and *logos* are partners in transmitting the Christian message,[71] a view Maguire fails to grasp. Accusing theists of mistaking metaphors for facts, Maguire argues that since Christian beliefs have questionable historical roots, we should return to the revolutionary moral epic of the Hebrew and Christian Bible. "Rescued from god, Christianity could offer a realistic global ethic for healing a planet sinking under the effects of human neglect." He claims that religions have a flawed immune system."[72] Our book respects Christianity's authenticity despite its flaws. Is Maguire in fact rescuing the essential Christian message from the mythological accretions that have distorted it? For Lonergan, anthropological and historical research has made us aware of the many varieties of human social arrangements, cultures, and mentalities. The church is now in a better position to understand the variations that occurred historically in expressing Christian doctrines.

> For if the gospel is to be preached to all nations (Matt 28:19), still it is not to be preached in the same manner to all. If one is to communicate with persons of another culture, one must use the resources of their culture. To simply use the resources of one's own culture is not to communicate with the other but to remain locked up in one's own. At the same time, it is not enough

---

70. Lonergan, *Method in Theology*, 106. Lonergan invokes Otto's mystery of fascination and Tillich's being grasped by "ultimate concern."

71. The *mythos-logos* "partnership" reinforces our view on the functional specialties-cosmopolis relationship. Lonergan's notion of cosmopolis is consonant with Armstrong's view. For us, GEM offers needed secular-religious bridging possibilities provided one does not resort to ideology. For Ricoeur, "We must understand in order to believe, but we must believe in order to understand" (*Symbolism of Evil*, 351). This is not a vicious circle, but a stimulating one.

72. Maguire, *Christianity without God*, 6. For Coyne, a Christianity without God would be similar to Buddhism or Taoism: a way of life without a god. Yet, many forms of Buddhism have developed their own versions of personal deities (Review of *Christianity without God*, 6).

simply to employ the resources of the other culture. One must do so creatively. One has to discover the manner in which the Christian message can be expressed effectively and accurately in another culture.[73]

This book promotes the "ideal" of mercy at the heart of spiritual traditions.[74] We should treat others as we wish to be treated ourselves. Spiritually-enriched persons embody God's kingdom—Lonergan is at their service. Unlike Maguire, he opens doors to interfaith dialogue by emphasizing faith, not outgrown beliefs. He helps question, as does Maguire, but he questions with a faith vision.[75] One cannot ignore historical or contemporary Christian, Muslim, and secular events. Although Lonergan's method is all-too-little-known, it clearly speaks to hearts. It encourages us to intervene in today's many problems[76] and motivates us to do so. It is not restricted to academic theories. Along with Lonergan, we seek a paradigm for community service applicable to all cultures. Unlike Maguire, we seek to bridge faith horizons, not retreat into academic niceties that would suffocate the Spirit in an age of transition.

The theologian Joe Martos believes that he and Maguire "have been sailing the same spiritual trajectory, although he and I have landed in different locations." Martos "deconstructs" sacramental theology so as to reconstruct Catholic rituals. In *Honest*, he argues that, by the fourth century, symbols that had arisen from the experiences of the first generations of Christians evolved from metaphors into a "metaphysical" system,[77] which

---

73. Lonergan, *Method in Theology*, 300.

74. Joseph Campbell, an ex-Catholic, believed in God as the *life force* behind the veil of all things, a metaphor for what transcends all levels of intellectual thought. He sacrificed the power of love to that of myth. See his *Hero with a Thousand Faces*, 33.

75. It may be that in caving in to atheism, Maguire wants to preserve the right of questioning—as does Lonergan who respects mystery and integrates individual hearts striving for the good. Prayer also underlies religion-inspired cosmopolis helping us to foster Christian unity, while providing ways to criticize Christianity so as to heal hearts.

76. Such interventions can be rooted, for instance, in authenticity that is common to Christianity, Islam, and ethical secular thought. GEM is a bridge that lends itself to the see-judge-act method of liberation theology—a "simplified type of GEM." See Raymaker, *Lonergan's Third Way*, 87–96. Maguire, by rejecting the divine, disqualifies himself as a Catholic and as a dialogue partner with Islam. Interfaith dialogue requires finding common ground and cultivating an awareness of one's own presuppositions. While for Lonergan knowing leads to loving—loving being a basic fulfillment of our conscious intentionality—and while Lonergan helps humans implement the good, Maguire shoots from the hip, undermining realistic ways to bridge Christian realism and interfaith dialogue (*Method in Theology*, 105).

77. As noted in our text, Lonergan totally revised medieval-modern notions of metaphysics to offset this anomaly.

dominated the imaginations of people in Europe until the twentieth century. It was perceived as being more real than many of the sordid aspects of everyday life, but since the end of World War II it has been disintegrating under the combined impacts of secularism, globalism, religious diversity, and religious tolerance (which used to be called indifferentism). Even though some of Christianity's supernatural aspects are being questioned, our bringing-Lonergan-down-to earth approach is one that is compatible with Karen Armstrong's faith-based search for a lived compassion.[78]

Armstrong has been influenced by the faith-belief distinction which pierces through a Maguire-like straw man that would throw out the baby with the bathwater. For his part, Martos agrees with Maguire "that emphasizing the symbols (the principal components of doctrines) is not the way to go in an increasingly secularized and addictive culture. Rather, we need to find ways to celebrate values such as belonging, forgiveness, fidelity, and service to others." Addressing social ills and working for systemic change, locally and nationally, is another way to embrace the prophetic vision of Jesus and to live the "social gospel." For us, being in love with God means practicing justice.[79] In well-led parishes, faithful to the church's social doctrine, parishioners are able to make the transition from restricting[80] themselves to works of mercy to actually fighting for a justice which is able to induce needed, systemic changes.

Emotional Intentionality and the Importance of Loving and Being Loved

For Lonergan, a loving emotional intentionality and being loved are crucial.[81] In her thesis, *Body-Psyche*, on the self-appropriation of the subject

78. Chittick prefers "mercy" to "compassion" ("Anthropology of Compassion," 2). Mercy has a broader range of appropriate connotations. In English, compassion and mercy are near synonyms, but mercy implies kindness rather than severity, a choice of clemency rather than strictness. The word "mercy" works nicely to render what he considers the most important theological principle in Ibn Arabi's writing after *Tawhid* ("There is no God but God").

79. Although Jack London was raised by a blasphemous astrologer and ended up an atheist, he wrote in *The Heart of the Soul* "If you are only able to enrich the love in the world with a small spark, then you haven't lived in vain." Quoted by Westhofen-Kunz, *Stars of Heaven as Messengers*. People today are still enthralled by 1 Cor 13, on love.

80. The Islamic notion of mercy, *wujud*, goes beyond particular works of mercy to include the justice we here stress.

81. Moloney, "Spirituality," 126. He notes that Lonergan narrows the centuries-old gap between theology and spirituality. "Lonergan's philosophy is very relevant in the practice of discernment. For many people, experience itself is a form of knowledge. For

in Lonergan's work, Mary McDonald shows how Lonergan builds bridges between minds. He offers us an abbreviated explanatory account of both an evolutionary world process and its unfolding in humans who know, feel, will, and love. He asks, "What in terms of human consciousness is the transition from the natural to the supernatural?"[82] In response, he gives an account of finality in an evolutionary view of the universe as correlated with the operators in human intentional consciousness. Such notions as emergence and development, which portray an evolutionary process, are paralleled with human intentional operations that are likewise dynamically related to one another in their self-assembling pattern. Lonergan's stress on the need for theology today to address the shift of meaning from classicism to interiority and to mediate "between a cultural matrix and the significance and role of a religion in that matrix"[83] means that theology is no longer a permanent achievement, but rather an ongoing process. Robert Doran's work on psychic conversion, which includes "body data" in the self-appropriation of the unconscious, can help believers integrate their organic and psychic "spontaneities" with conscious operations, thus increasing the probability of being authentic."[84] For Lonergan, in the relation of the natural to the supernatural—as infinite and absolutely transcending all finite being—one is in a realm beyond any created reality. Yet, addressing the natural in terms of its vertical finality to the supernatural helps us "understand humanity's relationship to God. Human nature is not merely subordinate to God but somehow enters into the divine life and participates in it."[85]

Lonergan, experience is only an infrastructure of the process of knowledge. Experience is indeed necessary for there to be knowledge, but experience only becomes knowledge in so far as it is illuminated by understanding and validated by judgment" (126).

82. Lonergan, "Mission and the Spirit," 23.

83. Lonergan, *Method in Theology*, xi.

84. McDonald, "Body-Psyche-Mind," 135. For McDonald, Gendlin's description of body knowledge (*Focusing*, 4) suggests that he is "struggling within the confines of theoretical meaning" but that he is not aware of the categories of interiority needed to explain his therapeutic experience of the body. His "focusing technique" (chapter four) explains the basic principles of focusing. It offers step-by-step instructions on how to utilize focusing for tapping into greater self-awareness and inner wisdom. As one learns to develop one's natural ability to focus, one becomes more in sync with both mind and body, filled with greater self-assurance, and better equipped to make positive changes ("Body-Psyche-Mind," 135).

85. McDonald, *Body-Psyche-Mind*, 3. Our focus on the kingdom of God emphasizes all types of valid mystic experience such as that of the Sufi Al-Ghazali who realized that the way to God is through love. In *Alchemy of Happiness*, Al-Ghazali writes: "The first step to self-knowledge is to know that thou art composed of an outward shape, called the body, and an inward entity called the heart, or soul. By 'heart' I do not mean the piece of flesh situated in the left of our bodies, but that which uses all the other

Lonergan matched Maguire's passion, but his passion was in tune with ancient and modern thought. The faith-belief distinction is crucial both for evaluating today's complex religious realities and for laying foundations that can reconcile the authenticity of both secular and religious principles. Instead of belittling beliefs in our pivotal era, or of caving in to postmodernist attacks on Christianity, he helps us reintegrate[86] ourselves through faith and universal values. His method probes the minds and hearts of believers throughout the ages. *Method*'s mediating-mediated[87] phases can help build religious-secular bridges. The beliefs of any religion can become divisive, whereas faith unites minds and hearts so that believers can find commonalities with one another and with secularists. We emphasize the role of the human heart in preparing a fertile ground for bridging what, on the surface, may seem like contradictory claims. We seek a middle way between faith, beliefs, and an ethics of the heart that is able to bridge differences in transformative ways. We rely on, and appeal to, common-good efforts within vibrant faith communities. Needed bridges[88] can best be found in hearts which are devoted to ethical, spiritual principles, or to the ethical

---

faculties as its instruments and servants. In truth it does not belong to the visible world, but to the invisible, and has come into this world as a traveler visits a foreign country for the sake of merchandise, and will presently return to its native land. It is the knowledge of this entity and its attributes which is the key to the knowledge of God" (18). He adds that those not firmly grounded in this science, nor visited by an ecstasy, cannot give a full description of what he experiences. Their utterances may border on "infidelity." We bring up mystic experience to complement McDonald and Doran's search for faith-reason's heuristic structures.

86. Postmodernists often deny reason's ability to conduct fruitful philosophical discourse; they use reason to deny its validity. Lonergan counters that one cannot use reason to claim it is unable to arrive at any certainty. While postmodernism contradicts itself if it appeals to truth, the world religions have an alternative to offer to arguments for unreason. Although postmodernism is a phenomenon trafficking under the secularist umbrella, it is a marginal position. For us, a prior condition for interfaith-secularist discussions is that all parties try to understand the other. One must also be able to give reasoned arguments to justify one's basic code of behavior as well as the traditions on which one bases one's behavior. Natural law is important in bridging heart and mind so as to arrive at a modicum of understanding and a tolerant peace. Postmodernists tend to swim in a nihilist bath of nothingness rather than accept the apophatic insights on which mystics have shared cross-culturally over the millennia. That is why we invoke the important apophatic-kataphatic distinction. One must not let one's beliefs (the kataphatic) obscure or even substitute for the generosity of a converted heart's apophatic underpinnings.

87. The mediated phase involves each one's personal foundations, his/her actual state as to needed conversions.

88. For Crowe, *Level*, 161, Lonergan provides a bridge from the universe of being to the universe of the subject by *reduplicating* the structure of knowing. One may compare this to the Buddhist view that all is interrelated.

principles guiding nonideological forms of secularism. Ethical commonalities that reach deep into the "unknowns" of human experience are a key to viably reintegrating ourselves personally and communally.[89] Addressing the foundations of true love based in religious experience, Lonergan writes:

> Olivier Rabut has asked whether there exists any unassailable fact. He found such a fact in the existence of love. It is as though a room were filled with music though one can have no sure knowledge of its source. There is in the world ... a charged field of love and meaning; here and there it reaches a notable intensity; but it is ever unobtrusive, hidden, inviting each of us to join. And join we must if we are to perceive it, for our perceiving is through our own loving.[90]

Lonergan adds that there are needed historical, psychological, and sociological studies of religious interiority that will help theologians enter into the experience of others and to frame the terms and relations that can express that experience. GEM helps us build bridges of understanding between religions for it does not neglect the heart in its faith-beliefs approach. As did other bridge-builders such as Suzuki and Merton, Lonergan sought to unravel the mysteries of our hearts, of our deeper selves.[91] By so doing, one finds keys to bridge-building that transcend divisive beliefs with faith and a universal viewpoint.[92] Even if in the manner of a Bernard of Clairvaux[93] or a Thomas Merton we cannot leave the world to pursue a more

---

89. Donald Ekstrand notes that although Jewish, at the age of 27, Weil began visiting the Benedictine Abbey of Solesmes—spending considerable time there when it was empty. In her writings "she states that it was at that point that Christ inhabited her soul and allowed her to see through His eyes. Weil saw Jesus as the perfect model of affliction. She believed God's love was so great that it journeyed across space and time to draw us closer to Him. If we refuse God's love, she said, 'God would come back again and again like a beggar'" ("Spiritual Insights of Simone Weil," 23).

90. Lonergan, *Method in Theology*, 290, referring to Rabut, *L'experience religieuse fondamentale*, 168. We develop this as a polyphonic field of love.

91. Christians have, since Vatican II, pioneered new paths to encounter the traditional beliefs of Africa, Islam, and Eastern religions. By way of examples, we note the influence of Zen Buddhism on Thomas Merton or of Islam on Charles de Foucauld, murdered while reaching out to Muslims in North Africa. Merton taught us how to pray through deep Zen meditation. On Western intolerance of Muslims, see Polakow-Suransky, *Go Back*.

92. On the universal viewpoint, see Lonergan, *Insight*, 587–91. Lonergan and Gadamer's hermeneutics can help us interpret religious texts so as to coordinate such with other disciplines. Gadamer had reacted to the "destructive aspects of the Enlightenment" and rehabilitated tradition (Lonergan, *Method in Theology*, 182n5).

93. Focusing on the Catholic tradition, Tamburello relates the spiritual wisdom of Bernard of Clairvaux, Teresa of Avila, and Meister Eckhart to the challenges of being

profound vision, we today can and should nevertheless explore the deeper aspects of affectivity and the undertow of the passions that may otherwise paralyze us and thus prevent us from acting creatively. A practical way to do so is exemplified in the see-judge-act method.

A Practical, See-Judge-Act Method: Implicitly Applying Lonergan's GEM

Just as persons integrate earlier stages of their life so as to transcend earlier stages, religious leaders should respond to social needs by endeavoring to change the *status quo* in case of need. An example of this is Joseph Cardijn, whose innovative see-judge-act method helped young Christian workers in Belgium in the 1920s. His practical, effective method at first encountered much resistance. His way of encouraging young workers to make their own decisions and act upon them frightened the authorities. Cardijn responded by accusing them of denying the legitimate rights of laborers to control their own destiny. With Cardinal Mercier's permission (1924), he was allowed to promote his Young Christian Workers Movement. In effect, he sought to dispel the communist influence on young workers; his practical see-judge-act[94] method partly exemplifies this book's bridge-building efforts. It is a practical how-to method advocating needed transformations. It is, in a way, a simplified version of Lonergan's complex method.[95] In the 1960s, Leonardo Boff and other Latin American theologians adapted the see-judge-act method to confront the continent's social divides.

Both Lonergan and Cardijn developed their methods while analyzing the confused and often violent situations facing the world and workers. Lonergan's method carefully analyzes the shortcomings of modern ideological thought—as we note in Part IV's Explorations. As with the eight specialties in Lonergan's *Method*, each step in the see-judge-act method must be

---

a Christian in the modern world. For him, intimacy with God is a corrective to the cerebral way many believers approach their faith. He emphasizes grace in everyday life (*Ordinary Mysticism*, 20–141). The resources of ancient Christian mysticism can undergird our attempts to understand God's wisdom as well as human contemplation, freedom, conversion, and action possibly informing human experience.

94. The use of the visual metaphor "see" for the act of understanding risks using the language of the counter-position. The see-judge-act method of liberation theologians should not omit experiencing or deciding ,which are two tacit personal acts *essential* to any adequate presentation of GEM's basic structural elements.

95. The see-judge-act method might help bring Lonergan down to earth since it addresses pressing social problems without going into the very complex philosophical problems Lonergan had to face as a professor and writer.

integrated with other steps. Each step retains its distinctive, complementary aspects of seeing a situation, judging its positive-negative sides, and then acting in accordance with the principles of justice. The distinctive yet complementary aspects of see-judge-act and of *Method*'s eight functional specialties—if properly assessed and acted upon—partly underlies our proposal in Parts II and III for a holistic interfaith and kingdom-oriented reintegration of evangelical values and community-building. Having analyzed in simplified fashion some of the needs of today's humanity and the threats confronting us, we turn in Part IV to analyze and document some of the complex philosophical, social, and religious problems Lonergan confronted.

PART IV

The Amplitude of Lonergan's Generalized Empirical Method—Addressing Important, Complicated Philosophical Issues in Twelve Explorations

THE RATIONALE FOR OUR TWELVE EXPLORATIONS

Lonergan realistically addressed ideals.[1] We argue that both mercy (compassion), an eye of love, and the ideals of community life inform and incarnate the messages of both Jesus and Lonergan. This is in line with our aim to make Lonergan's thought accessible to the average reader who is not well versed in philosophy or theology. Still, we owe it to the reader to suggest how Lonergan treated many of the complexities inherent in philosophy. The twelve Explorations in Part IV offer detailed explanations of arguments we briefly alluded to in the text. They are thus integral to our book, but dis-

---

1. Victoria Wulf argues that unless one adopts a GEM-type critical realism that "counters animal knowing, operating in the purely biological pattern of experience in which the world is experienced as a world 'out there,' confusion occurs." One must distinguish "two different types of dialectically-related knowledge." GEM is "not an idealism of the type Vernon Bourke fears" (*Bernard Lonergan's Transcendental Realism*, 1). For Bourke, according to Wulf, "philosophies that begin with consciousness do not take seriously the claim that knowing begins with experience." This results in idealism. But Wulf replies that since Lonergan's "account of consciousness explains it as an experience of oneself as acting in relation to a world of objects, Lonergan . . . does take seriously the claim that knowing begins with experience" (*Bernard Lonergan's Transcendental Realism*, 1).

pensing with them does not mean that a reader will fail to grasp the GEM essentials we previously outlined.

GEM provides realistic-idealistic solutions to what philosophers and sociologists have debated without end. Our stress on the human heart has prepared a fertile ground for bridging what may seem to be the contradictory claims of secularists and believers. Our middle-way ethics of the heart seeks to bridge what divides the two. As a "secular method,"[2] GEM can be applied to all fields of studies. It can help bridge an ethical secularity with the teachings of world religions by helping reintegrate what Western culture has to a large extent lost in its rush to secularism. The conversions at GEM's core have their redemptive role to play both in theory and in practice. Needed philosophical bridges are best grounded in hearts that are concerned about ethical, spiritual,[3] and secular goals. To his question as to whether historians follow a theory of history or have philosophical biases, Lonergan answers that such questions regard both "the historian's notion of history" and the way he/she writes history. Some "would modify this or that heuristic structure . . . this or that element in historical method."[4] He recalls that "heuristic" has the same root as *eureka*—a word which underlies much of his own work: "While Archimedes shouted his 'Eureka!' he was aware of a significant addition to his knowledge, but it is not likely that he would have been able to formulate explicitly just what a direct insight is."[5] Having so far avoided complicated philosophical topics, in Part IV we document Lonergan's ability to resolve many such topics—even some that had befuddled many great thinkers. The twelve Explorations are based on Lonergan's view of the heuristic-historical facets of his method. His method furnishes ways for thinkers in the domains of science and/or religion to communicate with one another. For us, Lonergan's dedication to scholarship is complemented by his stress on interiority, on an eye of love in one's life.

---

2. The loss of transcendence within secular societies and the rise of fundamentalism are both problematic. GEM is partly rooted in scientific-secularist reason: at its core, it is a secular method in dialogue with secularism and religions. Secularism can be a problem if and when it attempts to be dogmatic. See also Raymaker, *Third Way*, 80.

3. Thomas McPartland writes: "If Lonergan posits a level of symbolic consciousness because the psychic level of integration is precisely the link between unconscious energy and conscious intentionality, his positing of a spiritual level strains the metaphor even more" (*Lonergan and the Philosophy*, 20). Lonergan uses the spiritual operator of unrestricted loving which may remind one of Kierkegaard, Nietzsche, or de Chardin—driven by a distinct operator beyond that of the moral.

4. Lonergan, *Method in Theology*, 224.

5. Lonergan, *Method in Theology*, 304.

Exploration 1: Aristotelian, Hegelian-Marxist Influences on Lonergan's Dialectic

Aristotle's *Politics* stresses that we live in community. We are political animals who erect communities such as the household, the village, or the *polis* so as to attain a higher good: "A state exists by nature and is prior to each (of its parts); for if each man is not self-sufficient when existing apart from a state, he will be like a part when separated from the whole. . . . Other associations aim at some good. But a state aims at the supreme good."[6] Our book focuses on a dialectic of community. Through dialectic, people seek to discover clues "to the truth by reviewing and scrutinizing the opinions of others."[7] It is because of Aristotle that dialectic became a method for effectively discussing and drawing "conclusions from acceptable premises concerning any problems"[8] being proposed so as not to say anything inconsistent. "The same attribute cannot both belong and not belong to the same subject at the same time and in the same respect."[9] But such an argument has been disputed prior to Aristotle by Heraclitus and in modern times by Hegel. Still, both Heraclitus and Aristotle influenced Hegel's dialectics.

For Hegel, dialectic is not just a set of principles to be used to discuss various subjects, as with Aristotle.[10] Rather, with Heraclitus, Hegel applies dialectic both to thought and to the whole of reality. It is due to his principle of "contradiction as a unity of opposites" that Hegel differs from Aristotle. For Aristotle, the principle of noncontradiction must be maintained, but Hegel denies this since, in his view, contradiction constitutes all that has ever existed and will exist. Hegel traces the structures of family, civil society, and state, which are dialectically opposed but are then reconciled. There is, firstly, an immediate or natural ethical spirit—the family—but it is subject to division and to relativistic points of view. This is affected, secondly, by civil society—associations of self-sufficient individuals and entities in what is therefore a formal universality. Civil society must respond to social needs in accordance with legal statutes meant to secure both persons and their property.[11] And finally, the external state comes to focus on forms of public

---

6. While other works of Aristotle explore the meaning and community, *Politics* is best suited to our purpose, if only because of Aristotle's view that "man is by nature a political animal" (Aristotle, *Politics*, 1253 a 3; a 25–30).

7. Lonergan, *Insight*, 242.

8. Aristotle, *Topics*, 100 a 20–23.

9. Aristotle, *Metaphysics*, 1005 b 11–15.

10. Ferrarin, in *Hegel and Aristotle*, outlines the ways in which Greek thinkers influenced German thinkers.

11. Hegel, *Philosophy of Right*, 357.

life embodied within itself. In this process, Hegel applies his principle of sublating (*aufheben*), that is, the activity of negating and reconciling.[12] He compares *aufheben* with the life of a bud which disappears in the bursting forth of a blossom. The blossom then turns into a fruit, its true manifestation.

> These forms are not just distinguished from one another, they also supplant one another as mutually incompatible. Yet at the same time their fluid nature makes them moments of an organic unity in which they not only do not conflict, but in which each is as necessary as the other; and this mutual necessity alone constitutes the life of the whole.[13]

In Hegel's dialectic, one stage passes into the next, both negating and yet retaining elements of previous stages. For Lonergan, a dialectical sublation of this type is that of a genetic dialectic. For Hegel, who pours "everything into the concept,"[14] dialectic involves the triadic movement of "Spirit" (*Geist*), positing itself, negating, and reconciling both stages. For Lonergan, dialectic,[15] as a combination of the concrete, the dynamic, and the contradictory, "may be found in a dialogue, in the history of philosophic opinions, or in historical process generally."[16] Lonergan builds on both Aristotle and

---

12. *Aufheben* negatively means to cancel, negate, reject. Positively, it means to lift up, pick up, sublate.

13. Hegel, *Phenomenology of Mind*, 2.

14. Lonergan, *Insight*, 447. For Hegel, history is the unfolding of *Geist* (Spirit) who fashions history; humans are mere instruments. *Geist* is creative; it runs through stages until it reaches the stage of totality when *Geist* comes to recognize itself as free because it has been liberated from alienation. For Marx, the stage of alienation is the stage of capitalism in which workers are enslaved, forced to live inhuman lives (Williams, "End of History," 199). Like Hegel, Marx thinks of history as a dialectical process in quest of freedom, but for him, 1) there can only be freedom when capitalism collapses and communism take its place, and 2) history must be conceived as having an end. Lonergan counters, arguing that we make and refashion history through knowledge, action, technology, economy, politics. Thus, the economy and morality are interdependent movers of history. Morality is concerned with the good, but much of man's acting involves producing. Hence the need for an economy. Underlying both morality and an economy is our unrestricted drive to know which points to values as well as to God.

15. Lonergan's dialectic is not restricted to Hegel's triadic structure; it includes life's ambiguities: Intellectually, morally, and socially, "men are subject to ambiguous change, to development-and-decline" (Lonergan, "Role," 109). For Lonergan, morality is the consistency between essential freedom and effective freedom. The latter involves history. Unlike Kant, for whom freedom is a postulate of practical reason, Lonergan views it as constructed within history. Here, Lonergan is closer to Hegel and Marx, enabling him to supply a missing link between the two.

16. Lonergan, *Insight*, 242. The Hegelian dialectic is often referred to as thesis, antithesis, and synthesis—terms Hegel never used. Instead, he used "in-itself, out-of-itself and being-in-and-for-itself" in the sense that the synthesis of "the for-itself" is bound

Hegel. Aristotle views the *polis* as originating in nature but Lonergan adds historical contexts. Indeed, there is a social instinct implanted in us, but history is also important. It is here that one detects Hegel's influence on Lonergan. Just as there are tripartite occurrences in Hegel, so Lonergan speaks of a dialectic of complementarity, a genetic dialectic, and a dialectic of contradiction.[17] But he transposes Hegel's tripartite division. Hegel's mutual recognition between master and slave, for example, has affinities with Lonergan's dialectic of complementarity in that master and slave imply one another: "Action by one side would be useless because what is to happen can only be brought about by both."[18] Lonergan's three types of dialectic apply to human community, to the good, and to history. Our text focuses on dialectic because Lonergan uses it both as a method and as a constitutive element in the way knowledge arises and functions. He subscribes to Hegel's ideas of the dialectic as entailing a concrete, dynamic unity of opposites and also as an activity cancelling out and retaining—that is, in the form of a unity of opposites.

But Lonergan rejects Hegel's claim of necessary outcomes in dialectic due to his own notions of emergent probability and schemes of recurrence: "Hegelian dialectic is . . . necessitarian, and immanental. It deals with determinate conceptual contents; its successive triadic sets of concepts are complete; the relations of opposition and sublation between concepts are pronounced necessary; the whole dialectic is contained within the field defined by the concepts and their necessary relations of opposition and sublation."[19] In contrast, Lonergan's position is open, factual, and normative since it deals not with determinate conceptual contents, but with heuristically defined anticipations.

> Far from fixing the concepts that will meet the anticipations, it awaits from nature and from history a succession of tentative solutions. . . . The appeal to heuristic structures, to accumulating insights, to verdicts awaited from nature and history, goes outside the conceptual field to acts of understanding that rise upon experiences and are controlled by critical reflection; and so instead of an immanental dialectic that embraces all positions and their opposites, ours is a normative dialectic that discriminates between advance and aberration.[20]

---

to happen by necessity.
   17. Doran, *Theology and the Dialectics*, 14.
   18. Hegel, "Lordship and Bondage," 30.
   19. Lonergan, *Insight*, 446.
   20. Lonergan, *Insight*, 447.

Lonergan's position is intellectualist in the sense that it accommodates all that happens both in history and in the ongoing, personal itinerary of each person. One is accountable for his/her acts of knowing, but one's recurrent concepts do not suffice; we need new heuristic anticipations that are part of emergent probability wherein the schemes of recurrence may or may not be confirmed.

How Hegel, Marx, and Lonergan Differ in their Views of Family and Community

In *Philosophy of Right*, Hegel argues that an individual cannot decide what is true on one's own. One "must have standards of legitimacy against which to validate"[21] one's claims. The family, the basic unit of human association, is an instinctual relation. Everyone comes from a family and the family influences much of one's subjectivity; this involves a process founded on mutual love. "The first moment in love is that I do not wish to be an independent person in my own right (*für mich*) and that, if I were, I would feel incomplete. The second moment is that I find myself in another person. I gain recognition in this person, who in turn gains recognition in me."[22] For Hegel, private life is bound to chains of dependence among families and civil society ratified in various social contracts. Family relations are ideally based on love as instinctual, but civil society is contractual. As families make contracts and acquire goods, they need civil society. They thereby incur both rights and obligations. Actualizing one's selfish ends "establishes a system of all-round interdependence, so that the subsistence and welfare of this individual (*des Einzelnen*) and his rightful existence (*Dasein*)"[23] are interwoven with, and grounded in, the subsistence, welfare, and rights of all, and have actuality and security only in this context.[24] Notions of self or

21. Rose, *Hegel's Philosophy of Right*, 4.

22. Hegel, *Philosophy of Right*, 158A. Hegel's dialectic reduces differences to unity, but Lonergan retains the needed distinctions. Marx fell into a Hegelian-like determinist trap when arguing that the economic infrastructure determines the superstructure (politics, education, etc.). Lonergan rejects determinism; he invokes emergent probability which focuses on both the systematic and nonsystematic features of reality. This is a profound difference. The topics of work and production are central to both Marx and Lonergan's views on economics. Marx opposes capitalism for alienating workers. Lonergan's notion of common sense may recall a master-slave dialectic.

23. Hegel, *Philosophy of Right*, 221. Heidegger, a Nazi adherent, reinterpreted *Dasein* in a nontheological sense as a way of being involved with and caring for the immediate world in which one lives, while always remaining aware of the contingent element of that involvement, of the priority of the world to the self.

24. Hegel, *Philosophy of Right*, 183.

one's identity are also mediated by civil society. One identifies one's self with one's work, but "the State in and for itself is the ethical whole, the actualization of freedom; it is the absolute end of reason that freedom should be actual."[25] The State molds one's identity through and through.

For Lonergan, common experiencing, common understanding, common judging, and common deciding are at the heart of community-building. The structures of family and community are analogous. As human understanding is dynamic, so too are human communities. While Aristotle and Hegel consider the state respectively as self-sufficient or as godlike,[26] Lonergan stresses meaning and values. With Hegel and Marx, he sees history as moving through conflicts in search of freedom. He borrows Marx's idea of man's creative activity. Hegel and Marx both opposed Kant's notion of freedom.[27] For Kant, freedom as autonomy belongs to the realm of reason. For Hegel, history is the dialectical unfolding of reason. As for Marx, freedom develops in history. "For Kant, freedom is a fact of reason; for Marx, reason is socially constructed."[28] For Hegel, the key notion of *Geist* (Spirit) includes nature, persons, and society; it is a creative reality, one which is never at rest:

> Just as the first breath drawn by a child after its long, quiet nourishment breaks the gradualness of merely quantitative growth—there is a qualitative leap, and the child is born—so likewise the Spirit in its formation matures slowly . . . into its new shape, dissolving bit by bit the structure of its previous world, whose tottering state is only hinted at by isolated symptoms.[29]

For Lonergan, creativity is a historical fact.[30] Hegel appeals to the role of great men such as Napoleon who have shaped history: *Geist* keeps on ob-

25. Hegel, *Philosophy of Right*, 258.

26. For Hegel, "Man must . . . venerate the state as a secular Deity" (*Philosophy of Right*, 272).

27. McAllister, "Influence of Immanuel Kant's Concept," 44.

28. Ypi, "On Revolution in Kant and Marx," 263. As to emancipation and the interdependence between the world of life (infrastructure) and the world of theory (superstructure), for Marx, the latter depends on the infrastructure (life).

29. Hegel, *Phenomenology of Mind*, 789.

30. Lonergan disagrees with Marx's view that the economy is the sole contributing factor to tensions and conflicts. Connected with the notion of tensions and conflicts is the notion of emancipation or freedom. For Freud, what is needed is therapy; for Marx, communism; for Lonergan, the three conversions. As noted, freedom involves the self-determination of the human subject. Any choice involves the good of value. One makes the choice for this or viewing it as the best (morally). However, there are aberrations due to human failings. There are inconsistencies on the level of the individual, on the level of community as well as on the level of history.

jectifying itself in many ways, the goal being freedom. One reaches this goal through the clash of opposing forces. *Geist* unfolds dialectically, being in a state of alienation until it is reconciled with itself. Hegel is the first thinker to systematically speak of alienation as an externalization of *Geist*. As *Geist* incessantly objectifies itself, it becomes foreign to itself, unfolding toward freedom: "History, is a conscious, self-mediating process—Spirit emptied out in Time. This externalization as an externalization of itself leads to the negative of itself."[31]

For Marx and Engels, alienation[32] has to do with the clash of forces involved in production as has occurred throughout history, being a particular phenomenon within a precise form of economy: that is, wage labor and the transformation of labor products into objects. There are four phases whereby workers are alienated from 1) the products of their labors, 2) the forces of production, 3) themselves, and 4) the community. These capitalist evils leading to alienation carry the germs of their own destruction: "In place of the old bourgeois society . . . we shall have an association, in which the free development of each is the condition for the free development of all."[33] Capitalists seek to justify their actions, but need prompts workers to solve their problems in solidarity.[34]

Marxists argue that the clash of opposing forces is grounded in the forces of production inherent in man's essence.[35] As the forces of produc-

---

31. Hegel, *Phenomenology of Mind*, 789. Becoming is a slow-moving "gallery of images, each of which is endowed with the riches of Spirit. It moves slowly for the Self has to . . . digest this entire wealth of its substance" (789).

32. "Spirit is . . . a twofold activity, of creation or self-expression and of the reconciling self-interpretation of what it has created. The process through which Spirit actualizes itself therefore involves an intermediate moment of 'division' in which its objectivity has been posited as external to it but has not yet been reconciled or taken back into it. The immediate positing of the object is 'externalization', the experience of it as an . . . 'estrangement.'" Wood, "Alienation," I:179.

33. Marx and Engels, *Communist Manifesto*, I:127. See Musto, "Revisiting Marx's Conception," 79.

34. Hook, *From Hegel to Marx*, 39.

35. This is a crucial point analyzed by Kain: "Marx's concept of essence somewhat resembles Aristotle's. For Aristotle, the essence of a thing is formulated in its definition. The essence cannot be independent of its matter or substratum, but neither can it be defined in terms of its matter alone. The definition grasps the form of the thing. For Aristotle, the thing is more properly said to be what it is when it has attained to the fulfillment of its form than when it exists potentially. The essence of the thing is exhibited in the process of growth or development by which the form or essence is attained. Each thing has a process, activity, or function; and when it fully achieves its proper activity or function, it realizes its essence and achieves its end or good. For human beings, their proper activity—their end, their essence—is activity in accordance with reason, and the realization of this end implies happiness. In certain ways Marx's concept of essence

tion change, so does history. For Hegel and Marx, history develops through stages. For Marx, those stages are marked by the division of labor. A previous stage underpins following stages. In pre-class societies, there was "communal ownership of property and a simple division of labor."[36] Eventually, land was privatized, large cities were created, and a slave population came into being.[37] This resulted in large gaps between rich and poor. With the rise of commercial trading cities, capitalism replaced feudalism. For Marx and Engels, capitalism is the worst possible mode of production for it is there that man's alienation reaches its peak.[38]

Lonergan's notion of group bias corresponds to what Marx was opposing. Because the economy is part of the human good, we must not ignore Marx's verdict that political emancipation alone is insufficient. Since "civil society is the real basis of the state or political society, it is civil society that needs to be transformed, and it is only social emancipation that brings human emancipation."[39] When producing objects, "we are also producing and reproducing our economic and social relations. Economic relations are also products of human labor."[40] Hegel had spoken of the conditions needed for social reconciliation. Marx countered that the conditions of human alienation lead to a hostile social order, to mutual oppositions. Lonergan recovers for us notions of a just social order based on cooperation.

---

is closer to Aristotle's than to Hegel's. For Aristotle and Marx, things exist on their own and have their own essence. For Hegel, at least ultimately, there is a single essence and this essence is identified with the Idea or God: empirical things are products or manifestations of the Idea. Marx criticizes Hegel for turning things into attributes or predicates of the Idea, arguing that this robs individual things of their own reality. Nor does Marx accept Aristotle's notion that the form or end of a thing is unchanging. For him, as with Hegel, essences develop throughout history since man is free to a certain extent" ("Aristotle," 216).

36. Cited by Bottomore, *Dictionary of Marxist Thought*, 174.

37. Marx, *Capital*, 1:915. Class societies first appeared in Asia where powerful tyrants ruled. In Europe, after the fall of the Roman Empire, a large class of serfs began to work the land for a small class of aristocrats.

38. Marx and Engels, *Communist Manifesto*, 1.

39. Marx and Engels, *Communist Manifesto*, 1.

40. Sayers, "Individual and Society," 93.

EXPLORATION 2: DESCARTES' COGITO, AND LONERGAN'S NOTIONS OF CONSCIOUSNESS

The modern philosophical era opened with Descartes' *res cogitans* which replaced the "classical definition of a person as a 'rational animal.'"[41] Descartes and Lonergan both ask how one comes to know. For Hugo Meynell, whatever their differences, there is deep affinity between the two men. Both sought the ground on which to stand to move society forward. The needed ground is our consciousness. Descartes writes of his finding the Archimedean point of all knowledge[42] in *cogito*, the act of thinking. Unlike Aristotle, who relied on observing the external world, he adopts an introspective method of thinking. After considering everything thoroughly, he concludes that the proposition, "I am, I exist," "is necessarily true whenever it is put forward by me or conceived in my mind."[43] He takes that to mean that here he had discovered that this alone is certain, "inseparable from me."[44] But for how long?:

> For as long as I am thinking. For it could be that were I totally to cease from thinking, I should totally cease to exist. At present, I am not admitting anything except what is necessarily true. I am, then, in the strict sense only a thing that thinks; that is, I am a mind, or intelligence, or intellect, or reason—words whose meaning I have been ignorant of until now.[45]

Descartes asks himself: "What kind of a thing am I?" and answers that he is a "thinking thing,"[46] thus asserting that skepticism cannot shake his knowledge of self. He is "a thing that doubts, understands, affirms, denies, is willing, is unwilling, and also imagines and has sensory perceptions."[47] One is aware of one's acts of thinking, imagining, and feeling. One's certainty is based on one's being conscious of one's existence. Descartes's methodological doubt leads him to affirm himself as consciously existing. Lonergan rejects Descartes "universal doubt" in favor or his own criterion of "indubitability." This criterion "does not eliminate the experienced center of experience, the intelligible center of inquiry, insight, and formulations, the

---

41. Deely, "Defining the Semiotic Animal," 461.
42. Meynell, *Redirecting Philosophy*, 266.
43. Descartes, *Meditations on First Philosophy*, 25.
44. Descartes, *Discourse on the Method*, Part IV, 28.
45. Descartes, *Meditations on First Philosophy*, 22.
46. Descartes, *Meditations on First Philosophy*, 22.
47. Descartes, *Meditations on First Philosophy*, 26.

rational center of critical reflection, scrutiny."[48] Lonergan praises Descartes for his profound originality and enduring significance, for his "universal doubt was not a school of skepticism but a philosophic program that aimed to embrace the universe, to assign a clear and precise reason for everything to exclude the influence of unacknowledged presuppositions."[49]

Still, Descartes's breakthrough "should be disassociated from the method of universal doubt, whether that method is interpreted rigorously or mitigated in a fashion that cannot avoid being arbitrary."[50] His "thinking" includes everything of which we are directly conscious. For him, a subject becomes an object of introspection, a part of the spectacle one contemplates. Fred Lawrence comments that in the *cogito*, the Cartesian variant of thinking centers on the subject of consciousness conceived as "perceiving." This usage became fateful for modern parlance inasmuch as we are liable to say today that we are conscious of something if we perceive it expressly.[51] For Descartes, inner perception is conceived by taking a "good look" with one's eyes at something outside oneself. Quite inconsistently, consciousness is held to be a faculty of inward perception. The line of demarcation between Descartes and Lonergan is that Descartes thinks of a person as a spectator—not as a constructor.

The Cartesian approach to knowledge of taking a good look can be transposed, a la Lonergan, as that of a study of the dynamic structure of knowledge. When one talks about structure, one implies a kind of network with different operations leading to a unified outcome. For Descartes, the *cogito* submits the external world to a subordinate position. The body, as belonging to the biological realm, is best explained mechanically just as if it would be produced in a machine.[52] The mind is pure thought. A person is thus set over against the physical order, belonging to a separate ontological category, that of a thinking substance. His/her understanding of what a thing is—or even of the nature of truth—is supposedly derived simply from one's thinking about nature.

Despite his insistence on the importance of introspection in human thinking, Descartes does acknowledge the need for sense data if one is to attain knowledge. When inquiring into the nature of light, sound, or pain, he notes: "Despite the high degree of doubt and uncertainty invoked here, the very fact that God is not a deceiver, and the consequent impossibility of

---

48. Lonergan, *Insight*, 434.
49. Lonergan, *Insight*, 436.
50. Lonergan, *Insight*, 436.
51. Lawrence, "Fragility of Consciousness," 59.
52. Descartes, *Meditations on First Philosophy*, Meditation 6.

there being any falsity in my opinion which cannot be corrected by some other faculty supplied by God, offers me a sure hope that I can attain the truth even in these matters."[53] Descartes arrives at God's existence by asserting that an idea of an infinite being is embedded in the *cogito*. One acknowledges one's finite status, carrying within one's mind the idea of God as infinite being.

Lonergan rejects Descartes' claim that we arrive at certain knowledge by "taking a good look," for this sets up a mind-body dichotomy. For Lonergan, a knower is also a doer. In *Insight*, he reflects on a subject as a knower who experiences, understands, and judges. He then explores how a subject is also a doer who deliberates, evaluates, chooses, and acts. Such doing can modify or change the world of objects. But even more, it affects the subject himself. Human doing is free and responsible. Within it is contained the realities of morally developing or destroying character, of acquiring a sound personality or failing in these tasks. By one's acts a person constitutes self freely and responsibly. Indeed, one does so precisely because one's acts are the free and responsible expressions of self. As opposed to Descartes's views on doubt, understanding, and willing, Lonergan writes that "I am a knower, if I am a concrete and intelligible unity-identity-whole, characterized by acts of sensing, perceiving, imagining, inquiring, understanding, formulating, reflecting, grasping the unconditioned, and judging. But I am such a unity-identity-whole. Therefore, I am a knower."[54] It does behoove us to recall some commonalities and differences between Descartes and Lonergan. An obvious difference is that, for Lonergan, a person is a self-assembling consciousness in need of dialectic, but Descartes, as we have seen, divides all of reality into two incompatible modes of being: *res cogitans*, non-extended mind, and *res extensa*, unthinking matter. His is a dualism. In contrast, Lonergan argues that each of us is a concrete and intelligible unity-identity-whole. If Descartes doubts, Lonergan reinterprets tradition rather than doubting it.[55]

Descartes's ethics clearly acknowledges the significance of community. In a letter to Elisabeth of Bohemia (September 1645), he writes "The interests of the whole, of which each is a part, must always be preferred to those of our particular person."[56] This quote helps rectify some misunderstandings of Descartes. Lonergan follows Descartes's turn to the subject but

---

53. Descartes, *Meditations on First Philosophy*, 80.

54. Lonergan, *Insight*, 319.

55. "Descartes was unable to explain how the *res cogitans* and *res extensa* interact" (McCarthy, *Authenticity as Self-Transcendence*, 88).

56. Descartes, *Meditations on First Philosophy*, Meditation IV, 293.

rejects his claim that the mind is transparent. For Lonergan, community is primordial. One's internal life and life within a community both involve relationships. Descartes rejected Aristotle's view of the unity of matter and mind,[57] but in his *Meditations*, he seeks to establish some kind of unity. He thinks of knowledge not in terms of an activity, as does Lonergan, but in terms of mirroring. A person observes the external world so as to establish a correspondence between self and the external world. For Aristotle, there is a unity between body and soul. Lonergan upholds Aristotle's view that knowledge is an activity one performs. The external world provides images which the intellect processes. The intellect is that which is divine in man.[58] Descartes rejects Aristotle's matter-form interactions and the four causes, although he does recognize some kind of unity. For him, persons observe nature so as to discover correspondences. He differs from Aristotle in that, for him, matter is completely inert and passive, whereas for Aristotle, matter is animated. He is closer to Aristotle when he supports the idea of transcendence and of the infinite in man as originating from God. God is the guarantor of the idea of perfection in our minds.

The turn to the subject in both Descartes and Lonergan must be qualified. For Lonergan, a person dialectically engages in knowing activities through one's four complementary cognitional-volitional operations. These operations form a dynamic structure enabling humans to immanently reach toward God in search of transcendence. Any single operation does not exhaust what the human subject is. A person functions within communities, thus providing the horizon for his/her interactions with others. A person's whole being, including his/her knowledge, is constituted from the materials provided by one's life horizon. The horizon develops historically in any right-minded person. Community and dialectic both involve a multiplicity of mutually complementary operations. Both imply structure and depend on our knowing-doing operations. Levinas's ethics can be interpreted from such a point of view.

---

57. Aristotle's notion of development is largely confined to the vegetative state. For Lonergan, a person is situated historically: within history, a person's progress or decline depend on attentiveness, intelligence, reasonableness, or lack thereof. This idea is not developed by either Aristotle or Descartes. Aristotle describes man's faculties and properties from the standpoint of an outside observer. Lonergan, for his part, does so from the viewpoint of an insider. Descartes and Lonergan both view persons as conscious subjects, but Lonergan transcends Cartesian consciousness conceived as a mirror. Lonergan approaches human consciousness as that of a flow or activity.

58. Aristotle, *De Anima*, 3, 5.

EXPLORATION 3: HOW DIALECTIC DIFFERS IN HEGEL, LEVINAS, AND LONERGAN

Hegel ushered us into modern philosophy; for him, the link between two opposites is a rational one which is bound to happen. Lonergan's notion of emergent probability is characterized by openness. This marks a great difference between the two thinkers. Unlike Lonergan, Hegel views the state as a quasi-god. For Lonergan, culture may be a gateway to a transcendent being. He praises Hegel's historical-mindedness,[59] but his own dialectic rejects a Hegelian totalitarian turn. This exempts him from Levinas's criticism of Hegel for undermining transcendence:

> The relation with the other—the absolutely other—who has no frontier with the same is not exposed to the allergy that afflicts the same in a totality, upon which the Hegelian dialectic rests. The other is not for reason a scandal which launches it into dialectical movement, but the first rational teaching, the condition for all teaching. The alleged scandal of alterity presupposes the tranquil identity of the same, a freedom sure of itself which is exercised without scruples, and to whom the foreigner brings only constraint and limitation.[60]

Levinas and Lonergan both recognize difference but do not undercut transcendence. We may note that Lonergan is most relevant for Africans. Hegel claimed that Africans are short on rational thinking inasmuch as they live mostly in the commonsense world. He saw the peoples below the Sahara Desert as having remained shut out. "It is the Gold-land compressed within itself–the land of childhood, which . . . is enveloped in the dark mantle of Night."[61] With Lonergan, we hold that common sense and theory have complementary roles in arriving at valid knowledge. Hegel's notion of community in Africa has been denounced as reactionary and false.[62]

---

59. Thelma Lavine notes that Habermas has helped us see that philosophy from Descartes to Hegel's "Counter-enlightenment" has been trapped by a subject-object view of knowledge, "and a purposive, instrumental mode of relationship to things" ("Philosophy and the Dialectic," 2). A misguided principle of subjectivity devastated the whole of classical Enlightenment philosophy from Descartes to Kant and all idealistic philosophy itself, including Hegel's.

60. Levinas, *Totality and Infinity*, 203. While panentheists tend to emphasize God's presence in the world without losing the distinct identity of either God or the world, we appeal to the depths of mystic faith as an eye of love.

61. Hegel, *Philosophy of History*, 91.

62. Hegel saw Africa as having no historical part of the world. His claim has been denounced as underpinned by a
utopian, reactionary image of the African people and history. See Camara, "Falsity

EXPLORATION 4: KANT, SCHELER, AND LONERGAN ON DIALECTIC, VALUES,[63] AND THE GOOD

The Cartesian ego led to Kant's philosophy. For Kant, one cannot know the "I." In revising Descartes' method, Kant argues that "it is through enlightenment that man emerges from a self-imposed immaturity of being dependent in understanding due to a lack of . . . courage to use it without guidance from another"[64] In *Perpetual Peace*, he advises us: "Have courage, dare use your understanding."[65] He claims in his *Second Critique* (1788) that his morality is to be as much a Copernican revolution as was his 1781 theory of knowledge: "Thus far it has been assumed that all our cognition must conform to objects. . . . Let us try to find out by experiment whether we shall not make better progress in the problems of metaphysics if we assume that objects must conform to our cognition."[66] Kant argues that previous philosophers had assumed that physical objects exist independently of our minds' passive role and that knowledge consists of our accurately representing objects, but he proposes "that instead of our representations corresponding to objects, we should assume that in knowledge the objects must conform to our representations. . . . The mind is essentially active in cognition."[67] In *Insight*, Lonergan details how his epistemology avoids Kant's rigid view of the *a priori*. It is with the grasp of the unconditioned as essential to judgment that Lonergan goes beyond Kant. By identifying the notion of being with the drive of intelligent inquiry and critical reflection, and by defining metaphysics as the implementation of the integral heuristic structure of proportionate being, Lonergan develops philosophy as univer-

---

of Hegel's Theses," 82–96.

63. For Kant, a good will is always good: it maintains moral value even when it fails to achieve its moral intentions.

64. Kant, in the preface to *Grounding of the Metaphysics of Morals*, wants to establish morality's supreme principle.

65. Kant, *Perpetual Peace and Other Essays*, 41.

66. Kant, *Critique of Pure Reason*, B xvi.

67. Thorpe, *Kant Dictionary*, 55–56. Kant's ethics is a deontological moral theory: the rightness or wrongness of actions does not depend on their consequences, but on whether they fulfill our duty. Matthew Ogilvie notes that for Lonergan, Kant's "Revolution" was incomplete since his turn to the subject resulted in a relativism. Kant did succeed in bringing the subject into a technically prominent position in philosophy (*Faith Seeking Understanding*, 39). For Lonergan, after absolute idealism, the subject was well addressed by Kierkegaard, Newman, Nietzsche, and Scheler's emphases on feeling (*Method in Theology*, 264). These authors were united in the belief that "pure reason" does not exist. What counts is how a person's mind operates. This means that authenticity cannot be taken for granted; human activity is never pure. The struggle for authenticity can be won through practicing self-transcendent values.

sal knowledge without infringing upon the autonomy[68] of empirical science or common sense.

Kant and Lonergan's Complementary Notions of the Good

In morality, Kant's revolution was his rejecting traditional views that based morality on external sources such as obeying rules. He argued that people should decide for themselves[69] since moral principles reside in the will of persons—not in external sources such as revelation. What best establishes links between Kant and Lonergan in ethics is that they both legitimate ethics through their respective transcendental methods. For Kant, space and time (*a priori* forms of sensible intuition) and principles (such as causality or conditions of possibility)[70] must be in place before any experience or knowledge can occur. Kant's categorical imperative is the condition of the possibility of any moral act. Lonergan, using Kantian terms, establishes the condition of the possibility of ethics in these terms:

> Man is not only a knower but also a doer; the same intelligent and rational consciousness grounds the doing as well as the knowing; and from that identity of consciousness there springs inevitably an exigence for self-consistency in knowing and doing.[71]

For Kant, such questions as "What ought I do?" and "What can I know or hope for?" refer to the existential question of "Who am I?" For Lonergan, an authentic person does good by acting on the basis of what he/she knows. Kant's notions of the good are helpful. He defines the good in two ways: 1) "The will is a faculty of choosing only that which reason, independently of inclination, recognizes as being practically necessary, i.e., as good"[72]; and 2)

---

68. Faith and GEM's integral heuristic structure are two basic, foundational groundings that we use in this book. Faith underpins religious beliefs and is one of *Method*'s key points for addressing theology and interfaith dialogue

69. Like Adam Smith, who argued that social progress emerges as the unintended result of people's self-interested behavior, Kant held man's "unsocial sociability" promotes social progress (Thorpe, *Kant Dictionary*, 220).

70. Kant, confronted with new cultures, asked whether there was only variety. He wanted to know whether there were certain principles that run across this variety of cultures. That is why his Transcendental Aesthetic studies the conditions of possibility (*Bedingungen der Möglichkeit*) of knowledge (Thorpe, *Kant Dictionary*, 209).

71. Lonergan, *Insight*, 622.

72. Kant, *Grounding of the Metaphysics*, 412. In the third section of *Grounding*, Kant defines the will as "a kind of causality belonging to living beings insofar as they are rational; freedom would be the property of this causality that makes it effective,

"That is practically good which determines the will by means of representations of reason . . . not by subjective causes, but objectively, i.e., on grounds valid for every rational being as such."[73] For Kant, "the good is a necessary object of a rational will in accordance with a principle of reason. As the definition is purely general, we must take him to hold that to be good is to be the object of a rational will in accordance with a principle of reason; and that, vice versa, to be the object of a rational will in accordance with a principle of reason is to be good."[74]

In his quasi-definition of goodness, Kant is concerned with both the general and specific good which he categorizes as 1) my good (my welfare); 2) the good for (involving skills); and 3) the moral good in general (morality).[75] With some nuances, one can relate Kant's threefold division of the good to Lonergan's own threefold division, namely the particular good, the good of order, and the good of value. For Kant, when one acts, one must give the reasons motivating one's action. Action and the will imply one another. Herbert Paton outlines Kant's three arguments for this.

First, Kant's "my good," implies the need of prudence. For Paton, "Kant takes what I have called the good for me or my good to be my weal, my well-being (*Wohlsein*), my welfare (*Wohlfahrt*), or . . . my happiness."[76] For Kant, if it were

> easy to give a determinate concept of happiness, then the imperatives of prudence would exactly correspond to those of skill and would be likewise analytic. . . . The concept of happiness is such an indeterminate one that even though everyone wishes to attain happiness, yet one can never say definitely and consistently what it is that he really wishes and wills. The reason for this is that all the elements belonging to the concept of happiness . . . must be borrowed from experience, while for the idea of happiness there is required an absolute whole, a maximum of well-being in my present and in every future condition. Now it is impossible for the most insightful to be at the same time most powerful, but . . . finite, to frame a determinate concept of what it is that he really wills.[77]

---

independent of any determination by alien causes. Similarly, natural necessity is the property of the causality of all non-rational beings by which they are determined to activity through the influence of alien causes" (446).

73. Kant, *Grounding of the Metaphysics*, 413.
74. Paton, "Kant's Idea of the Good," ii.
75. Paton, *Categorical Imperative*, 103.
76. Paton, "Kant's Idea of the Good," viii.
77. Kant, *Grounding of the Metaphysics*, 418.

The perplexity alluded to here resides in the fact that happiness involves experience and reason, as well as the present and the future; this gives rise to tensions. These tensions can only be resolved in a moral world where the moral good reigns supreme which is also needed in the good of order. This is in some way reflected in the first section of Kant's *Grounding*, which opens with this striking statement: "There is no possibility of thinking of anything at all in the world, or even out of it, which can be regarded as good without qualification, except a good will,"[78] which can lead to happiness.

Second, Kant relates the "good for" to utility for it involves some end when dealing with problems. "All sciences have a practical part consisting of problems saying that some end is possible for us and imperatives telling us how it can be attained."[79] These involve so-called imperatives of skills.

Third, as to Kant's moral good without qualification, "a good will is good not because of what it effects or accomplishes, nor because of its fitness to attain some proposed end; it is good only through its willing, that is, it is good in itself."[80] Here Kant is anticipating Lonergan's notion of the good of value.

Each of the three types of good is guided by an imperative. Rationality involves counsels of prudence and guidelines for the useful or the laws of morality. Rationality places imperatives on the will, of which there are three kinds. The first kind of imperative might be called technical, "the second is pragmatic (belonging to welfare); the third kind pertains to free conduct as such, that is, to morals."[81] The first two imperatives are hypothetical, whereas the third is categorical. Kant's imperatives "are only formulas for expressing the relation of objective laws of willing in general to the subjective imperfection of the will of this or that rational being, e. g., the human will."[82]

A hypothetical imperative only says "that an action is good for some purpose, either possible or actual. In the first case it is a problematic practical principle; in the second case, one of assertion. Thirdly, a categorical imperative declares an action "to be of itself objectively necessary without reference to any purpose, i.e., without any other end."[83] It is an apodictic principle. Still, we must ask how does this imperative affect moral laws, free-

---

78. Kant, *Grounding of the Metaphysics*, 393.

79. Kant, *Grounding of the Metaphysics*, 415.

80. Kant, *Grounding of the Metaphysics*, 394.

81. Kant, *Grounding of the Metaphysics*, 417.

82. Kant, *Grounding of the Metaphysics*, 414. "The representation of an objective principle insofar as it necessitates the will is called a command (of reason), and the formula of the command is called an imperative" (413).

83. Kant, *Grounding of the Metaphysics*, 414.

dom, and human identity? For Lonergan, implicit in all we do there lurks the idea of the moral good. Thus, one should not postulate an oppositional dilemma, e.g. between economics and morality. Man is, in principle, moral, but depends on an economy. According to Kant's categorical imperative, one must act in conformity with the dictates of reason[84] in three ways: 1) "Act only according to that maxim whereby you can at the same time will that it should become a universal law"; 2) "Act in such a way that you treat humanity, whether in your own person or in the person of another, always as an end and never simply as a means"; and 3) "Act in accordance with the maxims of a member legislating universal laws for a mere possible kingdom of ends."[85] Kant tells us that, in fact, the three formulas (which are an effort to bridge the gap between the phenomenal and noumenal worlds) can be reduced to the one law of autonomy. Of the many possible formulas of a particular law, in fact, only one by itself

> contains a combination of the other two. Nevertheless, there is a difference among them, which is subjectively rather than objectively practical, viz., it is intended to bring an idea of reason closer to intuition (in accordance with a certain analogy) and thereby closer to feeling.[86]

For Lonergan, reflection leads to action. Kant's notion of freedom is intrinsically linked to his categorical imperative. Freedom of the will means autonomy (*auto*, "self"; *nomos*, "law"). Morality means that freedom is inseparably linked to an autonomous will. The Kantian universal principle of morality is the ground of all actions of rational beings, just as natural law is the ground of all appearances. To be autonomous means to be a law unto oneself. Autonomy implies self-determination and self-legislation, which are constitutive elements of freedom. For Kant, freedom and self-legislation of the will are both autonomous "and are hence reciprocal concepts. Since they are reciprocal, one of them cannot be used to explain the other or to supply its ground but can at most be used only for logical purposes to bring seemingly different conceptions of the same object under a single concept."[87]

For Lonergan, morality is relevant to politics' role in communities. It must be practical in the sense that it must direct individual behavior in

---

84. Notice here the similarity with Lonergan for whom there should be conformity of one's acting to one's judging.
85. Kant, *Grounding of the Metaphysics*, 439.
86. Kant, *Grounding of the Metaphysics*, 436.
87. Kant, *Grounding of the Metaphysics*, 450.

moral ways. Kant's categorical imperative extends to communities.[88] For him, morality, as applying to both individuals and to society, is

> the totality of unconditionally binding laws according to which we ought to act, and once one has acknowledged the authority of its concept of duty, it would be utterly absurd to continue wanting to say that one cannot do his duty. For if that were so, then this concept would disappear from morality.... There can be no conflict between politics as applied doctrine of right and morals as a theoretical doctrine of right.[89]

Lonergan specifies how he differs from Kant. "If we agree in affirming a categorical imperative, we disagree inasmuch as we derive it wholly from speculative intelligence and reason, from the dynamic structure of human cognition."[90] Lonergan wrote in the Cartesian tradition of the modern philosophical shift to the subject as revised by Husserl's notion of conscious intentionality. "In each of the major periods of Lonergan's work, a central role is played by a phenomenon found within human consciousness–an indubitable and existentially ineluctable desire, an immanent intentionality."[91]

For Lonergan, conscious and intentional operations exist. Anyone who would deny these operations' existence would merely disqualify one's self as being "a non-responsible, non-reasonable, non-intelligent somnambulist."[92] Just as a man cannot divest one's self of his animality, so one cannot put off the *eros* of the mind. Inquiring, understanding, reflecting, judging, deliberating, and choosing are as much an exigence of human nature as are

---

88. For Kant, an ideal community is the kingdom of ends: "The concept of any rational being as a being that must regard itself as giving universal law . . . so that it may judge itself and its actions from this standpoint leads" to the notion of "a kingdom of ends. By kingdom, I understand the systematic union of different rational beings through common laws. Because laws determine which ends have universal validity, if we abstract from personal differences of rational beings, and thus from all content of their private purposes, we can think of a totality of all ends in a systematic connection. . . . This is a kingdom of ends, which is possible on the principles stated above. For all rational beings stand under the law that each of them should treat himself and others never merely as means, but in every case also as an end in himself. There thus arises a systematic union of rational beings through common objective laws. This is a realm which may be called a kingdom of ends (surely only an ideal) because what these laws have in view is just the relation of these beings to each other as ends and means" (*Grounding of the Metaphysics*, 433).

89. Kant, *Perpetual Peace and Other Essays*, 94.

90. Lonergan, *Insight*, 624.

91. Morelli, "Reflection on Lonergan's Notion," 1.

92. Lonergan, *Method in Theology*, 17.

Part IV: The Amplitude of Lonergan's Generalized Empirical Method   151

waking, sleeping, eating, or loving.[93] On the empirical level, we sense, perceive, imagine, feel, speak, and move. On the intellectual level, we inquire, come to understand, express what we have understood, and work out the presuppositions and implications of our expression. On the rational level, we reflect, marshal the evidence, and pass judgment on the truth, falsity, certainty, or the probability of a statement. On the responsible level, we are concerned with ourselves, our own operations, and our goals; "we deliberate about possible courses of action, evaluate them, decide, and carry out our decisions."[94]

There is implied in our four levels of consciousness a hierarchy or scale of values whose range of application differs. The hierarchic scale of values[95] includes "vital, social, cultural, personal, and religious values in an ascending order."[96] Health pertains to vital values. Social values denote the good of order, while cultural values are the set of values within a particular culture. In general, the good of value satisfies some preferences but not others. We uphold "some systems for achieving the good of order and disapprove of others."[97] Personal value is the person in his self-transcendence, as loving and being loved, as "originator of values in himself and in his milieu, as an

---

93. Lonergan, *Insight*, 498.

94. Lonergan, *Method in Theology*, 9. The levels of consciousness are structured into a functional unity. In "The Subject," Lonergan notes that "The levels of consciousness are not only distinct but also related, and the relations are best expressed as instances of what Hegel named 'sublation,' that is a lower being is retained, preserved, yet transcended and completed by a higher" (80). Lonergan's realism includes every valid conclusion of empirical human science (*Insight*, 617); there is no alleged dialectical necessity as claimed in Hegel's idealism which pretends to be complete without delving into non-systematic matters of fact.

95. For Doran, "The ascending order of the scale—vital, social, cultural, personal, religious—is determined by the degree of self-transcendence to which we are carried in responding to values at each level. The exceptional validity of the scale and its heuristic fertility for understanding historical events are due . . . to its isomorphism with the levels of consciousness affirmed in self-appropriation. The scale of values is the social objectification of human authenticity collectively . . . be attentive, intelligent, reasonable, responsible, and loving human beings. Much work still needs to be done to fill in the formal structure with the help of ongoing work in philosophy and the human sciences, and especially to clarify the relations between cultural values and the 'dialectic of community' that structures social values: technological, economic, and political institutions in dialectical tension with spontaneous intersubjectivity. It is the integrity of that dialectic of community that alone will guarantee a recurrent equitable distribution of vital goods to the human community," in our changing world ("Vision," 11).

96. Lonergan, *Method in Theology*, 31.

97. Lonergan, *Lonergan Reader*, 431. Implied in the scale of values is the tension of a law of limitation and transcendence.

inspiration ... to others to do likewise. Religious values, finally, are at the heart of the meaning and values of man's living and man's world."[98]

Lonergan's Partial Reformulation of Scheler's Ethics

Lonergan clarified and expanded upon Scheler's view on emotional intentionality according to which feelings lead to values. For Scheler, values are *a priori*, not the secondary carriers of meaning implied in symbols or in intersubjectivity. But for Lonergan, the fact that a carrier is secondary does not threaten the status of values. Values remain even in the absence of a carrier. As to moral values, Scheler held that one errs when one chooses a lower value instead of a higher one. Lonergan approaches moral values by insisting on the consistency between one's judgment and one's acting. His rejection of *a priori* values stems from his principle of emergent probability and from his view that judgments are not static but are part of an invariant structure enabling us to judge. Here, we may recall Aristotle's working definition of the good within which Lonergan frames his hierarchic scales of values. Aristotle defines the good as "that at which all things aim."[99] The good occurs in many forms. For Lonergan, "good" is used in as many ways as the verb "is." It is used in such categories as "what" (God, mind); "what sort of" (virtues); "how much" (a right amount); what is useful; "time" (the right moment); and "location." "Good" does not signify a single reality. If it did, it would not apply to all categories, but only to one. Aristotle brought Plato down to earth.[100] Even if there is some good which is universally

---

98. Lonergan, *Method in Theology*, 32.

99. Aristotle, *Ethics* I, 1, 1094a 3–4.

100. Aristotle, *Ethics*, I, 1096b 30–35, constructs his theory of the good as an alternative to Plato's Idea of the Good summarized in the *Republic*, VI, 508d-509b. Aristotle writes: "What gives truth to the things known and the power to know to the knower is the form of the good. And though it is the cause of knowledge and truth, it is also an object of knowledge. Both knowledge and truth are beautiful things, but the good is other and more beautiful than they. In the visible realm, light and sight are rightly considered sunlike, but it is wrong to think that they are the sun, so here it is right to think of knowledge and truth as 'good(like)' but wrong to think that either of them is the good.... This is an inconceivably beautiful thing you're talking about, if it provides both knowledge and truth and is superior to them in beauty. You surely don't think that a thing like that could be pleasure. Hush! Let's examine its image in more detail.... You'll be willing to say, I think, that the sun not only provides visible things with the power to be seen but also with coming to be, growth, and nourishment, although it is not itself coming to be. How could it be? Therefore, you should also say that not only do the objects of knowledge owe their being known to the good, but their being is also due to it, although the good is not being, but superior to it in rank."

predicable of goods or is capable of separate and independent existence, clearly it could not be achieved or attained by man.

Aristotle sought the attainable, presupposing that there are virtuous people. For Lonergan, value presupposes self-transcending subjects. For Scheler, values can be "felt."[101] However, one does not feel a value until finding an appropriate occasion.[102] Kant had claimed that any nonformal ethics destroys the dignity of persons and their self-value which cannot be derived from anything.[103] Scheler rejects Kant's *a priori* ethics for failing to address the emotional side of life. For Scheler, good and evil originally stem "from acts of willing. That which can be called originally 'good' and 'evil' . . . is the being of persons themselves."[104] Consciousness is directed to values by way of our feelings: All values (including the "good" or its rejection) "are non-formal qualities of contents possessing a determinate order of ranks with respect to 'higher' and 'lower.'"[105] Scheler's distinction between value perception and purely mental or spiritual values anticipates Lonergan's scale of values, but Scheler's elevation of feelings and values above cognition points to a line of demarcation between the two men. For Lonergan, value constitutes the fourth level of intentional consciousness. For Scheler, all primordial comportment toward the world (vis-à-vis both the outer world and one's own ego), although not precisely one of representational perceiving, does imply a *primordial* emotional comportment of value-perception.[106]

Scheler distinguishes two broad groups of values (ethical, aesthetic) as being either positive or negative. This is an "essential quality of values—independent of our being able to feel specific opposites of values such as beautiful-ugly, good-evil, agreeable-disagreeable."[107] For Lonergan, values, the true, the good, are prior to and *independent of our perceiving* them or of affirming their status or worth.

---

101. Scheler, *Formalism in Ethics*, 16. Husserl focused on the lived-experience in relation to the intellect, while Scheler focused on lived-experience in relation to value. The intellect and affective values constitute two poles of our consciousness. Descartes and Husserl emphasized the intellect, but Scheler and Augustine stressed the affective.

102. Manfred Frings writes that "whereas intentional referents of 'thinking acts' of human consciousness are concepts, for Scheler, volitional acts are 'the intentional referents of acts of feeling.' . . . Values are foundational for all acts of consciousness in the wide sense of this term, independent" of prevailing laws ("Max Scheler," 136).

103. Scheler, *Formalism in Ethics*, 370.

104. Scheler, *Formalism in Ethics*, 28.

105. Scheler, *Formalism in Ethics*, 18.

106. Scheler, *Formalism in Ethics*, 197.

107. Scheler, *Formalism in Ethics*, 81–82. See also Mombula, *Human Community and Dialectic*, 99.

EXPLORATION 5: LONERGAN'S DEBT TO, AND TRANSFORMATION OF, HUSSERL'S PHENOMENOLOGY[108]

Lonergan adopted Husserl's concern for the *Lebenswelt* (living world) but gave it his own nuance. Husserl had inherited notions such as intentionality, consciousness, and subjectivity from Franz Brentano.[109] He treats consciousness in relation to the objective reality that must be analyzed in light of one's existential subjectivity. In turn, in adapting Husserl's view of consciousness, Lonergan attributes a more objective quality to consciousness than does Husserl. Subjectivity, a basic element in Husserl's phenomenology, is rooted in Europe's philosophical tradition. "Besides and beneath ... individual points of similarity, there is contrast at the level"[110] of Husserl's and Lonergan's basic views. Husserl stressed that a human subject's consciousness is open to the world and is intentional by nature. There need not be a disjunction between science and the living world within which persons are born and raised. Science is an achievement of persons living in communities. In *Crisis*, Husserl blames a one-sided notion of rationality. The problem "lies not in the essence of rationalism itself but solely in its being rendered superficial, in its entanglement in naturalism and objectivism."[111] Lamenting the artificial disjunction between science and the *Lebenswelt*, Husserl asks whether the world and human life within it would not be more

---

108. For Uljana Feest, in Husserl's *Crisis of the European Sciences*, two concepts predominate: that of life-world and history. But much attention is also paid to discussing "the relationship between Husserl's own phenomenological psychology" and the kind of naturalistic psychology practiced in "philosophy departments around him" ("Husserl's Crisis as a Crisis," 43).

109. Brentano (1838–1917) adapted Aristotle's works for modernity, emphasizing the Scholastic notion of intentionality. Phenomenologists attempt to describe human experiences without theoretical speculations. Husserl concentrated on the intentionality of our cognitional operations. Husserl notes that Brentano had attempted to reform psychology by investigating the psychic rather than the physical. Intentionality was one of these characteristics: "The science of the 'psychic phenomena' has to do everywhere with conscious experiences" (*Crisis of the European Sciences*, 233).

110. Ryan, "Intentionality in Edmund Husserl," 173. Gurwitsch formulates the problem of consciousness to which Husserl's theory of intentionality provides an inchoate answer. He sketches "the general conception of consciousness which dominated modern philosophical thought since its beginning with Descartes. According to this conception, which may be accurately termed the theory of Ideas, the only objects to which the mind or the conscious subject has direct and immediate access are its own mental states. Consciousness is conceived as a self-contained closed domain ... of interiority, completely severed" from the domain of externality ("Toward a Theory of Intentionality," 354).

111. Husserl, *Crisis of the European Sciences*, 6.

meaningful if science would recognize as true only what is objectively established. History, for its part, should teach us the shapes of the spiritual world, the ideals, norms upon which man relies. The danger is that presently the norms and ideals of a spiritual and ethical life seem to be dissolving as if they were mere fleeting waves.[112] The present perceived disjunctions need not be so since science and the life-world (*Lebenswelt*) are inextricably linked. Diachronically, the *Lebenswelt* comes first:

> The knowledge of the objective-scientific world is "grounded" in the self-evidence of the life-world . . . pregiven to the scientific worker, or the working community, as ground; yet . . . what is built is something new, something different. If we cease being immersed in our scientific thinking, we become aware that we scientists are, after all, human beings . . . components of the life-world which always exists for us, ever pregiven; thus, all of science is pulled, along with us, into the—merely "subjective-relative"—living world.[113]

Husserl insists that persons as scientists do not change their worlds or their consciousness when they leave the breakfast table and walk into their laboratories. Somehow, they have to integrate what they believe as scientists and what they believe as wives and husbands at the breakfast table. "It is both the supposed unity of consciousness and the supposed fundamental self-givenness of a transcendental ego in Husserl . . . that forces us to search for a connection between facts and values."[114] For Husserl, persons are holistic; they do not play different language-games. Like Husserl, Lonergan stresses intersubjective community: "As intersubjective community precedes civilization and underpins it, so also it remains when civilization decays."[115] In sum, the *Lebenswelt* is ubiquitous. We cannot do without it. To some extent, Husserl feels a kinship with Marx on this point. However, Husserl focuses on man's consciousness, whereas, for Marx, man wants action. Lonergan reconciles Marx and Husserl by insisting on both consciousness and action since a person has both intellectual and practical needs motivated by one's intellectual and practical patterns of experience. For Husserl, moderns erred in the ways they submitted themselves uncritically to the scientific method. In his view, the *Lebenswelt* is the foundation of all meaning and science; there should be no antagonism between the *Lebenswelt* and science. The presumed antagonism springs from faulty rationalist, positivist ideas

112. Husserl, *Crisis of the European Sciences*, 6.
113. Husserl, *Crisis of the European Sciences*, 130.
114. Hampe, "Science, Philosophy of Knowledge," 155.
115. Lonergan, *Insight*, 238.

according to which only facts matter. For him, science does not spring out of nowhere: it *is rooted* in the *Lebenswelt*. Positivists have underestimated the contribution of the humanities to science. Science and technology are not to be isolated from human interests, placed in an ivory tower, as it were. This would be pure alienation. By excluding the humanities, positivists induce meaninglessness within persons and among humans. In fact, present problems demand universal reflections based on rational insights. Lonergan's adaptation of Husserl's views on intentionality and *Lebenswelt* helped him fashion his views on common sense.

Both men insisted that unity does not mean sameness. There is unity in diversity between the life-world and science, between common sense and theory. In addressing the seeming radical opposition between the world of community, common sense, and the visible world, Lonergan stresses that by those three terms, he means, "exactly the same thing: the world that is familiar to all of us–and on the other hand the world of theory."[116] For Husserl, any conscious experience is directed toward an object. Corresponding to all points in "the manifold data of the real (*reelle*) noetic content, there is a variety of data displayable in really pure (*wirklicher reiner*) intuition, and in a correlative 'noematic content,' or briefly 'noema.'"[117] Conversely, everything that we call an object and that we

> regard as possible or probable . . . is thereby an object of consciousness. This means that, irrespective of what the world and reality are or may be, the framework of real and possible consciousness may be represented by corresponding fulfilled meanings or judgments with more or less intuitive content.[118]

Pannenberg argued that the Husserlian theory of meaning as intentionality is related to Lonergan's notions of historical and particular horizons which are needed to apply meaning-finding or meaning-making "to the study of which phenomenology is dedicated."[119] By one's historical horizon,

---

116. Lonergan, "Time and Meaning," 111.

117. Husserl, *Idea of Phenomenology*, 238.

118. Husserl, *Logos of Phenomenology*, 445.

119. Pannenberg, "History and Meaning," 90. "One of the key terms in phenomenology is 'intentionality,' which Husserl . . . describes as the connection between the mind and the world of objects. Human consciousness is intentional in that it is a consciousness of something. The move from directly experiencing the world around us to focusing on our consciousness of that world is called the phenomenological *epoché* or parenthesizing. . . . With this parenthesizing, or bracketing, we temporarily put aside the world of objects and focus on our cognitive apprehension of that world. This transition allows us to reflect on our own conscious activities and can help us achieve a greater sense of self-reflection. Husserl proposes that such a self-reflection might be the

we mean experiences lived within human communities. For Husserl, waking life is "always a directedness toward this or that, being directed toward it as an end or as means, as relevant or irrelevant, toward the interesting or the indifferent . . . toward what is daily required or intrusively new. All this lies within the world-horizon."[120] While it is true that consciousness is always consciousness of something, it is also constituted by human history, within which our viewpoints are defined and our life-world is constituted. For consciousness, "the individual thing is not alone; the perception of a thing is perception of it within a perceptual field."[121] Meaning is possible only through and within a person's lived horizon:

> The world as it is for us becomes understandable as a structure of meaning formed out of elementary intentionalities. The being of these intentionalities themselves is nothing but one meaning formation operating together with another, "constituting" new meaning through synthesis. And the meaning is never anything but in modes of validity, that is, as related to intending ego-subjects which effect validity. Intentionality . . . stands for the only . . . genuine way of explaining.[122]

For Husserl, the world as we know it is a tangle of meanings. When an infant is conscious, he/she sees buildings, roads, etc. Adults constitute meaning and its sedimentations which in turn help shape the appropriate correlations between intentional act and intentional object. Just as there is no consciousness and concomitantly no meaning without a pregiven world, so there is no world without a person constituting it. A passage from the *Crisis* suggests Husserl's influence on Lonergan:

> Beyond the world we know about, there is the further world we make. But what we make we first intend. We imagine, we plan, we investigate possibilities, we weigh pros and cons . . . we have countless orders given and executed. From the beginning to the end of the process, we are engaged in acts of meaning; and without them the process would not occur.[123]

---

key to not only knowing ourselves but to enriching our cognitive abilities." He suggests that there is a quality within human cognition that allows it to improve itself and that consciousness can perceive itself "as an experienceable object, accessible to a possible self-experience that can be perfected, and perhaps enriched" (90). Lonergan's approach helps realize the critical self-reflection anticipated by Husserl. See Perry, "Transcendental Method for Research," 264.

120. Husserl, *Crisis of the European Sciences*, 281.
121. Husserl, *Crisis of the European Sciences*, 162.
122. Husserl, *Crisis of the European Sciences*, 168.
123. Husserl, *Crisis of the European Sciences*, 233.

Although Husserl and Lonergan were both deeply interested in conscious intentionality, Lonergan charged that Husserl's project "is under the shadow of the principle of immanence, and it fails to transcend the crippling influence of the extroversion that provides the model for the pure ego."[124]

EXPLORATION 6: LONERGAN, WITTGENSTEIN, AND IDEALIZATIONS OF LANGUAGE AND MATHEMATICS

Lonergan built bridges between the various islands of knowledge focusing on meaning and time. Scientists approach time as a mechanical succession of events. Lonergan, following St. Augustine, links time to humans as a "stretching of the soul."[125] Let us give three examples of how Lonergan's realist idealism complements or corrects contemporary views on time, reality, and idealizations of reality.

First Example: Wittgenstein and Lonergan on Language, Mind, Values, and Reality

Wittgenstein reinforces in at least two ways Lonergan's view that meaning and reality are correlatives.[126] First, both opposed a notion of self as an isolated center of consciousness, detached from the body and the external world which it comes to know by some form of mental picturing. Second, language molds developing consciousness by structuring "the world about the subject."[127] For Lonergan, meaning is pervasive; it molds our daily lives; we attain meaning through our conscious, intentional operations using

---

124. Lonergan, *Insight*, 440. Lonergan faults phenomenology for being too focused on scientific *description* at the expense of a valid scientific *explanation*. This resulted in a phenomenological "abstract looking from which the looker and the looked-at have been dropped because of their particularity and contingence" (440). Lonergan helps us understand how inquiries in any field of study can be related to actual conditions of life. Description relates things to ourselves and to our senses while explanation relates things to one another within a universal view point. Explanatory understanding demands the creation of a theoretical language based on the various differentiations of human consciousness. This basic distinction between description and explanation is central to Lonergan's thought.

125. Augustine, *Confessions of St. Augustine*, XI:226.

126. Paul Ricoeur notes that Wittgenstein's writings bear comparison with the Husserl of the *Investigations* which takes the measure of language using a clearly defined logical ideal and the later Husserl of *The Crisis* which approaches language from the point of view of a meaningful potential implied by *Lebenswelt* ("Later Wittgenstein," 1).

127. Lonergan, *Method in Theology*, 71. See also Fitzpatrick, "Lonergan and the Later Wittgenstein," 42; Mombula, *Human Community and Dialectic*, 90.

Part IV: The Amplitude of Lonergan's Generalized Empirical Method   159

language. In *Insight*, without mentioning Wittgenstein, he addresses the roles of language in relation to knowledge and philosophy. Commonsense language is largely avoided by technicians and philosophers in their professions. It clings to the practical, the concrete; "it remains within the familiar world of things for us."[128] Language is indeed linked to the development of knowledge, to the meaning of words, to their sources, and their expressions. Opposing Wittgenstein as to the relationship between language and reality,[129] Lonergan insists that meaning is not of secondary importance, as some contend, so that what counts is only the reality that is meant and not the meaning that refers to it.[130] By means of his intentional acts that envisage ends, man transforms both self and his environment. Acts of meaning are not merely directive, but they are vital in constituting one's self.

> By its embodiment in language, in a set of conventional signs, meaning finds its greatest liberation. For conventional signs can be multiplied almost indefinitely. They can be differentiated and specialized to the utmost refinement. They can be used reflexively in the analysis and control of linguistic meaning itself. . . . (Language) molds developing consciousness, it also structures the world about the subject.[131]

Wittgenstein's *Tractatus Logico-Philosophicus* (1922) and his *Philosophical Investigations* (1953) have made him a renowned philosopher of the nature and limits of language, "a central theme of which is the question of

---

128. Lonergan, *Insight*, 104. "Language is an enormously complicated tool with an almost endless variety of parts . . . . Insight is needed to use language properly" (Lonergan, *Lonergan Reader*, 35).

129. For Lonergan *on* mental acts and language, see *Method in Theology*, 25. He wrote *Method in Theology* in the 1960s when the philosophy of language was in vogue. James Sauer writes that analytic philosophy had distant roots in eighteenth-century empiricism, its proximate source in logical atomism. It stands in the empirical tradition of Western philosophy "Most analytical philosophers claim to be epistemological empiricists and metaphysical materialists," arguing that philosophy's task is to clarify the use . . . of language. For them, a word's meaning "is its use in contexts" (*Commentary on Lonergan's Method*, 77). While Lonergan grants that meaning centers on how we use particular words, he refutes the analysts' rejection of the true role of the mental aspects of meaning. In Frege's distinction between sense and reference, one notices that his example of the morning star and evening star *does* involve interpretation. Lonergan insists that any interpretation involves mental acts: "meaning . . . intends something meant" (*Method in Theology*, 62).

130. Lonergan, "Dimensions of Meaning," 252. That contention "overlooks the fact that human reality, the very stuff of human living, is not merely meant," but is also in "large measure constituted through acts of meaning."

131. Lonergan, *Method in Theology*, 70–71.

the relationship between language and reality."[132] His *Tractatus* had sought to "explain how language attains meaning and relates one to the world. He had hoped that understanding language would help one understand philosophical problems."[133] The *Tractatus* opens with the words: "The world is everything that is the case. The world is the totality of facts, not of things."[134] Wittgenstein's picturing theory of language does *implicitly* recognize the significance of the mind since "picturing" takes place in the mind. Later he came to criticize his own earlier theory.[135]

In *Investigations*, Wittgenstein argues that speaking a language is like playing a game.[136] Here, his view partly converges with Lonergan's. For Wittgenstein language functions when, for example:

> Giving or obeying orders, recounting the appearance of an object or measuring it, reporting an event, forming and testing a hypothesis . . . cracking a joke, solving a problem in arithmetic, translating from one language into another, cursing, greeting, or praying.[137]

This view supports Lonergan's claim that meaning is ubiquitous. Wittgenstein in *Investigations* associates a desire for idealized clarity partly

---

132. Harris, "Language, Language Game," 41. For Mirela Arsith, "We use language to support the social order, to give us the common conventions that define the communities in which we live" ("Ludwig Wittgenstein and Language-Games," 21).

133. See Roach, "Early and Later Philosophy," 2.

134. Wittgenstein, *Tractatus Logico-Philosophicus*, 1.

135. Wittgenstein held that, the "key" of language is not in the mind, but a way of life that pushes us towards certain ways of using signs, which are the language games" (Arsith, "Ludwig Wittgenstein and Language-Games," 14).

136. Wittgenstein uses two metaphors to clarify his view—a metaphor of language as game and a metaphor of language as tool. "Language-game" stresses "that speaking of language is a part of an activity" (*Investigations*, 15e). "To imagine a language means to image a form of life" (19). As to how one learns a game, he writes that one does so by watching how others play it. It is played "according to particular rules because an observer can read them from the way a game is played—like a natural law governing the play" (31).

137. Wittgenstein, *Investigations*, 23. Victor Krebs writes that what separates Wittgenstein's "two great works is his discovery of a kind of intellectual blindness produced by the almost exclusive predominance of one single conception of knowledge . . . in our culture. For Wittgenstein, our identification with the cognitive ego is tantamount to a blindness to our own nature—blindness that is entrenched in our present culture. The task of philosophy is thus transformed into a form of cultural therapy that seeks to awaken in us a sensitivity to different modes of awareness than the merely intellectual. Its substance of reflection becomes not only the field of conscious rational thought, but the tension in our nature between reason" and feeling, between culture and life" ("Mind, Soul, Language in Wittgenstein," 1).

based on his admiration for St. Augustine. For all their affinities, Lonergan and Wittgenstein do differ in significant ways. If the issue is that of self-appropriation in GEM, the shortcomings in Wittgenstein's legacy are his attacks on the notion of the subject conceived as a disembodied center of consciousness.[138] For Lonergan, exploring the subject's self-appropriation is of the first importance. Wittgenstein rejected private language as well as interiority,[139] but for Lonergan, private mental acts are prerequisites for any linguistic expression; they are not merely derived—as Wittgenstein claims. For Lonergan, language "consists in the sedimentation of the developments that have occurred and have not become obsolete. New developments consist in discovering new uses for existing words, in inventing new words, and in diffusing the discoveries and inventions. All three are a matter of expressed mental acts."[140] With this assertion, Lonergan is refuting Wittgenstein's claim that philosophical problems are essentially linguistic problems: "If one conceives language as the expression of mental acts, one will conclude that philosophic problems have their source not only in linguistic expression but also in mental acts, and it could happen that one would devote much more attention to the mental acts than to the linguistic expression."[141]

---

138. Fitzpatrick, "Lonergan and the Later Wittgenstein," 49.

139. Ludwig Wittgenstein wants to refute Augustine's view of language: "Augustine describes the learning . . . of language as if the child came into a foreign country and did not understand the language of the country" (*Philosophical Investigations*, 19e). He knows only his own, but he can think by talking to himself. Since the notion of interiority is the centerpiece of Augustine's writings, it is easy to see why he would write that "It was not that grown-up people instructed me by presenting me with words in certain order by formal teaching, as I was to learn the letters of the alphabet. I, myself, acquired this power of speech with intelligence which you gave me, my God" (*Confessions*, I.8.13). Wittgenstein rejects this approach since he is not concerned with interiority but with ordinary, public language. For David Stern, Wittgenstein reminds us that language is a practice that "cannot be super-private" (*Wittgenstein's Philosophical Investigations*, 181).

140. Lonergan, *Method in Theology*, 255. He rejects Wittgenstein's inner/outer distinction. He further notes, "In the concrete physical, chemical, vital reality of human living, there also is meaning. It is at once inward and outward, inward as expressing, outward as expressed. It manifests need and satisfaction. It responds to values. . . . It orders means to ends. It constitutes social systems and endows them with cultural significance. It transforms . . . nature" (*Method in Theology*, 211).

141. Lonergan, *Method in Theology*, 256.

Second Example: Lonergan, Turing, Smale on Technical-Developmental Idealizations

How may we best correlate the methods of science and mathematics? Mathematics is embedded in science and is used to describe and understand many aspects of scientific discovery. The mathematician Steve Smale has studied the crossover between mathematics and biology. He asks whether mathematics

> is realistic or idealistic? Do the mathematical models we use to . . . understand the universe give a realistic picture of how the world works? Or do they have elements of fantasy that ignore the fine details in order to get a model that works nicely?[142]

Smale instances Alan Turing's theory of computation, which inspired the age of the Internet but was an ideal. "Even though Turing's mode is 'correct,' some counter that . . . it does not in fact model the real world. It is an idealization"[143] Newton's work on differential equations and mechanics is also an idealization to the extent that his calculations didn't even include friction; these were added to his theory some 100 years later.[144]

Third Example: Historical Idealizations by Scientists that have Changed History

John von Neumann's insights into quantum mechanics and his use of Hilbert space were also idealizations.[145] Such idealizations are possible as we see in the work of such geniuses as Newton or Turing who made their discoveries without the benefit of lab experiments. They used experimental data from other scientists' work which had already "been 'digested' by the scientific

---

142. Smale, "Is Mathematics Realistic or Idealistic?," para. 3. In computational complexity theory, a nondeterministic polynomial time (NP) complete decision problem is one belonging to both the NP and the NP-hard complexity classes. In this context, NP stands for nondeterministic polynomial time. Because "NP-completeness in computability assumes an infinite amount of input," it does not, in fact, model the real world. .

143. Smale, "Is Mathematics Realistic or Idealistic?," para. 4. He adds in paragraph 6: "Even in other fields such as Watson and Crick's discovery of the structure of DNA, no mention is made of the protein core of chromatin which was later discovered to be a fundamental part of the more detailed structure."

144. Smale, "Is Mathematics Realistic or Idealistic?," para. 5. Around 1800, Laplace began recasting Newton's mechanics by idealizing its problems so as to better express them by partial differential equations. These were later refined by more precise measuring instruments.

145. Smale, "Is Mathematics Realistic or Idealistic?," para. 6.

community."[146] We stress that our *realist-idealist* approach correlates with Lonergan's *critical* realism. Just as Smale studies dynamic mathematical systems to point to their limitations, so Lonergan's critical realism points to systems' limitations while advocating the ideals developed by ethicists and mystics of many persuasions.

EXPLORATION 7: LONERGAN ON COSMOPOLIS, EMERGENT PROBABILITY, AND ECONOMICS

Lonergan first began to study economics in the early 1930s. In 1974, he praises Cardinal Daniélou's interest in the poor, but adds that the basic step in aiding them is a matter of "spending one's nights and days studying economics,"[147] so as to formulate "the laws of an economic mechanism more . . . fundamental than the pricing system."[148] His economic theory is influenced by his knowledge of history and his ability to discern the role of common sense in economics. Authentic common sense can help an economy develop properly, but when common sense is mutilated by biases, it may go so far as to cause an economic depression. When all are attentive, intelligent, reasonable, and responsible, an economy can thrive. This is in line with what we have noted in our text on the role of cosmopolis which complements and helps clarify Lonergan's radically original proposals on economics.

While Marx had opposed capitalism for alienating humans from their true nature, for Lonergan, an economy should not primarily focus on profit, but on sensible, equitable forms of production. The young Marx, having read Feuerbach's criticism of persons' alienation within society,[149] argued that alienation is due to the malfunctioning of the economy. "The philosophers have only interpreted the world; the point is to change it."[150] Alien-

---

146. For Lonergan, "the scientific community is of fundamental importance. It is a sociological concept of science, locating the science not, . . . in the mind of this or that man, but in the group of men at the cutting edge of a developing science and gradually moving from the tension and opposition of disagreement to the unison of a consensus" ("Analogy of Revolution," 2). With Lonergan, we seek to bridge civil tensions, relying on the church's social teaching which seeks to build a just, holy society amidst the vast challenges of modern times.

147. Lonergan, "Sacralization and Secularization," 280.

148. Lawrence, "Editors' Introduction," 15.

149. In *Essence of Religion*, Ludwig Feuerbach writes that man "projects his being into objectivity, making himself an object to this projected image thus converted into a subject" (29). He accuses Christianity of depriving man of his temporal life.

150. Marx, "Theses on Feuerbach," 423.

ation occurs when workers are estranged from the products of their labor, from self, and from the community.[151] The relations of production to which Marx refers are social, economic, and technological relationships, plus the superstructure.[152] To Hegel's and Feuerbach's claims that humans can be emancipated by enlightening their consciousness,[153] Marx replies that they could only be emancipated by changing the material modes of production. For him, religion, science, and political society are a superstructure. In the *Communist Manifesto*'s second chapter, he and Engels ask how a worker's outlook is influenced by the conditions of his material existence and his social life. They answer that the history of ideas proves that intellectual production changes to the extent that material production changes. They fault the ruling classes for falsifying the problem.

Marx partly bases his argument on man's economic condition upon Hegel's view that man is essentially a worker. For Marx, this was the true birthplace of the Hegelian philosophy. In the *Phenomenology*, Hegel argues that a subject and an object necessarily intermingle. Self-consciousness entails the presence of the other—be it of persons or of nature. By involving oneself with nature through work, one becomes oneself; a bondsman realizes that it is precisely in his work in which he seemed to have only an alienated existence that he acquires a mind of his own. The two moments of fearful servitude and of an underlying formative activity are necessary; both operate universally. Without disciplined service and obedience, fear remains at the formal stage, and does not extend to the known real world of existence. Consciousness would not overcome fear: it would not become

---

151. Marx, "Economic and Philosophical Manuscripts," 329. Alienation estranges man from himself, from his own active function, from his vital activity. "It also estranges man from his species. It turns his species-life into a means for his individual life. Estranged labor therefore turns man's species-being—both nature and his intellectual species-power—into a being alien to himself . . . estranged from his own body, from nature, . . . from his spiritual and human essence" (300).

152. As to Marx and Lonergan on production and the superstructure, see Marsh, *Lonergan in the World*, 174. For Marx, superstructure refers to juridico-political institutions; infrastructure is the base for an economic structure. For Lonergan, "The material fabric of culture's living home is economic, and underlying this superstructure there stands as foundation the purely economic field concerned with . . . shelter, clothing, utilities" (*For a New Political Economy*, 12).

153. In his "Theses on Feuerbach," Marx writes: "Feuerbach wants sensuous objects, really distinct from the thought objects, but he does not conceive human activity itself as objective activity. . . . He regards the theoretical attitude as the only genuinely human attitude, while practice is conceived and fixed only in its dirty judaical manifestation. Hence, he does not grasp the significance of 'revolutionary', or of 'practical-critical activity'" (1).

explicitly "for itself."[154] Marx and Lonergan shared a common concern in reacting against Hegel, but for Lonergan, "Not only are men born with a native drive to inquire and understand; they are born into a community that possesses a common fund of tested answers, and from that fund each may draw his variable share, measured by his capacity, his interests, and his energy."[155] For Lonergan, Marx's crude economic "determinism" is mistaken. Still, "there *is* an economic determinism resulting from people not having any minds of their own, not insisting that human intelligence and reason and free choice be the ultimate determinant of what human life is to be. If that breaks down, then human life and human society become mechanical."[156] As to man being a producer, Lonergan invokes the practical pattern of experience: "In the drama of human living, human intelligence is not only artistic but also practical."[157]

Lonergan notes how pioneers in the New World "found shore and heartland, mountains and plains, but they have covered it with cities, laced it with roads, exploited it with their industries.... Yet the whole of that added, manmade, artificial world is the cumulative, now planned, now chaotic product of human acts of meaning."[158] A healthy, vibrant economy needs a critical mass of authentic persons. But a lack[159] of authenticity gives rise to biases and alienation, leading to a disregard of responsible living. Lonergan's views on production as a moving force of history stem partly from Marx. In some ways, Lonergan's notion of bias parallels Marx's notion of alienation. But while Marx advocated a classless society in order to correct the disparities caused by the market economy, Lonergan's cosmopolis seeks to offset decline.[160] People personally appropriate meaning and the good which are

---

154. Hegel, *Phenomenology of Mind*, 196. For Marx, *Phenomenology of Mind*'s dialectic of negativity (as the moving and producing principle) "lies in the fact that Hegel conceives the self-creation of man as a process, objectification as loss of object.... He grasps the nature of labor and conceives objective man to be true" ("Economic and Philosophical Manuscripts," 385–86).

155. Lonergan, *Insight*, 198.

156. Lonergan, *Topics in Education*, 45. This book's realist-idealist interpretation-application of GEM includes an espousal of Lonergan's "idealized-realist" economics. While the socialist Eduard Bernstein (1850–1932) sought to revise Marx's tenets of the imminent collapse of capitalism and the seizure of power by the proletariat, our heart-communal approach emphasizes a reconciliation of peoples, nations, and religions at a deeper level of faith-love discernment.

157. Lonergan, *Insight*, 232–33.

158. Lonergan, "Dimensions of Meaning," 254. Mombula, *Human Community and Dialectic*, 126.

159. Lawrence, "Editors' Introduction," lxix.

160. For Lonergan, the overall lack of ingenuity on the part of both liberal capitalism

communally shared. Although the structure of self-appropriation is universal, it occurs differently according to persons' backgrounds. For Lonergan,

> in the drama of human living, human intelligence is not only artistic but also practical. Man's practical intelligence devises arrangements for human living; and in the measure that such arrangements are understood and accepted, there ... results the intelligible pattern of relationships that we have named the good of order.[161]

The economy is one of those arrangements.[162] Two central ideas of Lonergan's economics are "the functional distinction in production and spending between investment and consumption," and "the pure cycle of innovative growth, which is Lonergan's equilibrium theory of macroeconomic dynamics."[163]

Due to the fact that an economy is embedded in society, it is important to relate Lonergan's economics to both the good of order and his normative notion of a sociocultural cosmopolis.[164] Economics and politics are vast, interdependent structures invented by practical intelligence. For Philip McShane, economists such as Joseph Schumpeter, Michael Kalecki,[165] and Joan

---

and socialism causes the general stagnation of an unintelligible social situation grounded in dramatic, egoistic, group, and general biases.

161. Lonergan, *Insight*, 232, 239.

162. "An economy is an example of the good of order." As a cooperative scheme producing a standard of living, it enables many to find employment "to buy the bread to satisfy the demands of hunger." Sauer, *Commentary*, 77.

163. De Neeve, "Income Distribution in Economic Growth," 4.

164. De Neeve aptly relates Lonergan's notion of cosmopolis to Marx. "Cosmopolis is a normative process that synthesizes liberal thought of the nineteenth century with Marx's social philosophy." Those liberals believed "that some automatic economic mechanism would ensure progress." But Marx was anticipating social disintegration in a revolution that he believed "would bring a utopia . . . Lonergan assures us that, because of our practical intelligences, there will always be technologies, economies, and politics, and we must work with the data as we find them" ("Income Distribution in Economic Growth," 16). Lonergan rejects excessive bureaucracies whose planning restricts the introduction of innovations that do not fit their plans and tend to restrict the freedom of citizens to create social development.

165. During the 1970s, Keynesian economic policies seemingly caused stagflation, a combination of rising prices and rising unemployment. The usual remedies did not work. These crises and the structural changes in the world economy focused economists' attention again on cycles. Some returned to the work done in the 1930s by members of the Austrian school such as Hayek and Schumpeter. Lonergan, encouraged by this renewed interest in studying cycles, as well as by the republication of Kalecki's essays, returned to studying economics in his retirement years. He did hope that his "Circulation Analysis" would find an audience of specialized economists.

Part IV: The Amplitude of Lonergan's Generalized Empirical Method 167

Robinson knew that there are deep flaws[166] in modern efforts at economic analysis. Schumpeter argued that economic crises have to be addressed as a "Crossing the Rubicon,"[167] but his dynamic analysis failed to develop refined scientific distinctions in the productive process. Kalecki and Robinson came nearer to such a refinement, but the question remained as to what is lacking in economic theories. McShane draws a parallel between Newton's transformation of astronomy through his theory of gravitation, and Lonergan's approach to the two flows (basic and surplus) that inevitably occur in the productive cycle. The culture of Europe at the time still subscribed to the theory of earthly and heavenly bodies, the latter being radically different, constituted by quintessential matter. This was accompanied by a mythology of two types of body. Newton reformulated the two types into just one. Economics today is conceptualized as a one-flow process,[168] symbolized by the Gross Domestic Product (GDP). Lonergan's key insight was to eventually identify the historical reality and scientific identity of two flows. "Very simply, where Newton leaped from 2 to 1, Lonergan leaped from 1 to 2. The operable heuristic comes from the clear leap from viewing economic output as GDP to arrive at an empirically defined GDP' and GDP," where the single prime points to consumer goods and the double prime points to producer goods. The leap requires precise thinking "about the relations between the two economic flows."[169]

Despite the vast scope of Lonergan's interests, there is a unity of thought in his overall corpus. His long interest in socioeconomic issues prepared him for writing *Insight*. Economists seek to understand how people

---

166. In *Why Liberalism Failed*, Patrick Deneen argues that when proto-liberals reconfigured the Western understanding of liberty in early modernity, one prong of their attack was directed toward overcoming the dominion and limits of nature. They believed in an expanding and potentially limitless human capacity to control nature. This was followed by an even more extreme view that human nature itself should be conquered, leading to our many present predicaments (59).

167. McShane, "Editor's Introduction," xxv, referring to Schumpeter, *History of Economic Analysis*, 1160. For Schumpeter, the main body of economics has been left on the riverbanks but what needs to be done is to find a "system of general economic dynamics into which statics would enter as a special case" (1160).

168. What is important in a flow is its differential. The differentials of what has flowed integrate "into the reality of the present and then it is of supreme concern to us. They are something beyond the elements . . . in the flow. People in the nineteenth century . . . were little concerned for the differentials of the flow" due to a misplaced confidence in political economists. This landed the 20th century in an earthly hell" (Shute, *Origin*, 74). As we do, Shute investigates historical contexts before addressing one's appropriation of his/her operational dynamics.

169. McShane, "Book Interview," 3.

behave as they produce, distribute, and exchange scarce goods and services.[170] Lonergan focused on the dynamic structure of macroeconomics,[171] on the interrelations of aggregate rates of production and payments, of expansions and contractions, of inflation and unemployment. He did this due to his interest in economic development and in increasing production as needed. He poses a question in his economics which is analogous to the questions he poses in *Insight* and in *Method*. In *Insight*, he asks: What are we doing when we know? In *Method*, the question is: What are we doing in theology? In economics, he asks: What should we be doing in this field? His macroeconomics seeks to explain the dynamics of business cycles, that is, of economic expansions and contractions.

For Marx, man as worker has to appropriate the means of production. For Lonergan, production stands at the center of his economic theory. Both men argue that economic conditions drive history—but their views of history differ. Lonergan sets the economy within the social context of the good of order to include the states of production, exchange, consumption, and finance. "The structure of productive process is a series of stages, where each stage is an aggregate of rates of production, and each lower stage receives from the next higher stage the means of long-term acceleration of its rates."[172] Lonergan qualifies this, noting that "productive process" is to be taken broadly:

> It denotes not merely "making things" but the extraction or cultivation of raw materials, their transportation and assembly, the planning and designing of products. . . . It includes not only activities upon material objects but also services of all kinds, not only labor but also management, and not only production management but also sales management. In brief, it is the totality of activities bridging the gap between the potentialities of nature,

---

170. De Neeve, "Income Distribution in Economic Growth," 12.

171. Lawrence notes that "Lonergan's avid reading of Jane Jacobs's books occurred in conjunction with a life-long interest . . . in the foundations of economics. Their works are complementary." She, wrote on the "micro-conditions" and he on the macro-phenomena. Both refused to yield "to the tyranny of planning in the sense of the word they both despised: using prediction and control to engineer results," (*Ethics*, iii–iv). For McNelis, "Theory," 1, Lonergan based his economics on the schemes of recurrence which challenge current economic research. His heuristics are an "ordered hierarchy of technology, economics, and politics; the distinction between the patterns of an economy and the coincidental motivations of participants" as well as the normativity affecting production.

172. Lonergan, *Macroeconomic Dynamics*, 33.

whether physical, chemical, vegetable, animal, or human nature, and, on the other hand, the actuality of a standard of living.[173]

It all starts with producing goods. In a capitalist economy, production is meant for sale. When one turns from production to exchange, Lonergan notes that products that fail to be sold are regarded as just waste. It follows that acceleration in production demands a proportionate acceleration in selling and buying. After distinguishing between the production of producer goods from the production of consumer goods, Lonergan distinguishes two distinct markets and explains the influence each exerts upon the other. Finance is the final stage in the productive cycle:

> The necessity of finance is twofold. First, there is the fact that the people with money have not the brains to use it, while the people with the brains have not the money to use; thus, finance transfers money from inoperative to dynamic positions in the system. Second, there is the fact that the economic process runs through a series of transformations and exploitations; the real flow varies, and the dummy flow has to vary concomitantly or else suffer inflation or deflation; moreover, the real flow attains volumes that greatly exceed previous maxima, and these peaks can be scaled only if the dummy has a notable elasticity. By finance we understand the effort made to solve these problems.[174]

Lonergan's views on economics are an extension of his cognitional theory, epistemology, and anthropology. In *Method*, he discerns in the procedures of the mind a transcendental method, a basic pattern of operations employed in every cognitional enterprise. This dynamic structure of

---

173. Lonergan, *Macroeconomic Dynamics*, 19–20.

174. Lonergan, *For a New Political Economy*, 41. McShane's *Piketty's Plight* sets out to show that without a better macroeconomic theory, Piketty's huge statistical analysis of the ruling "rent" economy guiding present global order is deficient. Lonergan's basic outline of an alternative theory begins from the fact that there are two economies—consumer and producer—which are intimately but not completely linked. Failure to understand why the two cannot work as needed is the reason that macroeconomic models have erred. For McShane, Piketty is unclear as to the deeper meanings of "capital" and "wealth." Piketty's r > g suggests a gap between the after-tax return on capital "r" and the economic growth rate "g," but it begs a further analysis about the origins and measurements of wealth inequalities. Differentiating between the two stages in the productive processes opens a door to evaluating today's wealth inequalities. The normative end of the productive process is the "wealth" that results when the potentialities of nature are transformed into a standard of living without booms or slumps. Piketty's analysis cannot restore a democratic control of productive processes. It lacks the interdisciplinary creativity to help transpose "r > g" problematics. It is a plight that McShane proposes to remedy with Lonergan's two-flows circuits.

the mind also operates in the field of economics. The productive process is "the aggregate of activities proceeding from the potentialities of nature and terminating in a standard of living."[175] For Lonergan, the dynamic process of consciousness "functions as a wheel: situation, insight, counsel, policy, common consent, action, new situation, new insight, new counsel, new policy, and so on. The wheel can turn indefinitely. Such an analysis of process is mainly in terms of experience and insight, and also choice."[176] Lonergan links our cognitional activities to economics within the larger perspective of emergent probability:

> In a universe such as ours, with ... enormous time intervals, one is led to think of schemes of recurrence, whose several carriers severally follow their own classical laws, whose assembly follows the probability of their emergence, and whose continued functioning follows the probability of their survival. Such in a nutshell is the evolutionary view that in *Insight* I sketched out under the name of emergent probability and, earlier in this essay, I have applied to economics.[177]

Our universe is a conditioned series of schemes of recurrence which may or may not happen:

> The notion of scheme of recurrence arose when it was noted that the diverging series of positive conditions for an event might coil around in a circle. In that case, a series of events A, B, C, would be so related that the fulfilment of the conditions for each would be the occurrence of the others. Schematically, then, the scheme might be represented by the series of conditionals: If A occurs, B will occur; if B occurs, C will occur; if C occurs ... A will occur. Such a circular arrangement may involve any number of terms ... and in general any degree of complexity.[178]

The process of emergent probability includes both systematic and nonsystematic aspects. The systematic features of reality have to do with the

---

175. Lonergan, *Macroeconomic Dynamics*, 20.

176. Lonergan, *Topic*, 51. For Mofid, our socioeconomic problems are a reflection of our attitude to life. Peace will occur only when the connection between the spiritual and practical in life is valued by each one of us. "This is beautifully expressed in a Chinese proverb: 'If there be righteousness in the heart, there will be beauty in the character. . . . When there is order in each nation, there will be peace in the world'" ("New Brexit," 2). Mofid inveighs against neoliberalist crony capitalism, adding: "It is not just 'they' who have to change. 'We' also have to change our attitude, (asking not) 'what's in it for me'" but rather how promote common good.

177. Lonergan, *Macroeconomic Dynamics*, 92–93.

178. Lonergan, *Insight*, 401.

Part IV: The Amplitude of Lonergan's Generalized Empirical Method 171

classical laws of empirical science, whereas the nonsystematic ones concern statistical laws. The actual functioning of earlier schemes in a series fulfills the conditions for the possibility of the functioning of later schemes:

> As such conditions are fulfilled, the probability of the combination of the component events in a scheme jumps from a product of a set of proper fractions to the sum of those proper fractions. But what is probable, sooner or later occurs. When it occurs, a probability of emergence is replaced by a probability of survival; as long as the scheme survives, it is in its turn fulfilling conditions for the possibility of later schemes.[179]

For Lonergan, what is true of the universe as a whole is analogously true for the mind and the economy, which both have regular and sporadic features. "Economic process was conceived by the older economists as a generalized equilibrium. However, we are concerned, not with single schemes, but with a conditioned series of schemes."[180] Lonergan does not reject wholesale the old economics; he wants to improve it. He rejects the old economists' claim that economics should operate independently of ethics. There is no dichotomy between morality and economics as free-market advocates and Marxists claim. As to whether there are tensions or even contradictions between economics and morality, for Lonergan, interiority, freedom, morality, and economics imply one another. A healthy economy and an adequate science both demand that one be attentive, intelligent, reasonable, and responsible. Responsibility requires that one's decisions and choices be unbiased as to evaluating short-term and long-term costs and benefits to oneself, to one's own group, to other groups, to all nations.[181]

EXPLORATION 8: HOW LONERGAN REFASHIONS FREUD'S VIEW OF A DIVIDED SELF

Lonergan sought to heal the divided self[182] so as to rescue it from Freud's atheistic, grim outlook on mankind. Freud subscribed to the ancient maxim

---

179. Lonergan, *Insight*, 145.

180. Lonergan, *Insight*, 141–42.

181. De Neeve, "Income Distribution in Economic Growth," 5. For Amartya Sen, in *Development as Freedom*, freedom means increasing citizens' access to what they have reason to value. Tragically, modern economics has been impoverished by cutting off economics from ethics.

182. Freud did not invent "the divided self," which dates back to Plato and appears in some Oriental doctrines. In his *Phaedrus*, Plato lets the psyche "resemble the combined power (*dynamis*) of a winged team of horses and their charioteer. Now in the

that "Man is a wolf to man," being convinced that humans can do terrible things. His concept of the unconscious assumed the presence in each of us of a kind of hellishness. He "ranks as a great unmasker, someone who was not easily taken in by the mere espousal of high-sounding principles. Pious intentions can after all lead to some of the worst social cruelties."[183] Unlike Freud, Lonergan held that our conscious operations harbor a systemic organization that is not a mere effect of one's unconscious. Rather, our cognitive-volitional operations integrate otherwise disparate potentialities. There is a "finality within human motivation drawing one from the disparate confusion of dreams . . . toward the partial clarity"[184] found through understanding, judgment, and decision. For Lonergan, the said finality enables a conscious, "higher" integration of the manifold of associative images—which he also called a "lower" or "underlying" manifold:

> To assert the higher integration does not require that one deny the reality of the underlying manifold that is integrated; that manifold remains as a reality and a condition for the integration. That is why Lonergan is able to accept so much of Freud in *Insight* without accepting any of Freud's habitual belittling of the autonomy of conscious intelligence. It also perhaps explains, however, why in works after *Insight* Lonergan was drawn to the humanistic and existential strains of psychology and psychotherapy, inasmuch as these movements are more compatible than are Freud's theories with commitments to the finality of human aspirations and the dignity of conscious life.[185]

For Lonergan, unconscious biases do contribute to community conflicts. He agrees in part with Freud's analysis of psychic structure and his views on repression and inhibition in relation to the censor function, to psycho-sexual development. Yet, Lonergan's and Freud's fundamental

---

case of the gods, horses and charioteers are all both good and of good stock; whereas in the case of the rest there is mixture. In the first place, our driver has charge of a pair; secondly one of them he finds noble and good . . . while the other is of the opposite stock, and opposite in its nature; so that the driving in our case is necessarily difficult" (246a 6b-4). The triadic psyche that Socrates likens "to a winged chariot ensemble is commonly interpreted as basically identical with the tripartite psyche of the *Republic*. The charioteer, his white and black horses correspond to the rational, spirited, and appetitive parts, respectively" (Buccioni, "Psychical," 331). Lonergan helps us revisit both Freud's and Plato's versions of the divided self.

183. Roazen, "What Kind of Man?," 75.

184. Kidder, "Hermeneutic and Dialectic of Community," 308.

185. Kidder, "Hermeneutic and Dialectic of Community," 308.

Part IV: The Amplitude of Lonergan's Generalized Empirical Method 173

conceptions of selfhood differ, especially as to the problem of psychical unity.[186] For Freud, the self is full of tensions and conflicts between the conscious and the unconscious resulting in an alienated, false consciousness. This results in conflicts between one's inner world and the demands of the outer world. Persons caught between their unconscious and conscious, are "engaged in permanent conflict due to the co-existence of life and death drives; the psyche is condemned to a battle, as is the human race."[187]

Lonergan addressed such problems with his notions of the biases and inauthenticity. Freud's divided self is the source of both internal and external conflicts. Divisions of the mind are postulated "in order to account for the mind's different aspects, which sometimes seem to be inconsistent with one another."[188] Lonergan knows that our unrestricted drive to know can be mutilated. What counts is being in love with God so as to transcend self. This demands the full involvement of the human subject and his/her capacities, but it is facilitated when one is in love with God in unrestricted fashion. "All love is self-surrender, but being in love with God is being in love without limits or reservations. Just as unrestricted questioning is our capacity for self-transcendence, so being in love in an unrestricted fashion is the proper fulfilment of that capacity."[189] In sum, Lonergan builds on Freud, but distances himself from him by focusing on love.[190] Since views on truth conflict, tensions are exacerbated by these biases. Lonergan acknowledges the hidden forces afflicting one's conscious life, but rejects Freud's way of projecting this fact onto either community or culture. In *Civilization and its Discontents*, Freud theorizes that civilization is a source of unhappiness. By inhibiting people's natural instincts, civilization drives people into a perpetual state of unhappy guilt. For Lonergan, communities and culture can have a positive influence on persons. If, for Freud, what is needed for emancipation is therapy, and if, for Marx, communism is the "answer," for Lonergan, the conversions are indispensable to viable solutions.[191]

---

186. Symington, "Unconscious and Conscious Self," 563.
187. Fuchs, "On the War Path," 569.
188. Tuske, "Being in Two Minds," 230.
189. Lonergan, *Method in Theology*, 105.
190. Lichtman, "Marx and Freud," 79.
191. For Drake, modern Marxism built on Nietzsche's proclamation that historicism threatened civilization and "that 'super-people' should rise above our animal instincts." While historicism believes that people change with time and can solve all our problems, in fact, "Nietzsche despised Marxism and historicism" ("Bernard Lonergan," 264).

EXPLORATION 9: LONERGAN'S ORIGINALITY

Lonergan praises Aristotle for his spirit of wonder and for opposing reductionism, but adds that he lacked an adequate understanding of human historicity and the provisional nature of both personal and communal achievement. Relying uncritically on a normative understanding of culture, he assigned a privileged status to the Hellenic artistic, educational, and political achievements. "In this way, Aristotle indirectly contributed to the interpretive outlook that Lonergan designated as classicism."[192]

Lonergan's originality is shown in the ways he adapted Aristotle and Aquinas to the present age, partly based on Augustine's treatment of human memory, intellect, and will. In *Method*, Lonergan follows Augustine in requiring a threefold (intellectual, moral, religious) conversion of the practicing theologian. Still, he criticizes Augustine's cognitional theory for "failing to correlate the inner words of conception and judgment with the direct and reflective insights that are their intentional causes. Augustine repeatedly relies ... on visual metaphors to account for human knowledge of truth and being."[193] He believes that objectively valid knowledge requires a direct intuition of the eternal reasons in the divine mind, a human intuition causally enabled by God's power of illumination. For Lonergan, this postulated intellectual intuition of divine ideas is "an epistemic fiction."[194]

Lonergan's originality can also be illustrated in his approaches to language, metaphysics, and economics. As to language, he shows why Wittgenstein's valuable insights "into ordinary linguistic meaning cannot account for significant linguistic innovation and originality without recognizing equally innovative intellectual discoveries (insights) on the part of intentional subjects."[195] In his metaphysics, Lonergan asks why have philosophical systems differed throughout history? He meets the difficulty not "by asking whether the views of any given philosopher follow from assumptions of a specified type," but rather by asking "whether there is a single base of operations from which any philosophy can be interpreted correctly."[196] His four chapters on metaphysics develop this base. His economics is original in that it offers an alternative to capitalism and socialism. "Economic process was conceived by the older economists as a generalized equilibrium. However, we are concerned, not with single schemes, but with a conditioned series

---

192. McCarthy, *Authenticity as Self-Transcendence*, 65. Mombula, *Human Community and Dialectic*, 60.
193. McCarthy, *Authenticity as Self-Transcendence*, 71.
194. McCarthy, *Authenticity as Self-Transcendence*, 71–72.
195. McCarthy, *Authenticity as Self-Transcendence*, 105.
196. Lonergan, *Insight*, 554.

Part IV: The Amplitude of Lonergan's Generalized Empirical Method 175

of schemes"[197] within complex schemes of recurrence. In sum, Lonergan's ability to survey, revise, and then integrate the thinking and methods of pioneers in many fields is truly original.

EXPLORATION 10: TOYNBEE AND LONERGAN ON HISTORY, CIVILIZATION, AND DECLINE

Arnold Toynbee's *A Study of History*, describes how civilizations develop and disintegrate. It focuses neither on individuals nor states, but on civilizations, defined in spiritual terms:

> A civilization might be defined as an endeavor to create a state or society in which the whole of mankind will be able to live together in harmony as members of a single, all-inclusive family. Civilization is due neither to the race factor nor to geographic environment as such but to a specific combination of two conditions: the presence of a creative minority and an environment which is neither too unfavorable nor too favorable. . . . The groups which had these conditions emerged as civilizations; the groups which did not . . . remained on the sub-civilization level. The mechanism of the birth of civilization . . . is formulated as an interplay of "Challenge-and-Response."[198]

Toynbee's guiding question was: Why do some societies or primitive groups become static at an early stage of their existence and not emerge as civilizations while others do reach this level? The environment constantly challenges a society. A creative minority can successfully respond to challenges but "a new challenge follows, and a new response successfully ensues. . . . In these conditions, no possibility of rest exists, the society is on the move all the time, and such a move brings it, sooner or later, to the stage of civilization."[199] Many historians criticized Toynbee's assumptions and theories. Pieter Geyl accused Toynbee of selectively using evidence to support his preconceived notions while disregarding evidence that did not support his thesis. He considered Toynbee's theory to be simplistic and a catch-all scheme. He opposed Toynbee's claim that Western civilization was in terminal decline.[200] On a positive note, Lonergan regarded Toynbee's *A Study of History* as a sourcebook of ideal types. Men such as Toynbee have

---

197. Lonergan, *Insight*, 141–42.
198. Cargas, "Arnold J. Toynbee's Philosophy," 516.
199. Pitirim Sorokin. Toynbee's Philosophy," 375.
200. Geyl, *Debates with Historians*, 2.

an essential function to fulfill. They provide "the materials from which carefully formulated ideal types might be derived."[201] While "ideal type" is a term used by Max Weber to refer to abstract, hypothetical concepts, this book's quasi-ideal type is a combination of kingdom-of-God and cosmopolis ideals. The kingdom of God is not abstract, but it asks for polyphonic conversions. Our text has sought to blend the different polyphonic intensities underlying both personal and social conflicts with a view to reconcile the unconscious, conscious, cognitive, and volitional aspects of our lives.

EXPLORATION 11: FREEDOM AND REALIZING THE GOOD

For Lonergan, consciousness is independent of biological and neural determinants. One cannot impose freedom or its attendant responsibilities on persons: "The excellence of man . . . is precisely doing what is right because he is free. His freedom is to realize the good."[202] Freedom is intrinsically linked with the dynamic structure of the four levels and activities of our consciousness. Contingence is involved in all of these activities, for were men "not free, there would be no question of their sinning."[203]

> The difference between our essential and effective freedom is that between a dynamic structure and its operational range. Man is free essentially inasmuch as possible courses of action are grasped by practical insight, motivated by reflection, and executed by decision. But man is effectively free inasmuch as this dynamic structure is open to . . . executing a broad or a narrow range of otherwise possible courses of action. Thus, one may be essentially but not effectively free to give up smoking.[204]

The negation of full effective freedom may seem to negate essential freedom if the proper grounds of the latter are not grasped clearly and distinctly. Thus, contingence of freedom arises

> in the order of spirit, of intelligent grasp, rational reflection, and morally guided will. It has the twofold basis that its object is merely a possibility and that its agent is contingent not only in his existence but also in the extension of his rational consciousness into rational self-consciousness. . . . It is one and the same

---

201. Lonergan, *Method in Theology*, 228.
202. Lonergan, *Topics in Education*, 38.
203. Lonergan, *Insight*, 714.
204. Lonergan, *Insight*, 643.

act of willing that both decides in favor of the object or against it and that constitutes the subject as deciding reasonably or unreasonably, as succeeding or failing in the extension of rational consciousness into an effectively rational self-consciousness.[205]

Being contingent, freedom can be restricted in many ways, as when effective freedom does not coincide with essential freedom because it is limited by illusions or other handicaps. There can be no valid argument from determinate knowing to determinate willing and doing. However, one is not to mistake the obvious for the essential. "The root of freedom lies in the contingence of the formal intelligibility of proportionate being. Because such intelligibility is contingent, it cannot guarantee its own existence or occurrence."[206] The contingence shows that it is not unique. Rather, manifold alternatives are possible. Because freedom is contingent, "it is known as merely possible, as in need of motivation, as needing motivation because it will exist or occur only if decision is forthcoming. Finally, because it is contingent, there cannot be valid motives for it that necessitate decision in its favor."[207]

Psychic illusions can prevent the consistency between knowing and doing, three of which are:

1) Flights from self-consciousness. Can one really flee from oneself? Yes, this does occasionally happen. Socrates counseled his hearers: "know thyself." This implies that self-knowledge is intrinsically linked with how one deliberates, how one freely acts upon knowledge of self and of others.

2) Rationalization, including the lies this may give rise to: "The average mind can invent lies about matters of fact; it can trump up excuses; it can allege extenuating circumstances that mingle fact with fiction. But hypocrisy is no more than the tribute paid by vice to virtue. It falls far short of the genuine rationalization that argues vice to be virtue, that meets the charge of inconsistency not by denying the minor premise of the fact but by denying the major premise of principle."[208]

3) Moral renunciation implies self-deception: "It is content with a speculative acknowledgment of the aspiration to make one's own intelligent

---

205. Lonergan, *Insight*, 642.
206. Lonergan, *Insight*, 644.
207. Lonergan, *Insight*, 644.
208. Lonergan, *Insight*, 623.

and reasonable. It is ready to confess its wrongdoing, but it has given up any hope of amending its ways."[209]

Aristotle, referring to Socrates asks about the type of judgment a man has if he behaves incontinently. "That he should behave so when he has knowledge . . . is impossible for despite his knowledge something else would master it and drag it about like a slave."[210] He concludes that there is no such thing as incontinence for no one should act against what he judges best; people act so only by reason of ignorance. For Lonergan, the human good and freedom are nonnegotiable moral elements. As did Aristotle, Lonergan speaks of the impediments that prevent effective freedom; his study of the biases helped him deepen Aristotle's insights on this point. He writes:

> All men are subject to bias, for bias is a block or distortion of intellectual development, and such blocks or distortions occur in four principal manners. There is the bias of unconscious motivation brought to light by depth psychology. There is the bias of individual egoism, and the more powerful and blinder bias of group egoism. Finally, there is the general bias of common sense, which is a specialization of intelligence in the particular, . . . but usually considers itself omnicompetent.[211]

Yes, man is essentially free, but blind spots interfere. Lonergan explains this analogically:

> If one were to represent a man's field of freedom as a circular area, then one would distinguish a luminous central region in which he was effectively free, a surrounding penumbra in which his uneasy conscience keeps suggesting that he could do better if only he would make up his mind, and finally an outer shadow to which he barely if ever adverts.[212]

Higher viewpoints can help one offset the outer shadow so as to help bring about liberation.

---

209. Lonergan, *Insight*, 623.
210. Aristotle, *Ethics*, vii, 1145 b 20–28.
211. Lonergan, *Method in Theology*, 231.
212. Lonergan, *Insight*, 650.

EXPLORATION 12: VOEGELIN AND LONERGAN ON DIFFERENTIATED CONSCIOUSNESS

Eric Voegelin argued that the historical dynamic of human living is universally experienced in consciousness. Lonergan wrote about the experience of the psychological present "reaching into its past by memories and into its future by anticipations."[213] Such experience and its implied universality suggest that historically it has been a basic conscious element of human living. Still this elemental experience is variously differentiated within humans. Reflection on the movement and direction of history differs according to the degree of differentiated consciousness—a phenomenon Voegelin addressed in his published works.[214] When Voegelin decided to discontinue his work on the history of political thought to concentrate on the history of experience and its symbolizations in *Order and History*, he was well aware of the implications of the shift. The abandoned work on political thought belonged to a way of thinking that conceived of history as driven by a dialectic between a fairly limited conception of experience and the unfolding logic of ideas. It then dawned on him that he had been stretching the framework of the old paradigm by trying to encompass within it a broader-than-usual conception of human experience since it included experiences of transcendence. With the new paradigm, Voegelin "burst the boundaries" of his previous framework. His new conception of history as a movement "had at its heart the unfolding not of ideas but of consciousness. . . . In the old paradigm, consciousness was not a variable. It was simply the constant medium of luminous transparency in which perceptions and impulses arose, left their traces, and faded out to be replaced by others."[215]

Voegelin had realized that the old paradigm had been confined to the horizon of self-interest as conceived by the Enlightenment. Just as Voegelin concluded that Gnosticism had misinterpreted the insights of myth, so Lonergan began to recognize the limitations of mythic consciousness. He opened ways for us to understand how language developed so that it came "to mediate and objectify and examine the linguistic process itself."[216]

---

213. Lonergan, *Lonergan Reader*, 496. McPartland, in "Meaning, Mystery and the Speculative," challenges the principles of contemporary intellectual culture. He searches for norms not in external perceptions or reified concepts, but in dynamic consciousness.

214. Ranieri, *Disturbing*, 72. Walmsley, *Pluralism*, 241, notes that, like Lonergan, the later Voegelin studied "the fundamental advance from compact to differentiated consciousness" as manifested in many ethnic cultures.

215. Webb, "Differentiations of Consciousness," 1.

216. Lonergan, *Method in Theology*, 92.

Changes in the stages or plateaus of meaning are determined by shifts in the fundamental control whereby meanings are grasped and accepted. "Changes in the control of meaning mark off the great epochs in human history."[217]

---

217. Lonergan, "Dimensions of Meaning," 256. For Thomas McPartland, "both viewed politics in a radically foundational manner, that differed from the reigning assumptions of modernity regarding epistemology . . . and metaphysics. Both dissented from the modern preoccupation of becoming masters of nature or, by implication, of human nature" ("Lonergan and Voegelin on Political Authority," 1).

Bibliography

Abbott, Walter M., SJ. *Documents of Vatican II*. London: Chapman, 1966.
Adams, Matthew. Review of *The Rime of the Ancient Mariner*, by Samuel Taylor Coleridge. *Irish Times*. May 11, 2017.
Aiken, David W. "Bernard Lonergan's Critique of Reductionism: A Call to Intellectual Conversion." *Christian Scholar's Review* 41.3 (2012) 233–51.
Al-Ghazali, Abu Hamid. *The Alchemy of Happiness*. Translated by Claude Field. Houston, TX: WLC, 2009.
———. *The Incoherence of the Philosophers*. Translated by Michael E. Marmura. Provo, UT: Brigham Young University Press, 2000.
Apostol, Tom M. *Calculus*, Vol. 2. Hoboken, NJ: Wiley, 1969.
Arcamone, Dominic. *Religion and Violence: A Dialectical Engagement through the Insights of Bernard Lonergan*. Eugene, OR: Pickwick, 2015.
Aristotle. *De Anima*.
———. *Metaphysics*. Translated by W. D. Ross. In *The Complete Works of Aristotle, Vol. 2*, edited by Jonathan Barnes, 1552–1728. Bolinger Series. Princeton: Princeton University Press, 1985.
———. *Nicomachean Ethics*. Translated by W. D. Ross. In *The Complete Works of Aristotle, Vol. 2*, edited by Jonathan Barnes, 1729–1867. Bolinger Series. Princeton: Princeton University Press, 1985.
———. *Physics*. Translated by R. P. Hardie and R. K. Gaye. In *The Complete Works of Aristotle, Vol. 1*, edited by Jonathan Barnes, 315–446. Bolinger Series. Princeton: Princeton University Press, 1985.
———. *Politics*. Translated by Benjamin Jowett. In *The Complete Works of Aristotle, Vol. 2*, edited by Jonathan Barnes, 1986–2129. Bolinger Series. Princeton: Princeton University Press, 1985.
———. *Topics*. Translated by W. A. Pickard. In *The Complete Works of Aristotle, Vol. 1*, edited by Jonathan Barnes, 167–277. Bolinger Series. Princeton: Princeton University Press, 1985.
Armstrong, Karen, *The Battle for God: A History of Fundamentalism*. New York: Random House, 2001.
———. *Twelve Steps to a Compassionate Life*. New York: Anchor, 2010.
Arsith, Mirela. "Ludwig Wittgenstein and Language-games (A Literary Application)." *Acta Universitatis Danubius* 5.2 (2011) 14–21.
Batterson, Steve. *Stephen Smale: The Mathematician Who Broke the Dimension Barrier*. Providence, RI: AMS, 2000.

Baumgartner, Wilhelm. Franz Brentano: "The Foundation of Value Theory and Ethics." In *Phenomenological Approaches to Moral Philosophy*, edited by Nicolas de Warren, 119–38. New York: Springer, 2002.

Baur, Michael. "Lonergan and Hegel on Some Aspects of knowing." *American Catholic Philosophical Quarterly* 88.3 (2014) 535–58.

Bawa Muhaiyaddeen Fellowship. "Sufi: A Brief Explanation." www.bmf.org/library/pamphlets/sufi-a-brief-explanation.

Beards, Andrew. *Lonergan, Meaning and Method: Philosophical Essays*. London: Bloomsbury, 2016.

Berthold-Bond, Daniel. "Hegel, Nietzsche, and Freud on Madness and the Unconscious." *The Journal of Speculative Philosophy* 5.3 (1991) 193–213.

Bock, Darrel L. "The Kingdom of God in New Testament Theology." In *Looking Into the Future: Evangelical Studies in Eschatology*, edited by David W. Baker, 1–20. Ada, MI: Baker, 2001.

Bonhoeffer, Dietrich. *London: 1933–1935*. Works Series, Vol. 13. Minneapolis: Fortress, 2014.

Bottomore, Tom. *A Dictionary of Marxist Thought*. Oxford: Wiley-Blackwell, 1991.

Brague, Remi. "The Impossibility of Secular Society." www.firstthings.com/article/2013/10/the-impossibility-of-secular-society.

Bretz, Mike. "Emergent Probability: A Directed Scale-Free Network." https://arxiv.org/ftp/cond-mat/papers/0207/0207241.pdf.

Bright, John. *Kingdom of God*. New York: Abingdon, 1953.

Brown, Colin. "A Man to Be Wrestled with." https://biblicalstudies.org.uk/pdf/churchman/088-01_047.pdf.

Brown, Patrick, D. "Lonergan and Berrigan: Two Radical and Visionary Jesuits." In *Faith, Resistance, and the Future*, edited by James Marsh et al., 183–208. New York: Fordham University Press, 2012.

Buccioni, Eva. "The Psychical Forces in Plato's *Phaedrus*." *British Journal for the History of Philosophy* 10 (2002) 331–57.

Camara, Babacar. "The Falsity of Hegel's Theses on Africa." *Journal of Black Studies* 36.1 (2005) 82–96.

Campbell, John. "Insight and Understanding in Bernard Lonergan." *Quarterly Journal of Speech* 71 (1985) 476–88.

Campbell, Joseph. *The Hero with a Thousand Faces*. Bollington Series, XVIII. Novato, CA: New World Library, 2008.

Cargas, Harry. "Arnold Toynbee." In *Great Thinkers of the Western World*, edited by Ian McGreal, 515–18. Mulgrave, VIC: Eastern, 1992.

Carmody, John. Review of *Mirror Mind*, by Bernard Lonergan. *Method: Journal of Lonergan Studies* 1 (1983) 89–92.

Cassel, Eric. "The Nature of Suffering and the Goals of Medicine." *New England Journal of Medicine* 8 (1998) 639–45.

Chittick, William C. "The Anthropology of Compassion." *The Muhyiddin Ibn Arabi Society* 48 (2010) 1–17.

Coleman, John A. "Thomas Merton." *America, The Jesuit Review* 98.3 (July 13, 2012) 5. https://www.americamagazine.org/faith/2012/07/13/thomas-merton-and-dialogue-buddhism

Conn, Walter. "Understanding the Self in Self-Transcendence." *Pastoral Psychology* 46.1 (1997) 3–17.
Coulter, Dale M. "Children of Light and Children of Darkness. *First Things* 5 (August 19, 2014) 2–3.
Coyne, Emmet. Review of *Christianity without God* by Daniel Maguire. In *The National Catholic Reporter*, March 25, 2015.
Crowe, Frederick. *Developing the Lonergan Legacy: Historical, Theoretical, and Existential Themes*. Toronto: University of Toronto Press, 1989.
———. *Lonergan and the Level of our Times*. Toronto: University of Toronto Press, 2010.
Dadosky, John D. "Desire, Bias, and Love: Revisiting Philosophical Anthropology." *Irish Theological Quarterly* 77.3 (2012) 244–64.
———. "Is there a Fourth Stage of Meaning?" *Heythrop Journal* 51.5 (2010) 768–809.
Deely, John. "Defining the Semiotic Animal: A Postmodern Definition of Human Being Superseding the Modern Definition 'Res Cogitans.'" *American Catholic Philosophical Quarterly* 79.3 (2005) 461–81.
Deneen, Patrick. *Why Liberalism Failed*. New Haven, CT: Yale University Press, 2018.
De Neeve, Eileen. "Income Distribution in Economic Growth: Ideas from Bernard Lonergan." www.eileendeneeve.com/Income%20Distribution%20in%20Economic%20Growth%20Complete.pdf.
———. "Lonergan's Economic Ideas Today: Functional Distinctions in Spending, the Pure Cycle of Innovative Growth, the Good of Order, and the Baseball Diamond." Lonergan Workshop #21, presented at Boston College, Chestnut Hill, MA, June 2008.
Descartes, Rene. *Discourse on the Method*. Translated by Donald A. Crest. Indianapolis: Hackett, 1998.
———. *Meditations on First Philosophy*. Translated by John Cottingham. Cambridge: Cambridge University Press, 1996.
Doctrine of the Faith and the Dicastery for Promoting Integral Human Development. "Considerations for an Ethical Discernment Regarding Some Aspects of the Present Economic-financial System." 2018.
Documents of Vatican II. London: Chapman, 1966, edited by Walter Abbott, S. J.
Doran, Robert, M. *Theology and the Dialectics of History*. Toronto: University of Toronto Press, 1990.
———. "A Vision." https://www.lonerganresource.com/pdf/lectures/Doran_-_International_Institute_for_Method_in_Theology.pdf
———. "Why Lonergan?" https://www13.shu.edu/catholic-mission/lonergan/upload/Why_Lonergan_Father_Doran_speech.pdf.
Drake, Lawrie. "Bernard Lonergan, Mechanism and Evolution." Lonergan Workshop, presented at Boston College, Chestnut Hill, MA, June 21, 1979.
Dunne, John. *A Search for God in Time and Memory*. New York: Macmillan, 1967.
Dunne, Tad. "Bernard Lonergan, 1904–1984." https://www.iep.utm.edu/lonergan/2003.
———. *Doing Better: The Next Revolution in Ethics*. Milwaukee: Marquette University Press, 2010.
Dupuis, Jacques. *Toward a Christian Theology of Religious Pluralism*. New York: Orbis, 1997.
Ekstrand, Donald W. "Spiritual Insights of Simone Weil." In *The Transformed Soul*. Maitland, FL. Xulon. 357–82.

Engels, Friedrich. "The Decline of Feudalism and the Rise of the Bourgeoisie." *Monthly Review* (1957) 445–54.

Featherstone, Mike. "Cosmopolis: An Introduction." *Theory, Culture and Society* 19 (2012) 1–16.

Feest, Uljana. "Husserl's Crisis as a Crisis of Psychology." *Studies in History and Philosophy of Biological and Biomedical Sciences* 43.2 (2012) 493–503.

Ferrarin, Alfredo. *Hegel and Aristotle*. Cambridge: Cambridge University Press, 2001.

Feuerbach, Ludwig. *Essence of Religion*. Amherst, NY: Prometheus, 2004.

Figueroa-Villarreal, Victor. "Gustavo Gutierrez's Understanding of the Kingdom of God in the Light of the Second Vatican Council." PhD diss., Andrews University, 1999.

Finamore, Rosanna. "Centrality of Consciousness." *La Gregoriana* XIX.47 (2014) 44–63.

Fitzpatrick, Joseph. "Lonergan and the Later Wittgenstein." *Method: Journal of Lonergan Studies* 10.1 (1992) 27–50.

Foucault, Michel. *The Order of Things: An Archaeology of the Human Sciences*. New York: Pantheon, 1966.

Francis, Pope. *Apostolic Constitution Faith, Reason Give Harmonious Witness to Truth*. https://press.vatican.va/content/salastampa/en/bollettino/pubblico/2018/01/29/180129c.html.

———. "Rejoice and Be Glad." http://w2.vatican.va/content/francesco/en/apost_exhortations/documents/ papa-francesco_esortazione-ap_20180319_gaudete-et-exsultate.html.

Frank, Anne. *The Diary of Anne Frank*. Edited by Otto H. Frank and Mirjam Pressler. Translated by Susan Massotty. New York: Everyman, 1947.

Fraser, Giles. "France's Much Vaunted Secularism is not the Neutral Space it Claims to be." *The Guardian*, January 16, 2005. https://www.theguardian.com/commentisfree/belief/2015/jan/16/france-much-vaunted-secularism-not-neutral-space-claims-to-be.

Frings, Manfred. "Max Scheler: A Descriptive Analysis of the Concept of Ultimate Reality." *Ultimate Reality and Meaning* 3.2 (1980) 135–43.

Fuchs, Jo-Ann. "On the War Path and Beyond: Hegel, Freud and Feminist Theory." *Women's Studies International Forum* 6.6 (1983) 565–72.

Fuellenbach, John. *The Kingdom of God: The Message of Jesus Today*. Eugene, OR: Wipf & Stock, 1995.

Gendlin, Eugene T. *Focusing*. New York: Bantam, 1981.

Gerhart, Mary. "Bernard Lonergan's 'Law of the Cross': Transforming the Sources and Effects of Violence." *Theological Studies* 77.1 (2016) 77–95.

Geyl, Pieter. *Debates with Historians*. Groningen: J. B. Wolters, 1955.

Good News Bible. New York: American Bible Society, 1976.

Gregor, Brian "The Critique of Religion and Post-Metaphysical Faith: Bonhoeffer's Influence on Ricoeur's Hermeneutics of Religion" edited by Matthew D. Kirkpatrick. Minneapolis: Fortress, (2016) 259–82.

Grudzen, Gerald, and John Raymaker. *Steps toward Vatican III*. Lanhan, MD: University Press of America, 2008.

Guardini, Romano. "The Power of Silence." In *Language, Poetry, Intepretation*, edited and translated by Louis Grech, 15–16. Brescia, Italy: Morcelliana, 2000.

Guite, Malcolm. *Mariner: A Voyage with Samuel Taylor Coleridge*. London: Hodder & Stoughton, 2017.
———. "Mariner: A Voyage with Samuel Taylor Coleridge." http://www.theimaginativeconservative.org/2017/04/mariner-voyage-samuel-taylor-coleridge-malcolm-guite.html.
Gurwitsch, Aron. "Toward a Theory of Intentionality." *Philosophy and Phenomenological Research* 30.3 (1970) 354–67.
Hampe, Michael. "Science, Philosophy of Knowledge: Husserl's Conception of a Life-World and Sellars's Manifest and Scientific Images." In *Science and Life-worl:. Essays on Husserl's Crisis of European Sciences*, edited by David Hyder et al., 150–63. Stanford: Stanford University Press, 2009.
Harris, James, F. "Language, Language Game and Ostensive Definitions." *Syntheses* 69 (1986) 41–49.
Harter, Joel. *Coleridge's Philosophy of Faith: Symbol, Allegory, and Hermeneutics*. Tübingen: Mohr Siebeck, 2011.
Hegel, Georg Wilhelm. "Lordship and Bondage." In *Dialectic of Desire and Recognition*, edited by John O'Neil, 29–36. Albany, NY: State University of New York Press, 1996.
———. *Phenomenology of Mind*. Translated by George Lichtheim. New York: Harper, 1967.
———. *The Philosophy of History*. Kitchener, ON: Botoche, 2001.
Hook, Sydney. *From Hegel to Marx: Studies in the Intellectual Development of Karl Marx*. New York: Columbia University Press, 1936.
Husserl, Edmund. *The Crisis of the European Sciences and Transcendental Phenomenology: An Introduction to Phenomenological Philosophy*. Hague: Nijhoff, 1954.
———. *Logos of Phenomenology and Phenomenology of the Logos*. Vol. 3. New York: Springer, 2006.
Ige, Simeon. "The Cult of Ancestors in African Traditional Religion." *An Encyclopedia of the Arts*, 10.1 (2006) 26–31.
Inglehart, Ronald. *Modernization and Postmodernization*. Princeton: Princeton University Press, 1977.
———. *The Silent Revolution*. Princeton: Princeton University Press, 1977.
Jackall, Robert. *Moral Mazes: The World of Corporate Managers*. Oxford: Oxford University Press, 1988.
Jenkins, Philip. *The Next Christendom: The Coming of Global Christianity*. Oxford: Oxford University Press, 2002.
John Paul II, Pope. "Christ Appeals to Man's Heart." http://www.ewtn.com/library/papaldoc/jp2tb23.htm.
Johnston, Paul. *The Contradictions of Modern Moral Philosophy: Ethics after Wittgenstein*. Abington-on Thames, UK: Routledge, 1999.
Johnston, William. *The Inner Eye of Love*. New York: Harper, 1978.
———. *The Mirror Mind: Spirituality and Transformation*. New York: Harper, 1981.
———. *Silent Music: The Science of Meditation*. New York: Harper & Row, 1974.
Kain, Philip. "Aristotle, Kant, and the Ethics of the Young Marx." In *Marx and Aristotle: 19th Century German Social Theory and Classical Antiquity*, edited by George McCarthy, 213–42. Lanham, MD: Rowman & Littlefield, 1992.

Kang, So-Young. "Why Integrate Diversity?" http://awakengroup.com/?ag_share=why-integrate-diversity.

Kant, Immanuel. *An Answer to the Question: What is Enlightenment?* Indianapolis: Hackett, 1973.

———. *Critique of Pure Reason*. Translated by Norman Kemp Smith. New York: St. Martin's, 1965.

———. *Grounding of the Metaphysics of Morals: On a Supposed Right to Lie because of Philanthropic Concerns*. Translated by James Wesley Ellington. Indianapolis: Hackett, 1993.

———. *Perpetual Peace and Other Essays*. Indianapolis: Hackett, 1995.

Kidder, Paul. "The Hermeneutic and Dialectic of Community in Development." In *International Journal of Social Economics* 24.11 (1997) 1191–1202.

———. "Lonergan's Negative Dialectic." In *International Philosophical Quarterly* 3 (1990) 299–309.

King, Catherine. *Finding the Mind: Pedagogy for Verifying Cognitional Theory*. Lanham, MD: Rowman & Littlefield, 2011.

Knitter, Paul F. *Without Buddha I Could not be a Christian*. London: Oneworld, 2013.

Krebs, Victor. "Mind, Soul, Language in Wittgenstein." www.bu.edu/wcp/Papers/Lang/LangKreb.htm.

Kreeft, Peter. "Comparing Christianity & Buddhism." www.peterkreeft.com/topics-more/religions_buddhism.htm.

Lamb, Matthew. "Praxis." In *The New Dictionary of Theology*, edited by Joseph Komonchak et al., 784–87. Wilmington, DE: Michael Glazier, 1988.

———. "The Theory-Praxis Relationship in Contemporary Christian Theologies." *Proceedings of the Thirty-first Annual Convention of the Catholic Theological Society of America* 32 (1976) 149–78.

Lavine, Thelma. "Philosophy and the Dialectic of Modernity." www.bu.edu/wcp/Papers/Soci/SociLavi.htm

Lawrence, Fred. "Editors' Introduction to *Macroeconomic Dynamics: An Essay in Circulation Analysis*, by Bernard Lonergan, xxv–lxxiv. Edited by Frederick G. Lawrence et al. CWL 15. Toronto: University of Toronto Press, 1999.

———. "The Fragility of Consciousness: Lonergan and the Postmodern Concern for the Other." *Theological Studies* 54 (1993) 55–96.

———. *Introduction to Ethics in Making a Living: The Jane Jacobs Conference*. Missoula, MT: Scholars, 1989.

Levinas, Emmanuel. *Totality and Infinity: An Essay on Exteriority*. London: Bloomsbury, 2015.

Lewis, C. S. *The Joyful Christian*. New York: Touchstone, 1977.

Lichtman, Richard. "Human Nature. Marx and Freud: Search for a Synthesis." *Capitalism Nature Socialism* 10.4 (1999) 77–96.

Liddy, Richard. "The Mystery of Lonergan." *America* 19.10 (2004) 16–20.

———. *Startling Strangeness: Reading Lonergan's Insight*. Lanham, MD: Rowman & Littlefield, 2007.

Lonergan, Bernard, "The Absence of God in Modern Culture." In *A Second Collection*, edited by William Ryan and Bernard Tyrell, 101–16. Philadelphia: Westminster, 1974.

———. "The Analogy of Meaning." In *Philosophical and Theological Papers 1958-1964*, edited by Robert C. Croken et al., 183–213. CWL 6. Toronto: University of Toronto Press, 1996.

———. "The Analogy of Revolution." In the Lonergan Archives. A2041. Located at the Toronto Lonergan Center and accessible at https://www.bernardlonergan.com/.

———. "Belief: Today's Issue." In *A Second Collection*, edited by William Ryan and Bernard Tyrell, 87–100. Philadelphia: Westminster, 1974.

———. "Christ as Subject: A Reply." In *Collection: Papers by Bernard Lonergan, SJ*, edited by Frederick E. Crowe, 164–97. Montreal: Palm, 1967.

———. "Consciousness and the Trinity." In *Philosophical and Theological Papers 1958-1964*, edited by Robert Croken et al., 122–41. CWL 6. Toronto: University of Toronto Press, 1996.

———. "Dialectic of Authority." In *A Third Collection: Papers by Bernard Lonergan, SJ*, edited by Frederick E. Crowe, 5–12. Mahwah, NJ: Paulist, 1985.

———. "Dimensions of Meaning." In *Collection: Papers by Bernard Lonergan, SJ*, edited by Frederick E. Crowe, 252–67. Montreal: Palm, 1967.

———. "Doctrinal Pluralism." In *Philosophical and Theological Papers, 1965-1980*, edited by Robert C. Croken and Robert M. Doran, 70–104. CWL 17. Toronto: University of Toronto Press, 2004.

———. *Early Works on Theological Method 1*, edited by Robert Doran, et al. CWL 22. Toronto: University of Toronto Press, 2010.

———. "Existenz and Aggiornamento." In *Collection: Papers by Bernard Lonergan, SJ*, edited by Frederick E. Crowe, 240–51. Montreal: Palm, 1967.

———. "Finality, Love, Marriage." In *Collection: Papers by Bernard Lonergan, SJ*, edited by Frederick E. Crowe, 16–53. Montreal: Palm, 1967.

———. *For a New Political Economy*. Edited by Phil McShane. CWL 21. Toronto: University of Toronto Press. 1998.

———. "Healing and Creating in History." In *A Third Collection: Papers by Bernard Lonergan, SJ*, edited by Frederick E. Crowe, 100–12. Mahwah, NJ: Paulist, 1985.

———. "Horizons." In *Philosophical and Theological Papers, 1965-1980*, edited by Robert C. Croken and Robert M. Doran, 10–29. CWL 17. Toronto: University of Toronto Press, 2004.

———. "The Human Good as the Developing Subject." In *Topics in Education: The Cincinnati Lectures of 1959 on the Philosophy of Education*, edited by Frederick Crowe, 79–106. Toronto: University of Toronto Press, 1993.

———. "The Human Good, Meaning, and Differentiations of Consciousness." In *Early Works on Theological Method 1*, edited by Robert Doran and Robert Croken, 30–55. CWL 22. Toronto: University of Toronto Press, 1967.

———. *The Incarnate Word*. Translated by Charles Hefling, Jr., edited by Robert Doran et al. CWL 8. Toronto: University of Toronto Press, 2016.

———. *Insight: A Study in Human Understanding*. Edited by Frederick E. Crowe and Robert Doran. CWL 3. Toronto: University of Toronto Press, 1997.

———. "Insight Revisited." In *A Second Collection*, edited by William Ryan and Bernard Tyrell, 263–79. Philadelphia: Westminster, 1974.

———. "Isomorphism of Thomist and Scientific Thought." In *Collection: Papers by Bernard Lonergan, SJ*, edited by Frederick. E. Crowe, 142–51. Montreal: Palm, 1967.

———. Lonergan Archives. http://www.bernardlonergan.com/pdf/62200DTEL60.pdf.

———. *The Lonergan Reader*. Edited by Mark D. Morelli and Elizabeth A. Morelli. Toronto: University of Toronto, 1997.

———. *Macroeconomic Dynamics: An Essay in Circulation Analysis*. Edited by Frederick Lawrence et al. CWL 15. Toronto: University of Toronto Press, 1999.

———. "Mathematical Logic and Scholasticism." In *Phenomenology and Logic: The Boston College Lectures on Mathematical Logic and Existentialism*, edited by Phil McShane, 115–38. CWL 18. Toronto: University of Toronto Press, 2001.

———. "Metaphysics as Horizon." In *Collection: Papers by Bernard Lonergan, SJ*, edited by Frederick E. Crowe, 202–20. Montreal: Palm, 1967.

———. *Method in Theology*. New York: Herder and Herder, 1972.

———. "Mission and the Spirit." In *A Third Collection: Papers by Bernard Lonergan, SJ*, edited by Frederick E. Crowe, 23–34. Mahwah, NJ: Paulist, 1985.

———. "Moral Theology and the Human Sciences." In *Philosophical and Theological Papers 1965-1980*, edited by Robert C. Croken and Robert M. Doran, 301–12. Toronto: University of Toronto Press, 2004.

———. "Natural Right and Historical Mindedness." In *A Third Collection: Papers by Bernard Lonergan, SJ*, edited by Frederick. E. Crowe, 169–83. Mahwah, NJ: Paulist, 1985.

———. "Openness and Religious Experience." In *Collection: Papers by Bernard Lonergan, SJ*, edited by Frederick E. Crowe, 198–201. Montreal: Palm, 1967.

———. "A Post-Hegelian Philosophy of Religion." In *A Third Collection: Papers by Bernard Lonergan, SJ*, edited by Frederick E. Crowe, 202–23. Mahwah, NJ: Paulist, 1985.

———. "Prolegomena to the Study of the Emerging Religious Consciousness of Our Time." In *A Third Collection, Papers by Bernard Lonergan, S. J.*, edited by Frederick E. Crowe, 55–73. Mahwah, NJ: Paulist, 1985.

———. "Questionnaire on Philosophy: Response." In *Philosophical and Theological Papers 1965-1980*, edited by Robert C. Croken and Robert M. Doran, 352–83. Toronto: University of Toronto Press, 2004.

———. "Redemption." In *Philosophical and Theological Papers 1958-1964*, edited by Robert Croken et al., 3–28. CWL 6. Toronto: University of Toronto Press, 1996.

———. "The Relationship between Philosophy of God and the Functional Specialty Systematics." In *Philosophical and Theological Papers 1965-1980*, edited by Robert C. Croken and Robert M. Doran, 199–218. CWL 17. Toronto: University of Toronto Press, 2004.

———. "Religious Knowledge." In *A Third Collection: Papers by Bernard Lonergan, SJ*, edited by Frederick E. Crowe, 129–45. New York: Paulist, 1985.

———. "The Response of the Jesuit as Priest and Apostle in the Modern World." In *A Second Collection*, edited by William Ryan and Bernard Tyrell, 165–87. Philadelphia: Westminster, 1974.

———. "The Role of a Catholic University in the Modern World." In *Collection: Papers by Bernard Lonergan, SJ*, edited by Frederick E. Crowe, 114–20. Montreal: Palm, 1967.

———. "Sacralization and Secularization." *Philosophical and Theological Papers 1965-1980*, edited by Robert C. Croken and Robert M. Doran, 259–81. CWL 17. Toronto: University of Toronto Press, 2004.

———. "The Subject." In *A Second Collection*, edited by William Ryan and Bernard Tyrell, 69–86. Philadelphia: Westminster, 1974.

———. "Theology and Man's Future." In *A Second Collection*, edited by William Ryan and Bernard Tyrell, 135–48. Philadelphia: Westminster, 1974.

———. "Theology in its New Context." In *A Second Collection*, edited by William Ryan and Bernard Tyrell, 55–68. Philadelphia: Westminster, 1974.

———. "Time and Meaning." In *Philosophical and Theological Papers 1958-1964*, edited by Robert Croken et al., 94–121. CWL 6. Toronto: University of Toronto Press, 1996.

———. *Topics in Education: The Cincinnati Lectures of 1959 on the Philosophy of Education.* Toronto: University of Toronto Press, 1993.

———. "The Transition from a Classicist World-view to Historical-mindedness." In *A Second Collection*, edited by William Ryan and Bernard Tyrell, 1–9. Philadelphia: Westminster, 1974.

———. *Understanding and Being: The Halifax Lectures on Insight*, edited by Elizabeth Morelli and Mark Morelli. CWL 5. Toronto: University of Toronto Press, 1990.

———. *Verbum: Word and Idea in Aquinas.* Notre Dame, IN: University of Notre Dame Press, 1967.

———. "The World Mediated by Meaning." *Philosophical and Theological Papers 1965-1980*, edited by Robert C. Croken and Robert M. Doran, 107–18. CWL 17. Toronto: University of Toronto Press, 2004.

Maguire, Daniel C. *Christianity without God: Moving Beyond the Dogmas and Retrieving the Epic Moral Narrative.* New York: SUNY Press, 2014.

———. *Whose Church: A Concise Guide to Progressive Catholicism.* New York: New Press, 2008.

Marsh, James, *Lonergan in the World: Self-Absorption, Otherness, and Justice.* Toronto: University of Toronto Press, 2014.

———. "Postmodernism: A Lonerganian Retrieval and Critique." *International Philosophical Quarterly* 35.2 (June 1995) 159–73.

Martini, Carlo Maria (Cardinal). "Bernard Lonergan at the Service of the Church." *Theological Studies* 66.3 (2005) 526–66.

———. "The Value of the Thought of Bernard Lonergan Today." In *Going Beyond Essentialism: Bernard Lonergan, an Atypical Neo-Scholastic*, edited by Cloe Taddei-Ferretti, 21–24. Naples: Instituto Italiano per gli Studi Filosofici, 2012.

Martos, Joseph. *Deconstructing Sacramental Theology and Reconstructing Catholic Ritual.* Eugene, OR: Wipf & Stock, 2015.

———. *Honest Rituals, Honest Sacraments.* Eugene, OR: Wipf & Stock, 2017.

Marx, Karl. *Capital.* Translated by Ben Fowkes. New York: Penguin, 1977.

———. "Critique of the Gotha Program." *Die Neue Zeit* 1.18 (1891).

———. "Economic and Philosophical Manuscripts." In *Early Writings*, translated by Rodney Livingston and Gregor Benton, 279–400. New York: Penguin, 1975.

———. "Theses on Feuerbach." www.marxists.org/archive/marx/works/1845/theses/index.htm.

Marx, Karl, and Friedrich Engels. *The Communist Manifesto of 1848.* New York: Penguin, 2014.

———. *Selected Works in One Volume.* New York: International, 1968.

Maspero, Giulio, and Robert J. Wozniak, eds. *Rethinking Trinitarian Theology: Disputed Questions and Contemporary Issues.* New York: T. & T. Clark, 2012.

Mathews, William A. *Lonergan's Quest: A Study of Desire in the Authoring of Insight.* Toronto: University of Toronto Press, 2005.
McAllister, Joseph. "The Influence of Immanuel Kant's Concept of Liberty." *Proceedings of the American Catholic Philosophical Association* 16 (1940) 38–53.
McCarthy, Michael. *Authenticity as Self-Transcendence: The Enduring Insights of Bernard Lonergan.* Notre Dame, IN: University of Notre Dame Press, 2015.
McDonald, Mary Josephine. "Body-Psyche-Mind in the Self-Appropriation of the Subject: Complexifying Lonergan's Account of Nature and Supernature." PhD diss., Regis College, 2014.
McFarland, Jan. "Who is My Neighbor?: The Good Samaritan as a Source for Theological Anthropology." *Modern Theology* 17.1 (2002) 57–66.
McGill, V. J. "Scheler's Theory of Sympathy and Love." *Philosophy and Phenomenological Research* 2.3 (1942) 273–91.
McKenzie, John L. *Dictionary of the Bible.* New York: Macmillan, 1965.
McLuhan, Marshall. *The Gutenberg Galaxy: The Making of Typographic Man.* Toronto: University of Toronto Press, 1962.
McNelis, Sean. "Lonergan's Economic Theory." In *Fifty Years of Insight: Bernard Lonergan's Contribution to Philosophy and Theology*, edited by Neil Ormerod et al., 175–204. Adelaide, Australia: Hindmarsh, 2011.
McPartland, Thomas, J. *Lonergan and the Philosophy of Historical Existence.* Columbia, MO: University of Missouri Press, 2000.
———. "Lonergan and Voegelin on Political Authority." Paper presented at the annual meeting of the American Political Science Association, Washington DC, September 2010. https://papers.ssrn.com/sol3/papers.cfm?abstract_id=1642482.
———. "Meaning, Mystery and the Speculative Philosophy of History." *Revista Portuguesa de Filosofia* 63 (2007) 961–89.
McShane, Philip. "Book Interview." http://www.philipmcshane/profit-book/Interview
———. "Detoxing Lonergan Studies." http://www.philipmcshane.org/forum/forums/forum/detoxing/.
———. "Editor's Introduction." In *For a New Political Economy*, edited by Phil McShane, xv–xxxi. CWL 21. Toronto: University of Toronto Press. 1998.
———. "Implementing the New Science of Economics." http://www.philipmcshane.org/forum/forums/forum/interpreting-economics/
———. *Piketty's Plight and the Global Future: Economics for Dummies.* Vancouver: Axial, 2014.
———. *Profit: The Stupid View of President Donald Trump.* Vancouver: Axial, 2016.
Merton, Thomas. *Mystics and Zen Masters.* New York: Noonday, 1963.
———. *Zen and the Birds of Appetite.* New York: New Directions, 1968.
Meynell, Hugo. *An Introduction to the Philosophy of Bernard Lonergan.* New York: Springer Library of Philosophy and Religion, 1976.
———. *Redirecting Philosophy: Reflections on the Nature of Knowledge from Plato to Lonergan.* Toronto: University of Toronto Press, 1998.
Miller, Mark T. "Why the Passion?: Bernard Lonergan on the Cross as Communication." PhD diss., Boston College, 2008.
Mitchell, Donald, and James Wiseman, eds. *Gethsemani Encounter: A Dialogue on the Spiritual Life by Buddhist and Christian Monastics.* New York: Continuum, 1998.
Mofid, Kamran. "The New Brexit and Trumpian World Order: Will They Engulf Europe and the Rest of the World?" http://www.gcgi.info/index.php/blog/830-will-brexit-

trump-style-revolt-engulf-europe-and-the-rest-of-the-world#.WCcX-cuVJoo. gmail.

Mombula, Alekiabo Godefroid. "Human Community and Dialectic in the Thought of Bernard Lonergan." PhD diss., Pontificia Universita Gregoriania, 2017.

Moran, Dermot, and Joseph Cohen. *The Husserl Dictionary*. New York: Continuum, 2013.

Morelli, Elizabeth, "A Reflection on Lonergan's Notion of the Pure Desire to Know. Remarks on Fred Crowe's Essay Entitled 'Bernard Lonergan's Thought on Ultimate Reality and Meaning,'" *Ultimate Reality and Meaning* 13.4 (1990) 58–89.

Mudde, Anna. "Risky Subjectivity: Antigone, Action, and Universal Trespass." *Human Studies* 32.2 (2009) 183–200.

Musto, Marcelo. "Revisiting Marx's Conception of Alienation." *Socialism and Democracy* 24.3 (2010) 1–23.

Nicholls, Bruce. *A Theology of Gospel and Culture*. Downers Grove, IL: InterVarsity, 1979.

Nicholson, Reynold A. *The Mystics of Islam*. London: Routledge, 1914.

Nordquest, David. "Cosmopolis: Bourqet's and Lonergan's." *Method: Journal of Lonergan Studies* 11 (1993) 37–50.

Nullens, Patrick, and Ronald Michener. *The Matrix of Christian Ethics: Integrating Philosophy and Moral Theology in a Postmodern Context*. Downers Grove, IL: InterVarsity, 2010.

Oduke, Onyango. "Lonergan's Notion of Cosmopolis: A Study of a Higher Viewpoint and a Creative Framework for Engaging Individual and Social 'Biases' with Special Relevance to Socio-Political Challenges of Kenya and the Continent of Africa." PhD diss., Boston College, 2005.

Ogbonnaya, Joseph. *Lonergan, Social Transformation, and Sustainable Human Development*. Eugene, OR: Pickwick, 2013.

Ogilvie, Matthew C. *Faith Seeking Understanding. The Functional Specialty, 'Systematics,' in Bernard Lonergan's Method in Theology*. Marquette University Studies in Theology 26. Milwaukee: Marquette University Press, 2001.

Ormerod, Neil, et al. "The Development of Catholic Social Teaching on Economics: Bernard Lonergan and Benedict XVI." *Theological Studies* 73 (2012) 391–421.

Pannenberg, Wolfart. "History and Meaning in Bernard Lonergan's Approach to Theological Method." In *Looking at Lonergan's Method*, edited by Patrick Corcoran, 88–100. Eugene, OR: Wipf & Stock, 2007.

Paton, Herbert. *The Categorical Imperative: A Study in Kant's Moral Philosophy*. Philadelphia: University of Pennsylvania Press, 1971.

———. "Kant's Idea of the Good." *Proceedings of the Aristotelian Society* 45.2 (1944–1945) i–xxv.

Paul, Jan. "The Kingdom and the Common Good." Psephizo. December, 11, 2015. www.psephizo.com/life-ministry/the-kingdom-and-the-common-good.

Perry, Donna J. "Transcendental Method for Research with Human Subjects: A Transformative Phenomenology for the Human Sciences." *Field Methods* 25.3 (2013) 262–82.

Peters, James R. *The Logic of the Heart: Augustine, Pascal, and the Rationality of Faith*. Grand Rapids: Baker Academic, 2009.

Plato. *Republic*. Translated by G. M. A. Grub. Edited and revised by C. D. C. Reeve. Indianapolis: Hackett, 1997.

Polakow-Suransky, Sasha. *Go Back to Where You Came From: The Backlash against Immigration and the Fate of Western Democracy*. New York: Nation, 2017.

Rabut, Oliver. *L'experience religieuse fondamentale*. Tournai, Belgium: Casterman, 1969.

Rand, Ayn. *The Virtue of Selfishness*. New York: New American Library, 1964.

Ranieri, John. *Disturbing Revelation: Leo Strauss, Eric Voegelin, and the Bible*. Columbia, MO: University of Missouri Press, 2009.

Raymaker, John. *Bernard Lonergan's Third Way of the Heart and Mind: Bridging some Buddhist-Christian-Muslim-Secularist Misunderstandings with a Global Secularity Ethics*. Lanham, MD: Hamilton, 2016.

———. *A Buddhist-Christian Logic of the Heart: Nishida's Kyoto School and Lonergan's "Spiritual Genome" as World Bridge*. Lanham, MD: Rowman & Littlefield, 2002.

———. *Empowering the Lonely Crowd*. Lanham, MD: Rowman & Littlefield, 2003.

———. "Theory-Praxis of Social Ethics: The Complementarity of Bernard Lonergan's and Gibson Winter's Theological Foundations." PhD diss., Marquette University, 1977.

Raymaker, John, and Ijaz Durrani. *Empowering Climate Change Strategies*. Lanham, MD: Rowman & Littlefield, 2015.

Raymaker, John, et al. *Spiritual Paths to An Ethical & Ecological Global Civilization: Reading the Signs of the Times with Buddhists, Christians, & Muslims*. Washington, DC: Pacem in Terris, 2013.

Ricoeur, Paul. *Essays on Biblical Interpretation*. Edited by Lewis Mudge. Minneapolis: Fortress, 1980.

———. "The Later Wittgenstein and the Later Husserl on Language." *Ricoeur Studies* 5.1 (2014) 1–22.

———. *The Symbolism of Evil*. Translated by Emerson Buchanan. Boston: Beacon, 1986.

———. "Toward the Restoration of Meaning." *Anglican Theological Review* 55.4 (1973) 443–58.

Ritenbaugh, John W. "Bible Verses about Kingdom of God as a Spiritual Entity." www.bibletools.org/index.cfm/fuseaction/Topical.show/RTD/cgg/ID/ 14166/Kingdom-God-as-Spiritual-Entity.htm.

Rixon, Gordon. "Lonergan and Mysticism." *Theological Studies* 62.3 (2001) 479–97.

Roach, Jesse. "The Early and Later Philosophy of Wittgenstein," *Truth Conquers Darkness* (blog), August 17, 2014, https://sophoslogos.wordpress.com/2014/08/17/the-early-and-later-philosophy-of-wittgenstein/.

Roazen, Paul. "What Kind of Man was Freud?" *Culture and Society* 37.6 (2000) 74–81.

Romero, Jose. "Don Quixote Rides Again: Illusion and Delusion in Conrad's Lord Jim." http://www.clas.ufl.edu/ipsa/2005/proc/romero.pdf.

Rose, David. *Hegel's Philosophy of Right*. London: Readers' Guide, 2007.

Roy, Louis. "Religious Experience According to Bernard Lonergan." http://www.lonerganresearch.org/site/assets/files/1230/religious_experience_lecture_at_lri.pdf

Rusembuka, Muhigirwa F. *The Two Ways of Human Development According to B. Lonergan: Anticipation in Insight*. Serie Filosofia 17. Rome: Gregorian & Biblical, 2001.

Ryan, William F. "Intentionality in Edmund Husserl and Bernard Lonergan." *International Philosophical Quarterly* 13.2 (1973) 173–90.

Sauer, James B. *A Commentary on Lonergan's Method in Theology*. Edited by Peter L. Monette and Christine Jamieson. Ottawa: The Lonergan Website, 2001.

Sayers, Sean. "Individual and Society in Marx and Hegel: Beyond the Communitarian Critique of Liberalism." *Science and Society* 71.1 (2007) 84–102.

Scheler, Max. *Der Formalismus in der Ethik und die materiale Wertethik*. Halle, Germany: Niemeyer, 1921.

Schepers, Maurice. "Human Development: From Below Upwards and from Above Downwards." *Method: Journal of Lonergan Studies* 7.2 (1989) 141–58.

Schumpeter, Joseph. *History of Economic Analysis*. Oxford: Oxford University Press, 1954.

Schwartz, Stephen. *The Other Islam: Sufism and the Road to Global Harmony*. New York: Harmony, 2008.

Sen, Amartya. *Development as Freedom*. Oxford: Oxford University Press, 1999.

Shea, William R. "Horizons on Bernard Lonergan." *Horizons* 15.1 (1988) 77–107.

Shute, Michael. *The Origin of Lonergan's Notion of the Dialectic of History*. Lanham, MD: Rowman & Littlefield, 1993.

Snell, R. J., and Steven D. Cone. *Authentic Cosmopolitanism: Love, Sin, and Grace in the Christian University*. Eugene, OR: Wipf & Stock, 2013.

Soni, Jimmy, and Rob Goodman. *A Mind at Play*. New York: Simon & Shuster, 2017.

Sorokin, Pitirim. "Arnold J. Toynbee's *Philosophy of History*. *Journal of Modern History*. 12.3. September 1940. 374–87.

Stang, Charles. *Apophasis and Pseudonymity in Dionysius the Areopagite: "No Longer I."* Oxford Early Christian Studies. Oxford: Oxford University Press, 2012.

Stern, David G. *Wittgenstein's Philosophical Investigations*. Iowa City, IA: University of Iowa Press, 2004.

Symington, Paul. "The Unconscious and Conscious Self: The Nature of Psychical Unity in Freud and Lonergan." *American Catholic Philosophical Quarterly* 80.4 (2006) 563–80.

Tackney, Charles. "Redeeming the Academy: Empirically Assessing the Operational Effects of Grace in History." Presented at the Management Spirituality and Religion Interest Group Academy of Management Conference, Chicago, IL, August 2018.

Tamburello, Dennis. *Ordinary Mysticism*. New York: Paulist, 1996.

Teevan, Donna. "Meaning and Praxis in History: Lonerganian Perspectives." *Theology and the New Histories* 44 (1999) 150–64.

Thorpe, Lucas. *The Kant Dictionary*. Bloomsbury Philosophical Dictionaries. London: Bloomsbury. 2015.

Toulmin, Stephen. *Cosmopolis: The Hidden Agenda of Modernity*. Chicago: University of Chicago Press, 1990.

Toynbee, Arnold, and Jane Caplan. *A Study of History*. Oxford: Oxford University Press, 1972.

Turner, Denys. *The Darkness of God: Negativity in Christian Mysticism*. Cambridge: Cambridge University Press, 1999.

Tuske, Joerg. "Being in Two Minds: The Divided Mind in the *Nyayasutra*." *Asian Philosophy* 9.3 (1999) 229–38.

Tyrrell, Bernard. "On the Possibility and Desirability of a Christian Psychotherapy." Lonergan Workshop, presented at Boston College, Chestnut Hill, MA, June, 1974.

van Hooft, Stan. "Scheler on Emotions." *Today*, 38.1 (1994) 18–28.

Vertin, Michael. "Lonergan on Consciousness: Is there a Fifth Level?" *Method: Journal of Lonergan Studies* 12 (1994) 1–36.

———. "Review of *Theology and the Dialectics of History* by Robert M. Doran." *The Thomist: A Speculative Quarterly Review* 56.1 (1992) 160–61.

Voegelin, Eric. *Order and History: Volume 1: Israel and Revelation*. Edited by Maurice P. Hogan. Baton Rouge, LA: Louisiana State University Press, 1956.

von Kirchbach, Agnes. "The Kingdom of God . . . A Treasure: Gospel Reflection for the Seventeenth Century in Ordinary Time." https://international.la-croix.com/news/the-kingdom-of-god-a-treasure/5614?utm_source=Newsletter&utm_medium=e-mail&utm_content=29-07-2017&utm_campaign=newsletter__crx_lci&PMID=0964dbe689e61e2051685525365931 54.

Walmsley, Gerard. *Lonergan on Philosophic Pluralism: The Polymorphism of Consciousness as the Key to Philosophy*. Toronto: University of Toronto Press, 2008.

Webb, Eugene. "Differentiations of Consciousness." http://faculty.washington.edu/ewebb/EVitaly.pdf.

———. *Philosophers of Consciousness: Polanyi, Lonergan, Voegelin, Ricoeur, Girard, Kierkegaard*. Seattle: University of Washington Press, 1988.

Wee, Cecilia. "Self, Other, and Community in Cartesian Ethics." *History of Philosophy Quarterly* 19.3 (2002) 255–73.

Weinstein, David, and Avihu Zakai. "Exile and Interpretation: Popper's Re-invention of History of Political Thought." *Journal of Political Ideologies* 11.2 (2006) 186–209.

Westhofen-Kunz, Dorothea. *Stars of Heaven as Messengers of Love*. Hamburg: Books on Demand. 2012.

Williams, Howard. "The End of History in Hegel and Marx." In *The Hegel-Marx Connection*, edited by Tony Burns and Ian Fraser, 198–216. London: Macmillan, 2000.

Winter, Gibson. *The New Creation as Metropolis*. New York: Macmillan, 1963.

Wittgenstein, Ludwig. *Philosophical Investigations*. Oxford: Basil Blackwell, 1958.

———. *Tractatus Logico-Philosophicus*. London: Kegan Paul, 1922.

Wulf, Victoria M. *Bernard Lonergan's Transcendental Realism*. New York: Fordham University Press, 2000.

Ypi, Lea. "On Revolution in Kant and Marx." *Political Theory* 42.2 (2014) 262–87.

General, Selective Index

African contexts, x, 10, 68, 128
Al-Arabi, 118–19
Al-Ghazali, 117–18
Apophatic (wordless prayer), 6, 113
Aquinas, St. Thomas, 40, 72
Aristotle, 30, 52, 64–65, 94, 133–39, 153, 178
Armstrong, Karen, 19–20, 107, 109, 123
Augustine, Saint, 12, 46, 59
Authenticity, 26, 49, 174

Beards, Andrew, 58
Being, notion of in GEM, 49
Biases, fourfold, 10, 70–76, 96 passim
Bonhoeffer, Dietrich, 30
Brague, Remi, 116
Bridge-building ability of GEM, 103, 128
Brown, Patrick, 108
Buddhism, 26, 103, 113, 114, 128

Campbell, Joseph, 27
Cardijn, Pierre Cardinal, 129
Coleridge, Samuel Taylor, 108
Common good, 10
Common sense, 57, 61, 67–87, 96, 163 passim
Community, importance of in Lonergan's writings, 18, 25, 28, 34–51 passim
Conn, Walter, 46
Conrad, Joseph, 32–33
Consciousness as a Polyphony within a person, 49

Cooperation among the world religions, 116
Cosmopolis, 7, 12, 23, 87, 163 passim
Creative process, 94
Crisis, its various aspects, 50
Crowe, Frederick, 8, 127

Data of consciousness, 7–8, 44, 45 passim
De Neeve, Eileen, 105, 166, 168
Descartes, Rene, 19–20, 25, 29, 43, 140–43
Dialectic, 11–12, 28 passim
Doran, Robert, 9, 33, 126, 151
Duffy, James, 48
Dunne, Tad, 44, 49
Dupuis, Jacques, 121

Economics in Lonergan's writings, 27, 163–70
Ethical integrity and an ethical secularity, 50
Evil, 30, 81

Faith-belief distinction, 116, 125
Feuerbach, Ludwig, 163, 164
Finamore, Rosanna vii, 39
Foucault, Michel, 32
Francis, Pope, 29, 103
Francis, Saint, 34
Freud, Sigmund, 30, 76, 109, 171–73
Functional specialties, radical difference between, 46

Gandhi, Mahatma, ix

GEM as a theory-praxis, 105, 106
Generalized Empirical Method (GEM), 8, 10, 26, 35, 44 passim
God in our "midst," in our lives, 8, 49
Grudzen, Gerald, 184
Guardini, Romano, 114

Healing-creating vectors in Lonergan's view of history, 43, 46
Hegel, 30, 50, 72–73, 133–39, 164
Horizons in Lonergan's writings, 9, 29, 51
Human good, the, 25, 48, 53–66, 176 passim
Husserl, Edmund, 7, 34, 50, 154–58

Interiority: eye of love, 116
Islam, 26, 121, 128 passim

Jesus Christ, 4–20, 25 passim
John Paul II, Pope, 16–17
Johnston, William, 19, 115

Kant, Immanuel, 86, 134, 145–51
Kidder, Paul, 13
Kierkegaard, Soren, 48
King, Catherine, 42
King, Marin Luther, Jr., 62
Kingdom of God, 7, 15, 27–28, 58 passim

Lamb, Matthew, 106
Lawrence, Fred, 163, 168
Leo XIII, Pope, 27
Lewis, C. S., 107, 109
Liddy, Richard, 5–6, 69
Lonergan, Bernard, vii, ix, 3–12, 14–21, passim

Machiavelli, 19–20
Maguire, Daniel, 122–24
Martini, Cardinal, 46
Martos, Joseph, 111, 124–25
Marx, Karl, 89, 133–39, 164
McCarthy, Michael, 25, 174
McDonald, Mary, 126–28
McFarland, Jan, 17
McPartland, Thomas, 20, 90

McShane, Philip, 167, 169
Meaning, Analogy of, 57, 60
Meaning as mediated and mediating, 8, 25, 53, 55, 60 passim
Mediating-mediated phases in Method in Theology, 8
Mercy-Compassion, 5, 107, 124 passim
Merton, Thomas, 112–14, 128
Metaphysics as transposed by Lonergan, 28, 124
Mombula, Godefroid, 10, 49
Moral judgements being confused, 50
Mystical theology, mystics, 19, 103, 116, 117

Nietzsche, Friedrich, 9, 10, 30

Oduke, Onyango, 10
Ogbonnaya, Joseph, 68
Operational range (of GEM), 27–28, 34, 43, 44 passim
Operations, operator role of in GEM-FS, 28

Pascal, Blaise, 19, 47
Patterns of Experience, 68–70
Persons, Subjects in Communities, 53–66, passim
Phenomenology, 154–58
Piketty, Thomas, 169
Plato, 30, 64
Popper, Karl, 88
Postmodernism, 30, 35
Prayer, importance of, 26, 111, 113

Radical, various meanings used in GEM
Ricoeur, Paul, 16, 31, 158
Rixon, Gordon, 5
Roy, Louis, 46
Rumi, 120

Sauer, James, 59
Scheler, Max, 14, 146, 152–53
Scotus, 57
Secular(ism), secularity, 26, 116, 132
See-judge-act method, 129–30

Self-transcendence, 45, 174
Socrates, 29, 178
Sorokin, Pitirim, 175
Sublation, (*Aufhebung*), 52, 134
Sufis, Sufism, 117–20
Symbols, role of in GEM, 59–61

Tackney, Charles, 26
Taylor, Charles, 50
Tensions in human life, 34, 53–66, 95 passim

Teresa of Avila St, 114
Toynbee, Arnold, 94, 175–76

Values, their importance in GEM, 35, 64, 65
Voegelin, Eric, 179–80

Weber, Max, 176
Weil, Simone, 128
Wittgenstein, Ludwig, 158–61

www.ingramcontent.com/pod-product-compliance
Lightning Source LLC
Chambersburg PA
CBHW051739230426
43670CB00012B/2079